Management for Professionals

The Springer series "Management for Professionals" comprises high-level business and management books for executives, MBA students, and practice-oriented business researchers. The topics cover all themes relevant to businesses and the business ecosystem. The authors are experienced business professionals and renowned professors who combine scientific backgrounds, best practices, and entrepreneurial vision to provide powerful insights into achieving business excellence.

The Series is SCOPUS-indexed.

Lefei Li

The Era of New Services

New Services, New Infrastructure and Service Rules for the Future Society

中信出版集团
CITIC Press Group

Springer

Lefei Li
Department of Industrial Engineering
Tsinghua University
Beijing, China

ISSN 2192-8096 ISSN 2192-810X (electronic)
Management for Professionals
ISBN 978-981-99-9564-6 ISBN 978-981-99-9565-3 (eBook)
https://doi.org/10.1007/978-981-99-9565-3

Jointly published with CITIC Press Corporation
The print edition is not for sale in China (Mainland). Customers from China (Mainland) please order the print book from: CITIC Press Corporation.
ISBN of the Co-Publisher's edition: 978-7-5217-2023-5

This Springer imprint is published by the registered company Springer Nature Singapore Pte Ltd.
The registered company address is: 152 Beach Road, #21-01/04 Gateway East, Singapore 189721, Singapore

Foreword by Li Zheng

As a colleague of Mr. Lefei Li for many years, I was delighted upon seeing his latest work *The Era of New Services* and agreed readily with his invitation for a foreword. The reading experience of this book was a pleasure since the large number of vivid examples make it easy to understand and the core concepts and theories connecting the examples as underlying clues bring life to doctrines and help readers seize the patterns working behind. Mr. Li has always been active in thinking and high on cross-disciplinary exploration. This book, as a quintessence of his observations of practices and theoretical learning in different domains, is of excellent readability and academic significance.

More than 10,000 years ago, the human race entered into an agricultural civilization and formed the primary industry, which signifies a giant step forward for human civilization. Then, the Industrial Revolution since the 1760s unleashed a surge in productivity and constructed an industrial society represented by the manufacturing sector, crowning the industrial civilization on top of the tides of history. Entering the twenty-first century, the service sector rises to take up over 70% in the GDP of most developed countries and 52% in China 2018, accounting for half of the national total. In spite of such a significance of the service sector, the public still lack systematic knowledge about it. International Business Machines Corporation (IBM) proposed in 2004 for the first time that services should be deemed as an independent discipline, which, since then, has been referred to as the "Services Science, Management, Engineering and Design", or "Service Science" for short. In the past dozen years, scholars in varied domains have explored the rules and patterns of services and, thereby, laid the scientific foundation for Service Science. The development of information technology has, on the one hand, provided the service industry with unprecedented opportunities that bring forth a multitude of new services to practice; while, on the other hand, complicated the service systems so that the disciplinary foundation for Service Science is far from well established.

Any common reader of this book would find him or herself related to services, being their acceptor or provider. The large number of service scenarios included in the book are quite inspiring, exemplifying the continuously emerging service innovations. Through the four perspectives for service innovation—networks, resources, needs and culture, Li provides a good categorization of innovations in services. In my view, these perspectives divide innovations into two types: those on the supply side (the effective organization of services with higher efficiency and quality) and the demand side (i.e., the provision of new-type services). With an analogy to physical products, the former equals innovations in production process and the latter innovations in products themselves. Certainly, the front and back ends of services are usually coupled, instead of being separated in manufacturing.

For professional readers (in Industrial Engineering or any service-related subjects), including professors, college students and practitioners, this can serve as an ABC book for them to step into the domain of services. I believe your first impression will be similar to mine: The words are easy to understand, with abundant examples in a lively writing style. But a perusal would reveal difficulties in complete mastering, since theoretical methodologies in different disciplines like Design Science, Industrial Engineering, Systems Engineering and TRIZ (Theory of Inventive Problem Solving) are needed.

As an Industrial Engineering scholar, I see the author's exploration into this discipline in the book. When Industrial Engineering was born in the USA a century ago, the Industrial Revolutions were still in ascendance. As indicated by its name, Industrial Engineering is a subject that specializes in industrialization and has provided theoretical foundations for manufacturing throughout the world for 100 years. Both the assembly lines of Ford and lean production of Toyota are based upon Industrial Engineering theories. The decreasing proportion of manufacturing in GDP of developed countries uncovers the transformation dilemma faced in this discipline, with the USA bearing the brunt. Services, especially medical services, are now the new research direction for American Industrial Engineering researchers. Though manufacturing is still promising in China, the rapid development of the service sector makes it urgent for Industrial Engineering to rationalize its discipline layout in advance, reflecting on discipline construction and cultivation of the new generation of industrial engineers, with its theories and methodologies utilized in the service sector. In this regard, the book may serve as a paragon.

July 2020

Li Zheng
Professor, Department of Industrial Engineering
Vice President of Tsinghua University
Beijing, China

Foreword by Jinghui Guan

Services: Hope of the New Era

On a midsummer day, a friend brought me the manuscripts of *The Era of New Services*. The word "services" leapt to my eyes at first. Services, aren't they the sole starting point and ultimate destination of all our work?

"All economies are service economies"—Lefei's new book *The Era of New Services* brings us a brand-new perception concerning the boundary of services in its openings and "putting the customers at the center" reveals the essential attribute of services. The four insightful perspectives of "networks", "resources", "needs" and "culture", supported by hundreds of real cases, turn the rising wind and scudding clouds of service innovation into explicitly and thoroughly explained details. His interpretation of "new infrastructure" from the perspective of "new services" and definition of "future life" empower the readers with strong characteristics of the time and impel them to fulfill their potential.

Being a scholar in Systems Engineering, Lefei has manifested systematicness incisively and vividly throughout the book. His vision of the big picture and understanding of the full lifecycle, on the basis of a system-oriented mentality, makes the principles and logic of service innovation clear and distinct throughout his analysis of service systems starting from their complexity, his interpretation of service innovations from four perspectives and the methodology system he constructed for service innovation. The inter-disciplinary perspectives across Engineering Technology, Management Science, Psychology, Design Science and other subjects have not only maintained the grand scenery composed of great academic mountains in different disciplines that "look like a range when viewed in face and one peak when from the side", but also a holistic view that reveals both the wood and the trees in it.

My recent participation in China's Cultural and Rural Revitalization campaigns taught me the necessity to combine traditional culture with characteristics of the new era, as integration with new technologies like "Internet Plus" and Big Data would bring innovative business models.

Lefei demonstrates, with abundant domestic and international cases in his book, the potency of innovations integrating technology and models and shows to me the new approach of cultural service innovation through "original experience" and "re-design". It is my belief that, once we could tap into our profound cultural characteristics and work diligently to develop service design, we would be able to transform the country's traditional cultural power into a great impetus for its great rejuvenation.

The methods and tools Lefei develops in his practice turn service innovation into a systematic design and fill the innovation process with fun by virtue of the combination of science and arts. In his discussion of design thinking, he compares western thinking with traditions and classics in the East, teaching the readers to stand in others' shoes with an "empathy map" so that fun is also found in the study on methods for service innovation. What is more, the book also represents a fusion of Chinese and western methodologies, giving us more confidence in its practicability and applicability.

The in-depth observations and understanding of social trends in this book mark a reflection upon services beyond themselves. An analysis of the service economy represented today against the backdrop of national rejuvenation on a historical dimension makes it easier for us to perceive the significance of service innovation. This is not only a characteristic of the post-industrial age of economic development, but also an inevitable proposition in our exploration of the ultimate goals of mankind—a concrete path toward "satisfying the people's aspirations for a better life".

I recommend and expect that more administrators and innovators could, under the inspiration of this book, make reflections and step onto the path toward the practice of systematic service innovation, the path of bringing a better life through design. *The Era of New Services* reveals that, if the economy of a country runs into a bottleneck as resources are no longer dependable, services are the hope for a breakthrough.

I will stop here to keep this a prelude for your reading journey.

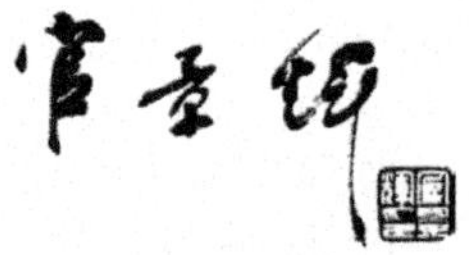

July 2020

Jinghui Guan
Vice President
Chinese Society of Ideological
and Political Work
Beijing, China

Foreword by Sheng Wu

Wonderful Services in the Digital Age

In the age when everything is an experience, services deserve a re-deliberation in all industries (because, in essence, services construct profound links to people), and a systematically effective design, more than ever before. Things to be designed are not only data and procedures, but, more importantly, the values rendered by such services and their sustainability.

Mr. Lefei Li has long devoted himself to the study of service experience and product innovation. This book can be considered a surprising publication of business thinking in 2020 that starts from the enabling logic of the Industrial Internet, and provides, on the basis of extensive case analyses and perspectives and tools refined, concrete base points and useful clues for its audience to tease out and reflect upon the previously "oversimplified" word—"service" in a refreshing and systematic manner.

It is precisely because that service has remained giant and correct in its connotation and denotation for a long time, we have to specifically perceive and construct its subtleties in digital economy.

People can see that, in the first half of 2020, the accelerated changes in the business world were by no means the results of cloudification forced by the "separation and isolation" caused by COVID-19 (the novel coronavirus disease). The fusion in between the real and virtual worlds prompts all businesses to think about how to achieve all-round, diversified and sustainable services. And, more importantly, the Digital Age, while incubating more productions, higher convenience and multiple connections in the process of "coping with changes" or "seeking for changes", is fermenting stronger randomness and hardness for businesses to seize the opportunities.

What made IKEA, a firm proponent of warehouse-size out-of-town malls, explore different e-business and retail forms, even opening a small-format inner city store IKEA City in downtown Shanghai? Why did the Chinese tea drink chain HEYTEA divide its stores into series like Pink Stores, HEYTEA Black, HEYTEA Daydreamer Project, HEYTEA Go unmanned stores and HEYTEA MIX Tea and Bakery, and establish sub-brands like HEYTEA Department Store and HEYTEA Mini? What are the reasons for the constant increase in market values of Software as a Service (SaaS) like ServiceNow and Workday, and for Salesforce to become the world's top software solution provider larger than Oracle?

As I proposed, when putting forward the "scenario-based algorithm of business for the young" in 2019, that the "inborn marginal and self-organized nature, and open coordination" represented among the new consumers can no longer be simply summarized as characteristics of the young in the new era, instead, they are the unprecedented and unstoppable underlying elements of the lifestyles in Digital Age.

What kinds of services should a business offer, and in what forms? Service design determines the "ecological niche" of the business's new battlefield. If demands and traffic volumes are hard to be captured precisely and timely in changing digital flows, at least, "scenarios" may serve as the interface for sustainable design. Among dispersed but fertile demands, pinpointed pain spots in segmented real scenarios along with systematically designed user-driven scenario-based solutions are opportunities for service innovations, brought by the digital business.

Wonderful services in the Digital Age refer to systematic solutions activated by scenarios. They are authentic, complete, extensible and meaningful.

All the things Amazon is doing not only are centered on its membership service Amazon Prime under the support of Amazon Web Services (AWS), but also depend on its ever-evolving retail solutions and newly divided service units, from Amazon Key to In-car Delivery ... which are far beyond simple replication and service translation.

Chinese video-sharing mobile app Kuaishou seems to have risen upon "marginal demands" to a recorder of infrastructures in a universally beneficial posture and satisfy efficiency needs in each scenario niche. In addition to low-threshold video creation and livestreaming, it keeps developing scenarios like education, food, fashion and pets so as to foster new products for different circles and scenarios. Food bloggers, teachers and artists can all have their demands satisfied at Kuaishou.

Services provided by these businesses cannot be directly defined or concretely concluded. We could only evaluate their authenticity and systematicness within each scenario. Services are now business models to be designed. In the Digital Age, each business or brand stands a chance and may find it necessary to transform into a "service provider" with elastic supply capacity to offer scenario-based solutions.

"Services change the world and design brings a better life." Manufacturing, sales, experience, software, hardware ... all are defined by services and turned into underlying capacities. Therefore, Lefei's insights in *The Era of New Services* from perspectives of "networks, resources, demands and culture" are groundbreaking revelations to us: to design services, in essence, is more than designing new business models, but to develop novel lifestyles.

Sheng Wu
Founder
Context Lab
Beijing, China

Preface

Services, the "first industry" by definition of its proportion in GDP, have never been so important as today, yet still lack a systematic understanding.

Sharing Economy, New Retail, (Software as a Service (SaaS) and all other models emerge endlessly while technologies like the Internet of Things (IoT), Artificial Intelligence (AI) and unmanned aerial vehicle keep dazzling our eyes. This Warring States Period of all kinds of service innovations is calling upon a return to reason, so we have to see through the phenomena of "changes" and perceive their "unchanging" essence.

It is hoped that, through this book, we can start from the dominant logic of services and introduce the increasing knowledge of Service Science worldwide into people's daily life. The book discusses the components and trends of service innovation from "the perspective of networks", "the perspective of resources", "the perspective of demands" and "the perspective of culture"; then analyzes the internal logic of service design and innovation from dimensions of "original experience", "redesign" and "diversification", and constructs tools for service innovation on the basis of research results of the SERVINO (Service Innovation System) and Parallel Services; and, finally, designs the future through an exploration of various desires of people, such as for "curiosity" and "fun".

"Design brings a better life and services change the world." May the eight years' iteration on the podium of Tsinghua University and interpretation of hundreds of real cases constitute this book into a well-laid staircase for us to seek, between the lines, the power to define the future!

Beijing, China Lefei Li

Contents

Part I Introduction

1 Services Everywhere 3
Reference 7

2 Services in Complexity 9
2.1 Coping with Complexity of Services 9
2.2 Thinking in a Continuum 11
2.3 Grasping History and Trends 13

Part II Four Perspectives of Service Innovation

3 The Perspective of Networks 17
3.1 Low-Cost Networks 17
3.2 Cross-Organization Networks 21
3.3 High-Efficiency Networks 23
3.4 Online or Offline? 35
3.4.1 Offline Towards Online 36
3.4.2 Online-Offline Integration 39
3.4.3 Online Towards Offline 40
Reference 42

4 The Perspective of Resources 43
4.1 Making Information An Asset 43
4.2 Secrets of Information Transfer 49
4.3 Tapping into Advantages to Expand the Market 51
4.4 Resources Sharing is not a False Proposition 52
References 56

5 The Perspective of Needs 57
5.1 From Needs to Demands 57
5.1.1 To Expand "Dimensions of Life" 59
5.2 From Satisfying to Surprising 59

5.3 Engaging "God" in Design 64
5.3.1 Customers' Needs and Design Thinking 64
5.3.2 How Far Should We Go in Customer Engagement 74
5.3.3 Functions and Beauty 75
Reference 77

6 The Perspective of Culture 79
6.1 Looking in the "Satisfaction Mirror" 79
6.2 Interactive Behaviors and Service Innovation 82
6.3 Excellent Organizational Culture 84
Reference 92

Part III Principles and Methods of Service Design and Innovation

7 Principles of Service Design and Innovation 95
7.1 Original Experience 96
7.1.1 Place of Origin 96
7.1.2 Original Culture 97
7.1.3 Original Craft 97
7.1.4 Original Memory 99
7.1.5 Original Genes 100
7.1.6 Original Materials 101
7.2 Redesign 102
7.2.1 Expand from Five Senses to More Perceptions 103
7.2.2 Power of Balance 106
7.2.3 World of Design and World of Art 108
7.3 Diversification 110
7.3.1 The Growing "Minorities" 112
References 113

8 Classical Tools for Service Innovation 115
8.1 Differentiation-Based Competitive Strategies 115
8.1.1 Differentiation is an Essential Need 115
8.1.2 Methods and Trends of Differentiated Competition 116
8.2 Service Encounters: Economic Efficiency, Effectiveness and Communicative Skills 125
Reference 129

9 SERVINO Methods 131
9.1 SERVINO System and Its Problem-Solving Process 131
9.2 Exploring the Overall System 133
9.3 Focusing on Problems in Design 134
9.4 Inspiring and Driving Innovation 134
9.5 Verifying and Implementing the Plan 135
9.6 Encouraging Service Experience: Starting from Observations 135

9.7 "Know Yourself": Decomposing the Service System 137
9.7.1 Case Analysis: Shangpu Home Design 140
9.8 Problem Analysis: Bridging Demands and Supply 141
9.9 How to "Invent" Services? 156
9.9.1 Separation Principle in Service 156
9.9.2 Inventive Principles for Service Innovation 157
9.9.3 More Methods to Inspire Innovation 158

10 Parallel Services 161
10.1 Parallel Services 162
10.1.1 Uniqueness of Parallel Service Management 163
10.1.2 The Three-Scale Model of Parallel Service Management 163
10.2 Services Empowered by AI Technology 164
10.2.1 Service Demand Cycle Model 164
10.2.2 Service Channel Choice Model 164
10.2.3 Parallel Learning and Optimization Model 165
10.3 The "Parallel" Age of Service Management 166
10.3.1 Service Channel Evolution Analysis 166
10.3.2 Micromarketing of Services 166
10.3.3 Intelligent Services 167
10.3.4 A Case Study 167
10.3.5 Constructing the Artificial Service System 168
10.3.6 Actual System Implementation 169

Part IV Service Innovation and Future Life

11 Service Innovation and Future Life 173
11.1 Curiosity 173
11.2 Fun 174
11.3 Passions Connected 176
11.4 No Need to Choose 176
11.5 Multifunctional Spaces 178
11.6 Tips 180
11.7 Scenarios Triggering Tender Feelings 180
11.8 New Interactions 181
11.9 Word-of-Mouth Economy 182
11.10 Service Boosts "Rural Vitalization" 184
11.11 "New Infrastructures" Boosted by "New Services" 185

Afterword 189

Part I
Introduction

Chapter 1
Services Everywhere

What are services? How important are they in people's lives? Let's start with the manufacturing sector and see the services in it, as shown in Fig. 1.1.

(1) Business services, including consultancy, audit, advertising and garbage disposal;
(2) Value-added services, such as finance, leasing and insurance, which are all important forces serving manufacturing;
(3) Circulation services, such as wholesale, retail, repair and maintenance and other services belonged to the back end of the supply chain;
(4) Fundamental services, for example, communications, transportation, public utilities and banking are all service providers for circulation businesses;
(5) Personal services, such as sanitation, healthcare, catering, accommodation and retail; and
(6) Governments, which actually constitutes larger service-providing entities offering military, education, justice, public security, fire protection and other services. So service-oriented governments are well grounded since governments are the largest service providers.

Now let's look into the manufacturing sector, where various links of finance, accounting, legal affairs, research and development (R&D) and design consist of different business segments within this sector. But these internal services are gradually outsourced to other companies, especially in segments like legal affairs, R&D and design. Guangdong Shunde Innovative Design Institute (GIDC) is a typical example in this regard. As a teaching, research and training base located in Guangdong Industrial Design City, GIDC provides local household appliance, machinery and other industries with comprehensive supporting services in R&D, design and talent training and recruitment. A Fortune 500 company in Shunde, Midea Group, is actively introducing external services so that much of its industrial design in product R&D has been outsourced to professional service providers in Guangdong Industrial Design City.

L. Li, *The Era of New Services*, Management for Professionals,
https://doi.org/10.1007/978-981-99-9565-3_1

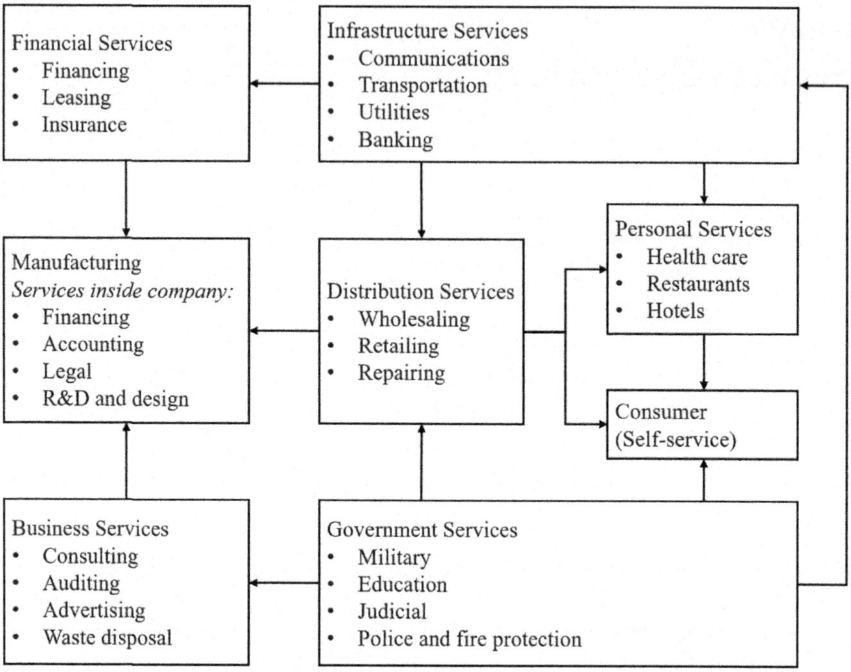

Fig. 1.1 Role of Services in an Economy. *Source* Guile and Quinn (1988)

So it appears that services are everywhere in our social life. In the United States, over 80% of the federal GDP in 2007 was contributed by the service sector. Of course, the two major contributors were finance and medicine, which were large proportion takers in this sector. As for China, in the first quarter of 2013, the GDP of the service sector surpassed that of the manufacturing sector, at 47.8% and, as shown by latest statistics in 2018, the ratio has grown to 51.6%, 11% higher than that of manufacturing. For megacities like Beijing, the service sector constituted more than 80% of GDP. Therefore, it is clear that China, too, has entered into a stage when the service sector is experiencing great development like in western developed countries.

Now, we have to discuss what are services. Following definitions are found from previous studies.

Firstly, "an activity or series activities provided as a solution to customer problems". This definition emphasizes that a service is an activity for customers, highlighting the relationship between the subject and the object.

Secondly, "economic activities whose output is not a physical product or construction", emphasizing the immateriality of services, which indicates that, sometimes, services are not visible nor tangible.

Thirdly, it is "intangible and perishable… an occurrence or process that is created and used simultaneously". This definition involves the nature of services by mentioning their natural attributes. Difficulties in management over the service sector actually arise from such natural attributes.

Fourthly, "a service is a time-perishable, intangible experience performed for a customer acting in the role of a co-producer". Here, the other natural attribute of services is mentioned—perishability.

Fifthly, "a service is a change in the condition of a person, or a good belonging to some economic unit, which is brought about as the result of the activity of some other economic unit". This one is somewhat obscure, emphasizing that services generate economic values through acting on entities.

I want to recommend a relatively broad and recognized definition: "a service is an interactive process between the service provider and its user that produces economic values. It exists not only in the tertiary industry, but also in the manufacturing sector".

Let's start with the first sentence. "Service provider" and "user" point out the two essential parties in service—the one that provides the service and the one being served. Then the interaction between them that generates economic value is known as a "service".

Now let's see the second sentence. What does it mean by "not only in the tertiary industry, but also in the manufacturing sector"? An important concept in recent years can be used here for explanation—"service-oriented manufacturing".

What is service-oriented manufacturing? Here is an example. Carrier Corporation, whose founder, Willis Carrier, acquired the patent for the world's first modern air-conditioning device in 1906, owns top-notch compressor and packaged refrigeration technology and has won a great many clients with its central air-conditioning facilities in the U.S. Then the corporation started thinking about a question—we may as well think about it: are people buying an air-conditioner out of the fondness of this machine?

It is easy to figure out that what people really want, instead of the machine itself, is the cooling function it provides. Then, can we change into another service mode if the cooling function is what they actually want?

In the conventional mode, if a user pays for an air-conditioner and Carrier installs it for him, this air-conditioner would belong to the user. Any failure in operation within the warranty period has to be fixed by Carrier, for free; while once the warranty period expires, the repair would become a paid service.

Since now we've realized what the users want is not the machine but its cooling function, how about trying this mode: the air-conditioner installed in a user's home does not belong to him, but Carrier, who signs a cooling service contract with this user, requiring him to pay Carrier for the cooling service it provides. Under this new mode, supposing the air-conditioner malfunctions, who would worry more, the user or Carrier? Obviously, Carrier would be the worrier, and that is the core issue. An air-conditioner bought under the conventional mode belongs to the user and would worry the user once it fails. However, under the new mode, with a cooling service contract signed, the air-conditioner is still the property of Carrier and Carrier would be the one that fixes the cooling function of the machine by all means upon its failure.

As we see, the core thinking of "service-oriented manufacturing" is well illustrated by this example. Even in the manufacturing sector, people are thinking about how to put the customers at the center, which is also the kernel idea of "service-oriented manufacturing".

This example is used to help clarify the relationship between services and products, and services and manufacturing. Next, I'll introduce a ground-breaking theory that has laid the foundation of Service Science—"Service-dominant Logic" (S-D Logic). It was proposed by two American professors, Stephen L. Vargo and Robert F. Lusch, in 2004 and has been continuously revised and improved since then. Here are the two important premises of this theory. First, "all economies are service economies". This is quite an aggressive premise. We used to believe that service provision belongs to the third industry, so when hearing that "all economies are service economies" all of a sudden, we may wonder: if so, what are products? The second premise answers this immediately: "goods are a distribution mechanism for service provision". We have to notice that, here, products (goods) are simple vehicles of services towards an essential goal, which is to satisfy people's demands.

These premises are the foundation that supports the so-called "Service-dominant Logic", indicating that we have to turn our mindset thoroughly around to be oriented towards services. The example of Starbucks is a good illustration of this.

Since founded by Howard Schultz in Seattle in the 1970s, Starbucks had kept operating in the model where roasted coffee beans were delivered to stores and then ground and made into coffee upon being ordered by customers. This is the classical Starbucks model. Whereas in the 1990s, Schultz handed Starbucks to his successor and this new CEO started a reform to lower costs and improve efficiency. One move of his was to stop delivering coffee beans to stores. Instead, all the beans were ground and vacuum-packed at one place and then distributed. Now, we may imagine, when a customer arrives at a Starbucks store and orders a cup of coffee, all the things that the barista has to do are to open the vacuum package, take the ground coffee and make the drink. Isn't this process shorter and more efficient? Obviously, the customer can have his cup of coffee sooner than before. What's more, grinding all coffee beans in one place can put the equipment to better use and achieve scale effects. It sounds good and like a paragon for cost reduction and efficiency improvement.

Around the year 2000, Starbucks met some difficulties in operation and Schultz had to take charge of the company again. The first thing he did was to resume the delivery of beans to stores. This sounded like a retroaction and obviously added to the costs. Then why did he do so? Let's think about what will happen when the beans are ground.

It is the aroma we smell when grinding coffee beans, an indispensable experience to be had at a coffee store! So the Starbucks case tells us: for the service sector, the manufacturing mentality—constantly reducing costs and improving efficiency—is not the best solution. We have to keep in mind that the real focus is customer experience, which is worth all our efforts. Of course, I am not advocating a blind pursuit of improvement in experience with no consideration on efficiency and costs. There is no end to experience, so the service experience should be set at a reasonable level.

After learning the S-D Logic, it is easy to understand why all customer-oriented innovations in products will finally settle into issues like management, experience and innovation of services—because the shift in mentality has resulted in changes in methodology.

Reference

Guile, B. R., & Quinn, J. B. (Eds.). (1988). *Technology in services: Policies for growth, trade, and employment* (p. 124). National Academy Press.

Chapter 2
Services in Complexity

2.1 Coping with Complexity of Services

Complexity is a challenging topic. A complex system is often taken as a typical system with complexity, featuring that, instead of adding all its single characteristics together and considering them the overall behavior of the system, emergent properties and nonlinear relations would be found, including self-adaptive behaviors of the system.

Generally, service systems are typical complex systems. The term "service package" is often used in Service Management to define a service system and a complete service package should contain five elements, namely, supporting facilities, auxiliary items, information, explicit services and implicit services. Therefore, all these five elements should be considered to have an understanding of service systems.

Furthermore, both the subjects and the objects of services are often human, which would bring the service systems greater uncertainty. How do we cope with such a complexity in service systems? From the point of view of systems engineering, to cope with complex systems, we should not merely simplify complex problems, but should use tools designed for complex problems to deal with such complexity. After years of study, Systems Engineering scholars have developed multiple analytical methods and tools, such as Complex Adaptive Systems (CAS) and multi-agent simulation and modeling. These methods and tools may help us in two ways: For one, they can provide a certain coarse-grained description and prediction of the overall behaviors of a complex system, based on behaviors of and interactions among individuals in this system. For the other, they can be used in probability analysis so that we can foresee the performance that the service system may have under certain operational scenarios, before putting it into use.

These tools have already been used in lab environment to analyze people's walk paths and consuming behaviors in complex retail scenarios and the results have been preliminarily verified. The next step is to establish parallel service systems with these results and use the system models as a foundation for virtual computing experiments so that considerable experiments can be carried out on computer to

L. Li, *The Era of New Services*, Management for Professionals,
https://doi.org/10.1007/978-981-99-9565-3_2

make projections on all possible consequences of these systems before any real service is provided. These projections may not be able to give us precise probabilistic conclusions, but at least, they can present all different probabilities so that we would have something in support or for reference when designing services, making remedy plans or even allocating systematic resources for service operational systems. In essence, it is quite similar to Cyber Physical Systems (CPS) or digital twins used in current industrial internet scenarios, while the digital twinning of service systems bear some other meanings. If the digital twin of a service system can well express and analyze human's behavioral models and differences among individuals, then hopefully, AI techniques can be used as auxiliaries for service processes to provide users with more customized service experiences, especially under catering, retailing and other public service scenarios.

Under the traditional service mode, it is hard for workers in the service sector to cater to personalized demands of all consumers since they have to serve a great number of consumers with only the memory held by the human brain. But AI is different. An ideal match of service contents, including customized setting of the service scenario, can be achieved by AI based on a comprehensive calculation of the personal information, consumption history, health condition and even current emotion of an individual consumer. In other words, the way we cope with the complexity in service systems may not only help improve the overall design and operation of a system, but also be applied in extended scenarios to provide precise services directly to individual consumers. In the future, AI assistants like Siri will act more than personal assistants of consumers, their twin brothers may assist service staff at work and, probably someday, replace these service staff and bring us unprecedented service experiences based on communication between machine assistants.

Of course, it is not easy to tell whether this actualization of AI technology would add to or reduce the complexity of service systems. But the precise control over deeper personalized demands, which is comprehensible to today's people, is truly beneficial to the improvement of efficiency and effectiveness of service systems, for which, precision medicine is the most illustrative case. Once a user's DNA information is known to the medical service provider, existing knowledge can be used to determine which type of medication would be more effective for the patient. This means a significant improvement in the customization capacity of current medical services, and consequently, the overall service quality in this domain.

In general, the relationship between the complexity and the design and management of service systems can be concluded as improving the overall service design and management with model-based computing experiments and projections. In order to transform the analytical methodology towards this direction, fundamental knowledge and models of people, their interactions and the surroundings are requisite, which in turn brings unprecedented opportunities to precision services aimed at individual people. The core of all these lies in the modeling and projection-making process, so a cross-disciplinary team with comprehensive capacities in psychology, consumer behavior, sociology, management, even brain science and life science will possess a stronger competitiveness.

In the meantime, diverse data acquisition equipment and tools for physiological characteristics identification and measurement will gain more opportunities for development since more high-quality data is needed for model training and verification. To integrate all the above components, organizations and individuals should bear profound understandings on business models and technology innovation as well as a strong sense of mission towards the building of a better life.

2.2 Thinking in a Continuum

The concept of "continuum" in complex system building serves as an indispensable paradigm in the construction of systematic global thinking, in particular, from a Progressive Perspective of System Thinking.

The continuum paradigm is also a powerful tool for service design within a system. Now that the space of service design is considered a continuum, the two poles of it should be defined first, with the broad space in between accommodating all kinds of possibilities. Both our existing services and potential ones in the future should find their places within this space.

To illustrate with travelling, if one pole of the transport continuum is transport modes with lowest rates and biggest carrying capacity, represented by public transport like subway and bus, the other pole would be point-to-point private vehicles used by individuals. According to current technological trends, the latter probably will develop into point-to-point UMVs that offer complete private spaces to passengers (high-end services in this mode might be the most expensive and least-carrying private aircrafts serving only one person).

If those are the two poles of transport, services in between may take changes in two ways. On the one hand, the carrying capacity of vehicles may vary. For example, carpooling serves a bit more passengers than one-to-one taxis; a minibus carries more than private vehicles; buses are even bigger, and subways possess the biggest carrying capacity.

On the other hand, the freedom and comfort people enjoy in the above transport modes decrease progressively, with the rates declining too. Therefore, a continuum of transport modes is now depicted on the basis of rates, comfort degrees, carrying capacities and other indexes. Each service mode observed currently has its place—a point—in the continuum and the space between any two points may contain possible new modes, which, for sure, have to perform better than existing solutions in one or several indexes so as to be accepted by passengers. In this view, the key validity measurements of the continuum of service systems have to be defined first, possibly supported by some essential technical parameters or performance indexes of related services. Values on two ends of these validity measurements may be used to determine the poles of the continuum, while the space in between is where providers could explore more economic and comfortable overall solutions.

This continuum paradigm can be used to interpret the relationship between art and design. Artists are exploring the boundary of fine art. The ultimacy of their personal expression would bring forth unique works appreciated by few, signifying one pole of the continuum. If the personality in such ultimacy declines along a certain direction towards another pole, the works may vary into designer brands, mass-market brands and eventually, normal goods used in people's daily life.

Similarly, services given by a certain provider can be fit into different modes in the continuum, and then provided to users with different demands or the same user in different scenarios, for example, all kinds of ride-hailing services offered by the Chinese platform Didi Chuxing, including DiDi Express, DiDi Premier, DiDi Taxi and even Bike-sharing. The extended coverage of demand points in a continuum not only embodies the diversification created by abundant choices, but also gives the broad masses in varied scenarios a unified interface, bring them ease and convenience in life. And the tenet of "making people's lives easier" is often a direction for innovation that endows enterprises with strong vitality.

Back to service design, the detection and definition of the continuum should start from the early design stage and often be related with the analysis on the company's business and mission, including its current services. Indeed, for many services, the market is not driven by a single index. When a complex space is constructed based on several indexes, a service cannot be simply defined as a point on a line segment with two ends. Instead, poles of more comprehensive indexes have to be considered to nail the multi-dimensional position of the service, which possibly contains essential information for its "positioning" in strategic analysis.

Taking the hotel industry as an example, sharing economy giants led by Airbnb have brought a great shock to hotels throughout the globe. These platforms maximize the utilization of resources like idle rooms, apartments and villas held by the public, by serving as a direct connection between one C-end (users) and the other C-end (consumers). Accommodations on Airbnb, instead of being uniformly furnished and equipped with standard facilities and services like chain hotels, are decorated in ways that the homeowners prefer, which ensures the guests fresh traveling experience. Also, the absence of standardized requirements of hotels allows the owners to show their sense of humor in communication so that the interaction between owners and guests can be filled with fun (the two-way comment system of Airbnb can avoid conflicts and guarantee both parties pleasurable experience). Of course, risks are inevitable in this model: it cannot rival traditional hotels in terms of precision in demands matching and consistency in service. Then, how about considering traditional hotels and various accommodations provided by individual homeowners on Airbnb as two poles of the hospitality continuum and finding points in the middle for differentiation? The "scattered hotels" newly emerged overseas are a beautiful middle point of this kind. As reported by Bloomberg Businessweek, roughly 2500 villages in Italy and almost 3000 in Spain are at risk of becoming ghost towns. In Japan, 8 million or so buildings sit vacant. How can we make use of these idle buildings? The answer is turning them into resort hotels! In Cyprus, entrepreneur John Papadouris rebuilt the abandoned properties in his hometown into a 40-room hotel and spa, which is fully reserved for all weekends this year for now. The hotel is so successful in profit-making that the president of Cyprus asked him to replicate his tourism scheme for 115 dying towns in the area. Italy has opened roughly 110 scattered hotels like this and the model has been proved applicable to oriental cultures by its success at Sasayama Castle Town Hotel nearby Kyoto, Japan. With a close analysis of characteristics of this model, we will find that, in addition to utilizing idle resources and tapping to unique flavor of life and historical accumulation of each room (perhaps with some touchable stories or anecdotes of famous people), it has maintained the advantage of traditional hotels, which is the uniformity in management and standardization, so that a middle point with beautiful sceneries is found on the continuum of hotel services.

2.3 Grasping History and Trends

In study of social trends, the foremost characteristic of an era can be marked as a rise or decline, from the dimension of history. A person in different states of mind or circumstances may shift his thoughts and focus. Like what Fan Zhongyan, the eminent minister of the Northern Song Dynasty, said, "When holding high positions at the court, they were concerned about the people; when afar from the center of power, they were concerned about the monarch". Prestigious scholars in the period of the Republic of China, eager to save the nation, focused on "using western learning in China" and comparing the contemporary era with the heyday of ancient China when close communication was maintained with foreign countries. The same trend was seen in other parts of the world. Rises in industry and design in Germany and Japan after World War II blazed with strong colors of redemption and rejuvenation, under the support of their national spirits. After over a century's vicissitudes, China and its people are also embarking on the road to rejuvenation, driven by their ideals and urgent needs to change the status quo.

Therefore, the judgment over any social trend has to be based on the study of national spirits and overall development stages; and the grand trend should be interpreted into segmented trends in society, which can be divided by sector, by the demand types of people, or the needs observed from people in different stages or classes.

While transferring these social trends into specific service designs, it is necessary to study the relationship between such transference and overall rise or decline of the society from a historical scale, to see, while conforming to segmented social trends, can it satisfy or even support the social reforms historically. This is an important indicator that will bring a system not only commercial success but also social significance in a broader sense over a long period of time.

For example, after a country steps, or basically steps, into a postindustrial era and people's material pursuits are almost satisfied, they would have higher demands over education. Such demands cannot be simply generalized as accessibility to and popularity of education, but have their extensity and profundity extended. The expansion of extensity is easy to understand: As influenced by the trend of lifelong learning, people are freer to explore their personal interests, such as painting and music, so that relevant supply gradually comes to their close reach and innovations in the segmented education market become promising. The extension of profundity requires education to tap into intrinsic needs deep in people's minds, as Mr. Qian Mu said in *My Ideal University*, "Things that the higher education has to transmit are no more than experience and ideals". The experience here includes knowledge, methods and skills, while ideals belong to demands at a higher and more profound level. To infuse these ideals with vital force, I reckon, the development status of society on a historical scale has to be taken into consideration.

In a brief summary, faced with "services" of such a complexity whose influence is constantly witnessed everywhere in our life, can we reel silk from cocoons to find some valuable patterns of service innovations? Before getting deep down to the principles, let's look at cases in different sectors and analyze from different perspectives. Here are the four perspectives I recommend for service innovation: networks, resources, demands and culture.

Part II
Four Perspectives of Service Innovation

Chapter 3
The Perspective of Networks

The first important perspective to be utilized in observing trends of service innovation is the perspective of networks in service and product development. Specifically, networks in four dimensions are included: low-cost networks, cross-organization networks, high-efficiency networks and online and offline networks.

3.1 Low-Cost Networks

Low-cost networks, to put it simply, mean that a brand-new mode with lower costs is adopted, at the level of networking structure, to serve existing industries and bring new service experiences.

A typical example of the low-cost network is FedEx, a benchmarking corporate for the express delivery industry. When studying at Yale University in the 1960s, its founder Frederick Wallace Smith proposed an interesting idea in a class paper, based on a simple device used in electronic engineering—junction box, which houses multiple electrical connections and allows any two of them to be wired.

In Smith's proposal, this device inspired him to find an American city to serve as the "junction box" that could accommodate parcels delivered by air from all other cities. With one transfer center built there, the exchange of parcels between any two cities can be realized and the exchanged parcels will take another flight to their destinations the next morning, with the delivery services throughout the United States accomplished overnight.

However, this brilliant idea got Smith a C for his paper, given by a professor at Yale. The grading was unsatisfactory, though, Smith still put the idea into practice. By April 1973, he had chosen Memphis as his junction box for parcel exchanges among merely 14 cities. Today, FedEx has grown into a delivery giant that covers more than 200 countries and regions in the world. What makes FedEx a typical low cost network? Supposing we are now covering all the cities in need in the most straightforward

L. Li, *The Era of New Services*, Management for Professionals,
https://doi.org/10.1007/978-981-99-9565-3_3

way, which is to connect any two cities with one flight, then it will take 91 flights in total. The costs would soar, compared with 14 flights. Then, think about the growth potential of this network. At the beginning, it has only to cover 14 cities, but what if we want to add one more city to the network? The solution would be easy in the FedEx network—to add one more flight to Memphis. While in the fully-connected network in our supposition, the newcomer has to be connected to all the former cities, which means that 14 flights have to be added. In a word, the underlying networking structure has determined that FedEx is a low-cost network and explains why it is the world's first deliverer that realized overnight delivery service and achieved rapid expansion. Therefore, the cost efficiency of the networking structure must be considered in the network building process, which may bring maximum economization.

Are there any similar cases in China? Actually, the four major express delivery players in the private sector (YTO Express, ZTO Express, Yunda Express and STO Express) were all typical low-cost networks upon their founding. The founders of all the four companies came from the same county named Tonglu in Hangzhou, Zhejiang Province. Because of this, Tonglu is known as the "hometown of private express delivery" in China, with more than 200,000 people working in this industry and a yearly turnover exceeding RMB 30 billion (USD 4.7 billion), taking up nearly 60% of the national market share. Founders of these companies used to discover the broad market space in the express delivery industry during their trips from Hangzhou to Shanghai to submit customs declarations, and started building their private delivery networks thereafter. A close look into their development process reveals to us a simple but efficient pattern that allowed them to rapidly construct a nation-wide express delivery network. All those founders were fellow townsmen from the same place. Let's say you and I are fellow townsmen. I am based in City A and you in City B. I would hand all parcels from City A to City B over to you and entrust you with the distribution; and likewise, you would do the same to me. On the basis of this pattern, with one fellow townsman in one city, an express delivery network was soon constructed to cover the whole country. Of course, there was another intriguing quality assurance system working behind this simple pattern. I once doubted, "It is easy to send a townsman to a city, but what if this man doesn't work well?" The answer was plain: "Anyone who slacks at work would be too ashamed to go back home for the New Year's reunion". Clearly, the QA system of such a network based on hometown ties and a reputation system was the reason for these companies' rapid expansion and nationwide networking success. Up to now, YTO, ZTO, Yunda and STO have strengthened their synergetic development in connecting upstream and downstream links and extending the industrial chain, and realized a precise, characterized and customized whole-chain management that "connects factories to users and farmland to dinner tables". In the meantime, scientific information technologies have permeated into every link in sectoral and industrial collaboration, to construct a delivery ecosphere with full vitality.

A new trend observed in another aspect in recent years is worth pondering. To illustrate it with an instance, a startup in the United States named Deliv is a representative of the great number of crowdsourcing platforms emerging recently. Figure 3.1 shows how Deliv works.

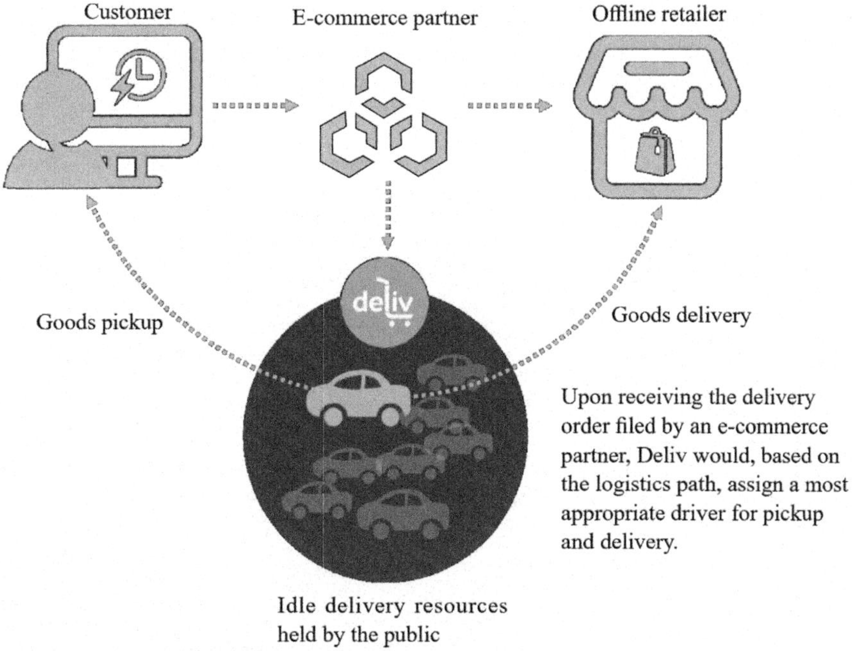

Fig. 3.1 Service process of Deliv

Anyone that has applied and passed the training and review of Deliv will become its registered driver. Upon receiving the delivery orders filed by its e-commerce partners, Deliv would, based on logistics paths, assign those orders to the most appropriate drivers, who will then complete the ordered delivery tasks by picking up the goods and delivering them to customers at the designated places and time, as shown in Fig. 3.2. Founded in 2012, Deliv has covered 35 American cities in merely 6 years and provides same-day delivery services to more than 5000 partners. This is quite similar to the popular Chinese ride-hailing application, Didi Chuxing, which, actually, is a utilization of idle resources in society. Such a utilization matters significantly since people, vehicles and time in idle are all mobilized to help satisfy delivery demands.

The mode of shared transport, represented by platforms like Didi Chuxing and Uber, seems quite reasonable. But we may as well ask, why didn't they emerge ten years ago? The prevalence of a certain technology—the mobile internet—was essential. It is the enabling technology for shared transport and the promising sharing economy, at large. In other words, the emergence of smart phones carrying GPS, 3G and 4G mobile networks has enabled us to find close-by passengers, drivers and their vehicles, and then match them through platforms.

While Didi Chuxing and Uber deliver people with the power of crowdsourcing, platforms like Deliv are delivering goods with this power. Uber has a spin-off

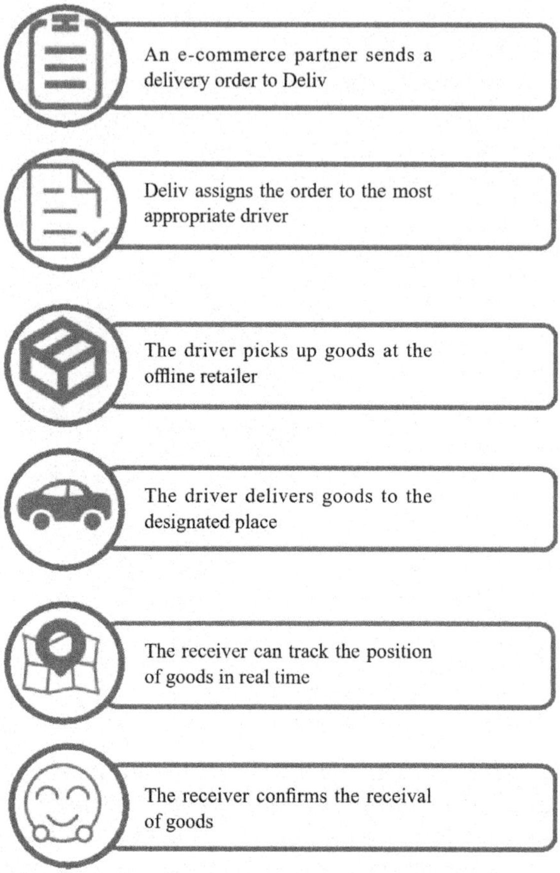

Fig. 3.2 Deliv's logistics and delivery process

for goods delivery in the United States, named Uber Rush. China, too, has a crowdsourced goods delivery platform, FlashEX, which operates in the same fashion.

The pattern that prompted the springing-up of similar crowdsourcing platforms can be concluded as "a strong platform makes it possible to unite and manage individual powers". By principle, there are two marvelous reformations: connecting supply and demands in the model and relying on intelligence for capacity.

What does "connecting supply and demands" mean? Taking Best Inc., the Chinese logistics company listed at New York Stock Exchange in 2017, as an example, it has a sub-brand "Best Store^{+}" which provides services to convenience stores in a very interesting model: Through a mobile phone application, Best Store^{+} serves convenience stores and family-run shops of all scales in cities—the tail ends of the urban retailing system. Storeowners acquire the membership of Best Store^{+} through registering on its application and can then make online orders for replenishment, with no need to visit the wholesale market in person. While at the other end, Best Store^{+} takes the advantage of its over 300,000 registered convenience stores and family-run shops to negotiate with upstream suppliers, so as to fetch goods directly from factories and use its own logistics network to distribute them to "capillaries" throughout the country. This kind of one-step service model that connects factories to convenience stores and family-run shops is an ideal use of the advantages of logistics systems under the support of intelligent information platforms that enable a direct connection between supply and demands. Once such a "direct connection" is established, its advantages are self-evident.

3.2 Cross-Organization Networks

The second dimension in the network perspective is cross-organization networking integration. Let's start with an example. S.F. Express cooperated with convenience store franchises like 7-Eleven to launch a 24-h pick-up service in Hong Kong and Taiwan, which means that, instead of handing parcels to customers in person, S.F. deliverers can leave the parcels at a 7-Eleven store in the neighborhood for customers' pick-up.

Up to now, more than 370 7-Eleven stores in Hong Kong are offering this self pick-up service in cooperation with S.F. Express, joined by other Circle K convenience stores, Shell Gas Stations, CR Vanguard supermarkets and some small franchise stores to provide customers with more service outlets. On top of this, to solve the last mile delivery problem, Hive Box Technology, with S.F. as its lead investor, has established a smart express locker system to provide self-service parcel pickup functions. By 2022 Hive Box Lockers have covered more than 200 major cities in China, with 270,000 outlets handling a daily average of more than 25 million parcels, and has taken over 60% of the market share in China.

This seemingly simple cooperation model deserves more scrutiny. First of all, what does S.F. Express get from this? Obviously, the overall delivery efficiency is improved. How is it improved? The kernel is in end distribution. With a further look into the time saved in end distribution, we will discover more from the comparison. For one, deliverers in the past had to contact receivers one-on-one, who, sometimes, were not available for the time being, making subsequent contacts necessary. For another, this type of one-on-one service is in a serial structure, requesting deliverers to not contact the next receiver before finishing contacting and serving the one at hand. But if the parcels are all deposited at a 7-Eleven store, the delivery for all receivers nearby could be finished once and for all, which means a considerable lowering of end-distribution costs and a great efficiency improvement for S.F.

Secondly, what are there for 7-Eleven and other convenience stores? It clearly brings them potential consumers. Consumer behavior theory divides the buying behaviors of consumers into planned and unplanned buying, with the latter accounting for a big portion beyond our imagination. For example, I once went to a supermarket nearby Tsinghua University to buy some batteries and ended up spending more than 30 dollars on snack food. Upon leaving there, I came to realize that all I wanted to buy at the beginning was batteries. An important pride of

7-Eleven is their brilliant category management capacity, which allows them to offer products in more than 3000 categories in a store with a business area of 100 m^2. The huge variety of products may stimulate consumers to carry out a large amount of unplanned buying when discovering delicious or amusing products as they pick up their parcels. Of course, this brings benefits to 7-Eleven.

Finally, what about us, the receivers who have to pick up parcels? The flexibility in time arrangement is certainly an important advantage. If it is inconvenient for a receiver for the moment, he or she could ask the deliverer to deposit the parcel at 7-Eleven and pick it up later. This actually is an excellent solution creating a triple-win result, benefiting all the three parties engaged. Cainiao Post is another example following the same principles, whose extended use of the approaches of community laundry and retail shops actually falls into the same model as S.F. Express.

Apart from the advantages above, there is another thing worth considering in this model—the construction of networking resources: Why can't S.F. run its own pick-up stations to improve its end distribution efficiency? It absolutely can, and does have some pick-up stations of its own. But land and properties in close neighborhood to most customers are usually costly, making it hard for the stations to survive solely on the pick-up business.

Why do we call for cross-organization networking integration? Because, exactly, the resources needed for our organization may be in the hands of others, there's no need for a rebuilding; while, on the other hand, we may also hold resources needed by others. These are the foundation for cross-organization cooperation. For this kind of two-way win–win mindset, its rationality derives from the trade-off between marginal costs and scale effects.

When I was at the University of California, Berkeley as a visiting scholar from 2014 to 2015, I lived in a small town northern to the university, where something interesting happened to me. A friend of mine back in China sent me a parcel by S.F. and I also ordered something on Amazon at that time. The two parcels turned out to be delivered to me by the same person. Please note that this deliverer sent me an S.F. parcel and an Amazon parcel at the same time, but neither of the two companies were his employers. This interesting experience made me wonder how it happened.

Please note, the background of the story was the town I lived in. What does this mean? The population there was small, so the demands for parcel distribution were low. In another word, it was unworthy for S.F. to assign a deliverer to such a place and this was also true for Amazon. As a result, a small local company popped out and integrated all the delivery demands of S.F., Amazon and Walmart together, which was certainly sufficient to support the survival and development of a newly-built small company. This is how the business model of cross-organization cooperation appeared. The aggregation of demands at some timing brings forth new business opportunities or models. We may as well think, are Hive Box Lockers a facility that created demands for aggregation in communities?

Through these cases, I want to discuss with you the following questions: Do we really need to build the resources we need? Do we also hold resources needed by others? This kind of cooperative model is worth being studied—the model of cross-organization networking integration.

3.3 High-Efficiency Networks

Apart from economic feasibility, the efficiency of the network is another important factor that distinguishes most service-providers from others and influences their customer satisfaction.

Amazon is an outstanding representative of high-efficiency networks. It started as an e-bookseller, building its success on supply chains. The founder of Amazon, Jeff Bezos, graduated from Princeton University and holds a degree in electrical engineering and computer science. After working years in financial investment on Wall Street, he moved to Seattle in about 1994 and started his own business—an online bookstore named Amazon. Amazon is definitely not the first online bookstore. Then how did it stand out among all its competitors? It even survived through the Dotcom Bubble Burst in the United States around the year 2000 and developed into the high-tech company with the highest market value in the world.

How did Amazon make a success based on its supply chains in the early days? Its first move was to launch a brand-new service model—an online book fair. What does this mean? The way books are sold in traditional B2C (Business to Customer) model is that, with books stored in the warehouse, the seller, upon receiving an order placed by a customer, picks the ordered books out and posts them to the customer (Bezos had to deliver parcels himself at the post office in the first years of Amazon). But Amazon switched its mentality: Since we now have millions of users buying on our website with their information registered, can we turn them from buyers into sellers? The answer is an absolute yes!

Once the role of users was swapped from buyers to sellers, the whole model of Amazon was reversed. This actually is the business model described in the bestseller *The Long Tail*, as shown in Fig. 3.3.

Suppose that Fig. 3.3 represents the whole book market, with the x-axis showing the categories of books and the y-axis their sales. If we define books with annual

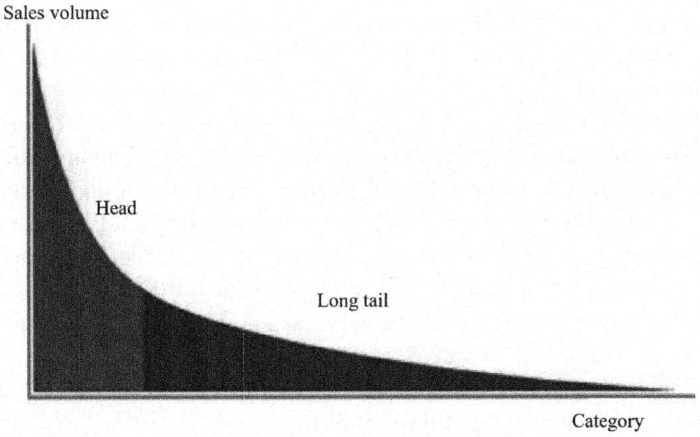

Fig. 3.3 The long tail in book market. *Source* Anderson (2015)

sales exceeding 10,000 copies as bestsellers, the rest, with sales below that, are less popular ones. Now the books are divided into two types. Obviously, physical bookstores tend to sell bestsellers, because obscure books entail huge risks with slow-moving inventories and fully packed bookshelves. Therefore, in the traditional model, booksellers, especially physical ones, offered mostly bestselling books, for fear of the risks caused by the less popular.

However, what does Long Tail Theory reveal to us? Please mind that the less popular books, with low single copy sales, though, altogether consist of a great variety, indicating a huge market space. Who would be able to cover such a huge market? One with operational costs low enough.

Back to the online book fair of Amazon. In the traditional B2C model, books are stored in warehouses of Amazon, while the new online fair model turned Amazon users into sellers on the platform. The books to be sold are now stored on the shelves at the users' home, taking up neither the warehouse nor any funds of Amazon, who just has to take commissions upon transactions. So for Amazon, a transaction is only a record entry, indicating the title and price of the book that the user wants to sell. The mere publishing of one piece of information costs Amazon nothing. Through lowering its operational costs by slashing inventories, Amazon has acquired the ability to take over the long-tail market.

In addition to benefiting Amazon with this long-tail market, such a model has resulted in a very interesting effect. When Amazon provides both popular and less popular books, it becomes an ideal channel for end users to get access to the whole variety of publications. Whenever a consumer wants to buy a book, he or she would try Amazon first. If it is not there on Amazon, it won't be anywhere else. The efficiency improvement brought by such variety is quite attractive to users, and also, is the attraction brought by the long tail.

Around 10 years ago, I wrote an article *A Few Words on the Long Tail of Logistics*. Does the same phenomenon exist in the logistics market? Large-scale factories and mines look very attractive to logistics companies for orders of one large mine will guarantee million tons of freight volume and all the logistics providers need to do is to organize the transport well. But never ignore small and medium-sized clients in the logistics sector. Although their freight volumes are low and unstable, the large amount of them still compose an enormous long-tail market.

Who would be able to cover this long tail of logistics, then? To explore into such a market, one needs low-enough costs and high efficiency in operation. Recent years have seen many crowdsourcing platforms or platforms of non-truck operating common carriers (NTOCC) in the ascendent, for example, KXTX and Full Truck. These platforms are exploring to win over the long-tail market of small and medium-sized logistics business. To extend the discussion a little further, how big is the market space created by logistics demands of individual consumers? Its great potency has been proved by the burgeoning express delivery industry.

So the long tail mentality not only works in publishing, but also in other markets, and Amazon has been a successful forerunner.

Apart from the online book fair, Amazon adopted two more innovative measures to completely take over the long-tail market. One of them is the print-on-demand business. Instead of holding physical copies of some books, Amazon stores its electronic copies in its server and, upon being ordered by a user, prints them with high-speed printers and delivers them to the buyer. We may ask, this would cost a lot and run slowly, right? No need to worry. Print-on-demand offers are not for bestsellers, they are usually obscure ones. When the customers could not find the book anywhere else, they would definitely be willing to pay more and wait longer. Therefore, the print-on-demand service, with conformity to the Long Tail Theory and strategy, is an approach to lower inventories and funds tied up.

The other innovation of Amazon is Kindle, the e-book reader it launched. This mobile device for book reading is terrific since it is connected to the e-library of Amazon through 3G/4G mobile data networks. With such a terminal at hand, users may select books online and have them transferred to this terminal through data networks, rid of all logistics links. This makes one more approach for Amazon's cost reduction.

It is said that Kindle offers an interesting function to American users. As a popular saying in China goes, "Only borrowed books will be read.", we often buy books for a display on the shelf while reading the borrowed ones because there is a time to return them. Kindle developed a mode based on this (which applies only to users in the United States now), in which, if you bought a book from Kindle to put on your e-shelf and your friend borrowed it from you, the book would disappear temporarily and show up in your friend's Kindle, and then return back to yours in two weeks. This software simulation of the book borrowing process is very interesting.

The combination of all the three approaches above consists of Amazon's model innovation on the basis of its supply chains. This new business model helped Amazon lower its costs and take over a brand-new market at one go. Upon succeeding in the book market, Amazon found that this model could be easily extended to other categories, so it almost sells everything today. On the one hand, Amazon is selling fresh food in many American cities. On the other hand, when we still took Amazon as a 2C (to Customer) platform, Amazon has launched the B2B (Business to Business) Amazon Business in 2015 and acquired an annual revenue of USD 10 billion, today.

These two business expansions challenged Amazon with the need to manage a sea of products. As the product categories kept growing, a problem became inevitable: was the picking efficiency of warehouses high enough? Nowadays, the picking capacity of warehouses still composes a core competitiveness for all B2C websites. To put it simply, now that an order is made, how quickly can the warehouse finish picking all the items ordered? In a feature report about an Amazon Fulfillment Center in Phoenix by Sina Tech, we can see the principles behind its system design and the light it sheds.

> Amazon's Phoenix warehouse was put into use in September, 2007, taking an area of over 50,000 m^2, as large as 10 football fields. The conveyors reach a total length of 9.6 km, fulfilling the delivery of hundreds of thousands of orders each day. Among Amazon's 50 global fulfillment centers back then, half were in the United States and the one in Phoenix was for small-sized goods. Firstly, Amazon's purchasing staff would make a purchase order

> in the computer system, then the supplier accepting the order would log on a designated website to make an appointment for delivery. After that, the system would make calculations based on previous distribution of clients' orders and available spaces in the warehouse, and decide on the exact destination for the supplier's delivery, which is the place where the goods are received and stored.

As we may notice, the supplier cannot make a delivery at any time as it wishes after accepting the purchase order. Instead, an appointment has to be made. The landing area familiar to us is often packed with trucks and drivers scrambling to unload goods, behind which is a tremendous waste of resources. Why do appointments have to be made for delivery and calculations are needed to determine where the goods to be placed? These are the kernel of Amazon's logistic model and worth a good considering, since, for warehouses of small-sized goods, the speed of order fulfillment is an important index.

This can be illustrated with an order placed on Amazon's website. A customer who buys a laptop would likely order a mobile mouse with it. If the laptop and the mouse come from different suppliers, they would be delivered by two separate trucks. Supposing the laptop supplier is asked to deliver it to the southernmost part of the warehouse while the mouse supplier delivers to the northern corner, you may imagine how much waste would occur when the picker has to find them from two far ends of the warehouse to fulfill this order. Now we'd understand the reason for Amazon to require delivery appointments and calculation for storage locations. The key is to save the picking time in the warehouse. To minimize the time spent on items picking upon receiving orders is Amazon's core objective and what the system calculation is for.

Loading docks at the warehouse receive goods 24-h. Staff open the cases and scan barcodes of goods to have them registered into the Amazon system. All scanned items will be placed on a blue table for stowing and the stowers will scan them for the second time, put in their carts and place them on shelves in hours. Once the items are on the shelf, users can see and buy them on the Amazon website.

Here comes the interesting part. Amazon adopts a unique method of random stow, in which people move but goods don't. Stowers shelve the items randomly wherever they see empty space as they walk, and then scan them into the computer system. The advantage of this method is to shorten the travel distance for pickers.

Here is a noticeable question: What keeps the items from being messed up in random stow? In fact, each slot bears a barcode in the system. When putting an item in a slot, the stower just has to scan their barcodes so that the system matches them clearly. Then why do they put it anywhere empty? Obviously, this is the quickest way for stowing. For stowers, the travel distance is minimized and they can soon have the job done by just putting things into the nearest empty slots. So here, we see the first important principle in the design of a logistics service system—unnecessary travel of people means huge waste, so it should be avoided with all efforts. Therefore, the essential goal of random stow is to shorten the process and make workers travel less.

Once all items are shelved randomly, they are ready for picking upon being ordered. The powerful system of Amazon will log the locations of all randomly placed items and calculate the shortest pick itineraries based on the items included in orders: The system will assign several orders to a picker and plan an optimal itinerary for him. This picker works with no paper but a handheld terminal. After this picker scans one picked item, the terminal will direct him the location of the next item. He doesn't even need to think about the information of the order.

Why does the system assign those specific orders to the picker? It must be that in the system's calculation, his travel distance for picking items in those orders is the shortest. In addition, the picker doesn't have to worry about the picking sequence, because it would be shown on the handheld terminal. Which slot first and which next, no experience is needed for determination, it is all calculated by computer, and the essence of which is to shorten the picking distance.

Similar consideration is often found in the design of background operating systems of services, whereby manual judgment and memorizing are minimized and, with the judgment task completed by the computer system, workers need only to finish the manual operation.

In addition, in the picking process at warehouses of small-sized goods, the system divides orders into two kinds: the kind with a single item and the kind with multiple items, and has them packed on different conveyor lines. Let's think about it. Which would be easier when single-item orders and multiple-item orders get onto the packaging lines? The answer seems to be the single-item ones since one item fulfils one order and is ready for packaging right away. However, for orders with multiple items, the packer can only start work after all the items are collected.

So the two kinds of orders differ in difficulty for subsequent operations. That leads to the second important principle in system design (not limited to logistics systems): Never mix simple procedures with complex ones, otherwise the capacity is wasted. This principle is quite significant, and has been sufficiently proven by my system design practice.

My team and I designed a transfer center for a delivery company in 2006. Before we started, it was a small center with over ten pickers operating manually to pick and sort 1000 parcels per day. In our design, we added a simple semi-automatic conveyor line and carried out an all-round revision to the procedures, information system and layout so that the handling volume reached 15,000 parcels, 15 times higher than before, with no single person added. The first important thing we did was to optimize the system by separating the mixed handling of parcels and documents. Under their old mode, pickers had to hold both documents and all kinds of parcels, and walk to different locations for picking and sortation. In our optimized plan, document pouches were singled out and stored in letter boxes, while all parcels were put on the conveyor for picking. This one optimization has resulted in a great improvement in the operation efficiency of the whole system. Therefore, separating simple procedures from complex ones is an important approach towards efficiency improvement.

Back to Amazon's Phoenix Fulfillment Center, in following procedures, the picker will fetch items for single-item orders according to the pick itinerary calculated by the system and transfer them to the packaging line once the cart is full. The staff at the packaging table will then scan an item, find the suitable package automatically selected by the system according to registered information on its size and weight, finish packing, taping and labeling, and then put the parcel onto the conveyor.

Please note, here, the selection of the suitable package is carried out by the system automatically according to the registered size and weight of the item. When we receive parcels delivered by e-businesses in our daily life, the embarrassment of finding a small item in a big container happens sometimes, not only resulting in a waste of resources by overpacking, but more importantly, taking up too much space in subsequent logistical links. But in an Amazon warehouse, workers don't even need to determine the size of package to be used, since the system knows the sizes and weights of items to be contained and will recommend the suitable package directly. This, again, is an embodiment of the idea of "No need for staff to decide".

The picking procedures of multiple-item orders start with a picking cart packed with randomly placed items. The shelf in front of the packer are divided into slots with adjustable volumes and for each item scanned, the system will designate a slot for it to be put in, so that items within the same order are put together. Then, the system will give a package recommendation based on the lengths and widths of all items, attach it to the order and deliver to the conveyor. The packer sitting in front of the slotted shelf, upon scanning every item, will see a slot lighted, indicating that this is the slot for the item. In the end, when all the items in the cart are scanned and well placed, each slot contains items for one order, with a corresponding package selected by the system. The sorter will then finish the packing and subsequent work at the delivery area. Apparently, the procedures for multiple-item orders are more complicated than those of single-item ones.

Now, an interesting thing again. All parcels will go through a special weighing procedure on the conveyor, whose aim is to check, are the contents within the parcel things we need. How do we know items in a packed parcel are exactly those ordered by the customer? Normally, we have to unpack it for an inspection, but for spot checks only, since if all the parcels are opened for inspection, it makes no sense to pack them before.

So, the traditional inspection is based on random selection, while a weighing device on the conveyor can check the weight of each parcel. As the system already knows the weight of all items within it, including the weight of the package, the total weight of the parcel is clear. Any deviation would point to a problem in picking, so the abnormal parcels will be kicked off to another line for manual operation, with all normal parcels conveyed to next procedures. A design thinking for the automation of manufacturing or logistics systems is revealed here: automatic handling for normal procedures and manual operation for abnormal ones.

Finally, the conveyor brings all eligible parcels to the delivery area so that sorters can assign them to different delivery vehicles according to order information and have them delivered to users at the time expected.

Now that the full process at Amazon's Phoenix Fulfillment Center is introduced, there are three more issues to be explored.

- ***Acquiring accurate data as driven by data-based decision-making process***

There is a premise supporting all the practice from automatic recommendation on packaging to quality assurance carried out by a weighing device: the accuracy of data. If they do not hold complete information and data of all items, or the data is inaccurate, the whole system would be prone to mistakes or would even crash down. So actually, this reminds us of the necessity to informationize our enterprises. However, our businessmen often get it wrong by pinning the hope of improving management on informationization. This is a problematic way of thinking.

The right way is that we have to, firstly, make up a clear mind about the design for management improvement, and then have them realized through information-based approaches. Many companies wish to make their management better through simply introducing some computer software, but the software may just not fit them. Looking around outstanding enterprises in the world, we'd see they all had clear management ideas first and then put them into practice with the help of software.

In other words, for companies complaining about the inaccuracy and uselessness of data, my suggestion is that please ask ourselves first: are we really using these data to make decisions? This probably is the more essential question. We used to make system design for a logistics company and collected a pile of paper waybills there, to check the time of receipt of their orders. However, the time filled in all the bills was 4.00 p.m., obviously unreasonable. Simply blaming the expressmen would make no sense and our investigation showed that this information on receipt time had never been analyzed, not to mention being used for decision-making. If the managers had no plan to use the data, the whole organization wouldn't be motivated to ensure their accuracy.

Accordingly, the usefulness of data does not depend on their accuracy. Instead, the managers play the determinant role in the first place. If they want to use the data in support of decision making, they have to be resolved and spend great efforts on data acquisition, including adopting auxiliary digital devices like handheld terminals.

- ***Designating a specific area for best-selling products and handling simple procedures in a simple way***

Amazon has an area designated for best-selling products. These products, such as Amazon's Kindle, are high in sales volume and fast in turnover, and therefore are placed separately.

The whole area is devoted solely to best-selling products, even rid of traditional shelving and picking procedures. Think about this. It actually conforms to an important principle of system design mentioned above: Never mix simple procedures with complex ones. Since best-selling products go quickly, and often as single-item orders, if shelved, they have to be picked out just minutes later, and go through all the procedures that bring a waste of system capacity. This reminds us to think about the management of our own service systems (including systems for universal use): which parts can be fulfilled through simple procedures—it is quite necessary to single them out and deal with separately.

- ***Creating expandable system capacities***

There is another interesting area in the Amazon warehouse, where many machines are covered by plastic sheets temporarily, to be used at peak times like the New Year, Christmas and other festivals. This practice is also seen in the passenger rail service system in China. During the Spring Festival travel rush, we'd see Regular speed green trains widely used 20 years ago bearing "Special Extra" plates shuffle to carry passengers back home. The China Railway and Amazon are using the same coping strategy. Actually, it is the thing to be considered in all system design in the broad sense—how to cope with the varying service demands at high peaks and low ebbs. It does not mean that the daily operation capacity should be enlarged to easily handle peak demands, which would definitely be a huge waste. Peak demands must be handled with special measures, instead of the normal service capacity.

This is the typical coping strategy for demands at peak and ebb in the management of service systems.

Werner Vogels, the CTO (Chief Technology Officer) and Vice President of Amazon once said, many people thought that Amazon was an online business, but behind it are huge complex systems, whose intelligent operations have made shopping experience on Amazon more convenient and considerate, which is also the result of Amazon's continuous efforts in innovation and optimization. As we noticed, in the system design of the Phoenix center, which orders should be assigned to which pickers are all results of calculation of the computer system. It essentially shortens the travel distance of people and ensures the picking efficiency at the Amazon warehouse.

Now, can we move faster? The Kiva Systems[1] must be mentioned here—it is Amazon's smart warehousing department now.

Years ago, Kiva had made its efficiency 2–4 times higher than in the traditional pick mode. What is the innovative principle that inspires them to handle items with walking robots? In the Phoenix warehouse mentioned above, Amazon's computer system keeps optimizing to reduce the travel of human staff since that means a huge waste. What could be the end of this reduction? Well, humans won't need to walk. The core idea of the Kiva Systems is that goods move while people don't. In the past, it was the other way around since the shelves were fixed and only people were movable. Now the shelves are moving instead, being a typical result of reverse thinking.

In addition to simply thinking reversely, Kiva Systems offers infinite flexibility, which poses great challenges to Operations Research. Imagine a shelf in the robotic warehouse travelling from Location A to a picker. Where will it go when the picking is finished? Returning to Location A? Obviously no, it can just go to the next picker or move to Location B, or even rest in the corner of the warehouse.

That is, for all shelves and robots, people can decide where they should go, at what time, through what itinerary and where to go next. But, with hundreds of thousands of robots walking in a warehouse, their dispatch would be extremely challenging when we want to improve the efficiency. Also, the distribution of orders has to be considered, along with the queuing of robots and other problems. These are why the Kiva department at Amazon has employed a great many algorithm engineers to keep optimizing their algorithm. Many Chinese companies are also capable of making similar warehousing robots (e.g., Geek + , Huaheng, etc.), but the difficulty is not in the mechanical part, it is the dispatching and control system, which pose great challenge but also contain great potential.

After being efficiently picked and packed all the way through the Phoenix Fulfillment Center to robotic warehousing systems like Kiva, the ordered parcels are now loaded on trucks for delivery. How can the trucks deliver faster? Or how can the parcels arrive at the users' hands more quickly after leaving the warehouse? We'll have to mention Amazon's drone delivery here.

[1] The company was founded in January 2003 and acquired by Amazon in March 2012 at the price of USD 775 million.

Several years ago, a professor from Massachusetts Institute of Technology came to Tsinghua University for a conference held by the Department of Industrial Engineering. Seeing that a colleague of mine ordered something on JD.com and received the parcel in the same afternoon, he was surprised and said that the e-commerce and delivery business in America was a generation behind China since they'd never deliver so fast. Not long after that, Amazon launched its Prime Air drone delivery service. It is said that in testing, the shortest delivery time was 12 min, from ordering to receiving the parcel by the user in Manhattan. Recently, Amazon even put forward the idea of launching mega-drones to serve as the "motherships" of its drones, turning urban delivery services into scenes in a sci-fi film.

How much further will e-commerce go if such a model is well promoted? Nevertheless, Amazon has not yet acquired the approval from the Federal Aviation Administration (FAA) for aerial operation. For one reason, flying parcels overhead do look a bit "terrifying" to citizens, with many safety problems to be solved. For another, what if someone intercepts any parcel maliciously? These are all things to be considered before the commercialization of any business model.

Of course, technology should depend on the needs of people and business—this is an important logic driving any service innovation. Drone delivery has already demonstrated unique advantages in some scenarios: skies are open to drones in island areas in New Zealand and Northern Europe, which are very ideal application scenarios. Among islands with low demand densities for parcels, the shipping efficiency is also bad so that transportation by ship barely forms any scale effect. But a drone can soon finish delivering a parcel. Presently, S.F. Express is also testing drone delivery. In mountainous areas of southwestern China, roads are often blocked. Therefore, drones can deliver S.F. parcels easier to their destinations, as compared with trucks. JD.com also has drones, but they are used only for dispatch among warehouses for now.

Accordingly, we may conclude a rule based on similar technological applications: technology serves value creation; we have to clearly know the values to be created first, and then find appropriate technologies to realize them. If the technology is there, we can take it and use it; but if it is not there or immature, we'll have developed some. Taking the drones of Amazon as an example, the values they serve are to accelerate the delivery of parcels. Once we are sure that trucks can't be faster, we'd naturally consider using drones.

As for innovation, there are more we can learn from Amazon, including some of its intelligent service design. For example, Amazon launched the function of "1-Click Ordering" on its website very early. When we shop on other websites, after clicking "checkout", we still have to confirm the address for delivery, payment method, invoice information, do we need a gift wrapping and is there any promo code before finishing the ordering process. What is Amazon's logic? Most of the time, the shopper has a default address and default credit card, which do not change frequently. As a member of Amazon, you'd store such default information to the website. If you do not plan to change your address or card information for this order, you can simply use the "1-Click" button on the right side of the webpage to finish ordering right away, which means a large amount of time saved for the user. Statistics show that this "1-Click" function has brought Amazon 5% additional revenues, creating annual earnings of nearly USD 2.4 billion.

Now that the "1-Click Ordering" has become a mature function of Amazon, the latest version of it is worth more consideration—Amazon Dash Buttons. For instance, an external button bearing the trademark symbol of Tide is added to a washing machine. A customer, finding that the detergent is running out when washing clothes, needs only to press the button and a Tide product will be shipped to the customer's home right away. This is another version of Amazon's "1-Click Ordering". Why is it so intriguing? Firstly, why must the Dash Button be installed on the washing machine? Because the time you wash clothes is when you realize the detergent is running low—also the moment you get the strongest motive for detergent shopping. Amazon's underlying logic is to offer consumers a barrier-free solution to help them finish the purchase at the peak of their shopping motive.

Let's look at the usual way we buy detergent. Firstly, when someone finds that the detergent is running out, he has to keep this in mind, to buy it next time he shops in a supermarket. Or he can open a mobile application like JD Supermarket and Tmall Supermarket, find a product in the exact brand and specifications he needs, click "checkout", confirm the address and pay for it. Such a process takes long and bears a risk of being forgotten. Instead, Amazon offers a barrier-free solution when the customer needs it most, one click solves all problems. It is not difficult technologically, though, this typical application of IoT is a smart home technology connected to a button in the consumer's home through Wi-Fi. All the system needs is his Amazon account information, while the specification of detergent is directly associated to the washing machine.

You may ask, what if my kid fiddles with the button? It is easy to imagine, if this happens frequently, the next generation of Dash Buttons would feature fingerprint ID. In other words, technology must serve the creation of values, so we have to firstly figure out what are the problems we want to fix and then find the appropriate technology for assistance.

Similar products appear in China, too. For example, external buttons are installed to water dispensers, allowing users to call for barreled water delivery with one press. No phone call or online shopping is needed. Its working principle is exactly the same as Amazon Dash Buttons. There are more products offering this function, not only washing machines, but also printers. With one press on the button installed on a printer, paper for replenishing would be on its way to the office. Solutions like this can be adopted to many scenarios, but the key questions are still: What are the values you want to create? What kinds of experience do you plan to bring to your customers? Are the implementation costs low enough?

Among the many imitators of Amazon, no one has ever transcended it, because Amazon never stops innovating and this is also an important reason why its market value is growing. As its founder Bezos once said, a developed company still has to carry on adventuring and innovating. Blindly following others and repeating existing successful practices are no options. Instead, sound self-positioning is the way towards opportunities. Thanks to this tenet, Amazon's services are always one to two years ahead of its competitors', and Amazon Web Services (AWS) even holds a 5 years' lead.

Another top seller of Amazon in recent years is its smart speaker named Amazon Echo, which used to hold 70% of U.S. consumer market share in its category, with Google Home taking 20% and Apple HomePod and other products sharing the rest 10%. In China, we also have many brands of smart speakers, featuring voice interaction and audio play functions.

However, Amazon Echo Show is equipped with a camera and a display, so that it can be used for video calls, as a digital picture frame, and as a remote monitor when there is no one home. The user can control Echo Show by voice to monitor his/her home through the camera. The user can also ask it to play certain types of music, in the meantime of which, it can recognize the user's voice by the built-in Automatic Speech Recognition (ASR) technology and figure out the meaning of the user's speech. Of course, all these features need the support of many patented technologies.

But, in addition to general functions like video calls, digital picture frame, video play and voice command, its main responsibility is to attract potential users for Amazon Prime, the premium paid subscription service of Amazon. The Prime membership offers subscribers additional discounts and delivery privileges, and is also requisite for buying an Echo speaker. An Echo costs only over 100 dollars, making it very clear that Amazon does not expect to make profits by selling hardware. Instead, the subscription fees of Amazon Prime are its major source of income. So this interesting hardware is used to attract service subscribers, and therefore, serve a larger ecosystem. This is what we should learn from.

The latest development of smart speakers has made them the "control center" of all kinds of smart appliances at home, performing like a housekeeper of the smart home. Amazon's virtual assistant Alexa is the first consumer-grade smart home platform that enables control over 20,000 smart appliances via Amazon Echo. Of course, all these appliances can be bought on Amazon. In comparison, the platform of Google Assistant, accessed through Google Home, supports only slightly over 5000 smart home devices, which is still more than Apple's HomeKit, accessed through HomePod with an inbuilt Siri. These are the "larger ecosystems" mentioned earlier.

In 2017, Amazon bought America's most famous organic food seller, Whole Foods Market, and led to a slump in the stock price of Walmart, because this march into physical markets marked that the combination of Amazon's online and offline resources would bring it a stronger competitive power. Likewise, Alibaba's joining into Intime, RT-Mart and other department stores as their shareholders were also moves to enter the offline market. The FreshHema supermarkets familiar to us is a striking example.

But what does Amazon's offline retailing have to do with Echo speakers? The future life in Amazon's plan may be like this: You just have to stay in your bed and speak to your Echo, "I'm thirsty. Give me a bottle of water". The supermarket or convenience store in your neighborhood would send you the water automatically. The 1-Click Ordering mentioned above still needs a click. But now with your smart speaker interlinked to offline retailers, all you have to do is lie in your bed and say the words.

That is to say, to satisfy people's demands of "staying lazy" is an important trend for innovation. It reminds me of a washing machine invented by Japanese people, which, in addition to the not-novel drying function of conventional washing machines, offers more by folding the dried clothes and putting them neatly in wardrobes. This is definitely glad tidings for housewives. There are more products following this innovative trend, bringing people more convenience. Back to the idea I keep repeating, "technology must serve to create the experience you want to bring to your customers"—that is the core principle.

Of course, technological advance, from another perspective, is an important driver for service efficiency improvement, which makes many unprecedented models possible today.

First of all, technological advance has facilitated the growth of cloud computing and the drop in bandwidth costs. A large number of business scenarios are transferring towards cloud technology in the future, and will soon overthrow some existing models. Not only Netflix has totally transformed itself from a DVD rental company into an online video provider, subscription services launched recently, like Google's Stadia and Apple Arcade, have raised the curtain of the battle between cloud gaming and Sony's and Nintendo's console games and high-end PC games. Faced with opportunities flooding this new market, Amazon and Microsoft, old players in the arena of cloud services, are also itching to join the fight with their upcoming cloud gaming products.

For sure, services based on cloud-centered storage methods points only one direction, among others. According to Gartner's prediction, as digital business and IoT keep developing, 75% of enterprise-generated data will be created and processed in edge scenarios outside a traditional centralized cloud or data center by 2022, compared with 10% in 2018. The common development of edge computing, 5G, cloud computing and other technologies will result in significant changes in micro service experience, with a series of smart algorithms sophisticatedly integrated into people's lives. To put it another way, cloud services and edge computing are two mutually supplementary gems casting beautiful reflections on each other since they are both infrastructure transformations towards leaner quick-response service systems whose essential goals are still to provide users with experience they have never had before.

Secondly, with the popularity of ultimate customization in services, the precise and efficient operation in "multi-category and small-batch" scenarios becomes highly challenging in terms of intensity and difficulty. To illustrate with an example, Dig Inn, a chain restaurant brand in New York, allows its online guests to order from a selection of three bases (greens or one of two grains), 10 sides and six proteins for a meal and that means 810 different combinations. How can they pack the right food into the right boxes when all the orders flood in during peak hours? How to maintain different temperatures for different food so that they won't be influenced by the room temperature? All are great challenges for management. Consequently, special custom software has become needed. Online food ordering systems like ChowNow appeared, along with other restaurant-empowering software providers. The Japanese leader in the bento box industry, Tamagoya, uses another way to tackle difficulties in customization. They deliver, with the bento boxes, paper menus for the next week so that ingredients preparation and food distribution can be done precisely. A Tamagoya store hit a miracle record of selling 130,000 boxes in one day.

Another case is Meituan, a Chinese internet retail company. Since its establishment in 2010, Meituan has been continuously promoting the digital upgrading of both service retail and commodity retail. To enhance delivery efficiency and provide a better working experience for its couriers, known colloquially as "riders", the company's food delivery service has been persistently refining its algorithms, allowing riders to enjoy more reasonable and relaxed delivery schedules. Moreover, Meituan publicly disclosed the "estimated delivery time" algorithm, and experimentally changed the estimated delivery time display from a specific point of time to an extended time period.

The food delivery scenarios are complex and variable, with encounters with exceptional circumstances being one of the main reasons for insufficient delivery time for riders. Addressing this issue, Meituan solicited suggestions for rule improvements from all sectors of society, including riders, traffic police, and experts, and proactively adjusted its algorithms. Starting from the entirety of the riders' delivery process, the exceptional scenario factor is integrated into the time algorithm mechanism, dynamically adjusting delivery durations. Furthermore, targeted optimization pilot tests of delivery rules have been conducted in various aspects, such as dispatch mechanisms, delivery times, and delivery subsidies, especially for the three categories of "large orders" characterized by "heavy weight, large volume, and high value". After implementing the new delivery rules, exceptional scenarios caused by rider delays and poor reviews decreased by 52%, the user complaint rate dropped by 67%, and the experiences of both users and delivery personnel were significantly improved.

"High efficiency" has become a sector spined off from the value chain. Obviously, high efficiency would not be easily achieved with some software. It is small wonder that production lines are set in kitchens solely for delivery (e.g., in an American fast food salad chain, Sweetgreen) and pizzas are made in running trucks on their way to customers' homes (e.g., by Zume Pizza, although experienced other technical difficulties later on). Therefore, the science of Industrial Engineering, which was born in the manufacturing sector, is now marching into the service sector in an all-round way, so you can find practices of improving service efficiency and quality through methods of Operations Research and Lean Management everywhere.

3.4 Online or Offline?

The wrestle between online and offline business has fueled much attention. In China, online platforms have successfully "created" shopping festivals like "Double 11" (on November 11) and "6.18" (on June 18) and seriously stricken offline physical stores. However, the offline stores have not yet disappeared today.

If the two are compared, what are the advantages of online retailing? The most prominent one is the convenience and ease for shoppers to make orders at any time. Second, online goods are cheaper, but why? Because no physical room or even salespeople are needed for an online store. The third advantage is the rich options available to customers. A conventional physical store can only accommodate limited items, so customers have to shop around many stores to get enough choices.

However, the web pages of Tmall Supermarket are developing towards precise categorization, broad coverage and personalized recommendation, by putting categories on the left side of the page and a search box on the upper-right corner. The fostering of real experience is rather slow.

What keeps physical stores from vanishing under such huge strikes? What are their advantages? The most important one is the better shopping experience they offer. In a physical store, you can touch the items with your own hands, see if they fit you after trying on and then determine whether to buy or not. That is the superiority of physical stores. This comparison of advantages of online and offline channels can help us predict their development trends better.

In the U.S., online bookstores like Amazon have left fine traditional bookstores, such as Barnes & Noble, in great difficulties for operation. If Barnes & Noble opens its own online store like Amazon, which it actually did, its customers may get their ordered books sooner than using other platforms. Why? Because if a Barnes & Noble store in the customer's neighborhood happens to have those books, it can deliver them directly to him or her, which works a lot faster than delivering from a central warehouse of Amazon.

To sum up, online and offline channels are doomed to move towards and integrate with each other. The clear distinction used to divide them into absolutely different camps will no longer exist. Therefore, we may discuss them in three kinds of models: offline towards online, online-offline integration and online towards offline.

3.4.1 Offline Towards Online

Offline business wins by the substantiality and experience it provides. Is there any way to enrich the offline experience with abundant online information? The advance of technology has brought us new opportunities for breakthroughs.

The first case is Google Glass. In spite of its failure to step out of Google, the R&D team of Google Glass still carries on their work. Right now, Microsoft, HTC and other companies have also joined in the development of smart glasses, since they are the most typical application of Augmented Reality (AR) technology, which is especially favored by venture capitals in recent years.

What does AR do? Supposing we are passing by a restaurant we have never been to, how do we know should we try it or not? The usual way in China is to check in the restaurant review application (for example, Dianping) on our mobile phone to see the ratings, reviews and recommendations of the restaurant, and make decisions afterwards. It has become a habit of normal people. When I traveled in South Korea and stood in front of a restaurant, I did the same thing with Dianping but found nothing there. I was suddenly at a loss. That was the influence this habit had on me. Now, with the help of AR technology on devices like Google Glass, we won't need to take so much trouble. When we find a restaurant, the glasses would recognize it with the camera, capture information similar to those provided by Dianping and display them in front of our eyes. That is to say, when we see the restaurant for real, the virtual information about it is also presented to us through the glasses, including people's ratings and recommendations. It sounds like some fancy power owned by robots in sci-fi films—information-bearing digits are displayed in front of them whenever they see something. Actually, this is AR: grabbing information from online sources to augment our offline perception and experience.

Another important technology that may revolutionize services around us is the Indoor Positioning System (IPS), represented by Apple's iBeacon, as shown in Fig. 3.4. The current Global Positioning System (GPS) is used mainly for outdoor positioning, for its indoor performance is far from people's expectations. AutoNavi in China is also developing the technology for indoor positioning. The mainstream IPSs today are based on Bluetooth or Wi-Fi connection. The core of such technology is a chip in the mobile phone that communicates directly with receivers, rid of the interference of any substance, such as a wall or pillar.

The IPS technology can greatly improve the experience in offline stores. Without it, a retail store or eatery has to put a greeter at the door so that guests can be ushered in. Otherwise, people in the store wouldn't know that somebody is passing by, not to mention what this person likes, Sichuan cuisine or Japanese food.

Now that an IPS is there, as long as your mobile phone has the Wi-Fi switched on, the stores you pass by could communicate with you, send you customized advertising, learn about your preferences, and provide pertinent discounts to attract you to walk in. This is an inevitable stage of intellectualization the IPS technology will go through

Fig. 3.4 iBeacon positioning technology. *Source* http://sohu.com/a/63665578_120731

in the future, enabling offline stores to interact with customers in information-based approaches, instead of any physical contact. This is a typical scenario where offline business is approaching towards online sources. Information online can be used by physical stores offline to provide precise services and augmented experience. This is of great importance.

A railway station is another more realistic scenario for application, where infrequent visitors will find themselves confused about "where am I? where's the person supposed to meet me?". Especially in large multi-storey composite buildings like Shanghai Hongqiao Railway Station and Beijing South Railway Station, it is even difficult for passengers to figure out which floors they and their pickers-up are on. Now, mobile applications like WeChat allow us to send our positions so that we can find each other, but this only works if we are on the same floor, outdoors. The problem in railway stations cannot be figured out. The IPS technology plays a critical role in such a scenario.

Hence, indoor positioning and navigation is, same as AR, a critical technology that enables offline entities to approach online resources.

At first glance, Fig. 3.5 looks like a window by a beautiful coastline to us. The exquisite scenery of rolling tides and euphonic waves seems as if live-action alongside California State Route 1. But, in fact, this is a display developed by Haier that resembles a window. If such a "window" is installed on a wall of a restaurant, with a table put beside it, the guests would feel like eating nearby California State Route 1. If they prefer ancient buildings over a sea view, the site can be changed into Piazza di Spagna in Rome or the night view at Eiffel Tower in Paris.

Fig. 3.5 A Haier display

This technology belongs to "Ubiquitous Display", which is also used to improve offline experience. All the information comes from online, meaning that online information is used to boost offline experience via these devices.

3.4.2 Online-Offline Integration

The second type of solutions integrate online and offline resources.

This is what Chinese retail enterprises Suning has been doing. Through combining Suning.com and offline stores of Suning, its physical stores have been transformed into experience centers. Consumers can choose products in a physical store and make orders on Suning.com. I once went to a Suning store to buy an air purifier on a smoggy day in Beijing, but when I finished choosing and was checking out, the shop assistant told me that I couldn't take it away since they didn't have any inventory at the store, so I had to order it online and wait for the delivery. Suning no longer keeps inventories in its physical stores, which, instead, only function as experience centers for customers. All the orders have to be placed online. This is a novel model that aligns prices and synchronizes paces online and offline.

Similarly, an American apparel brand, Bonobos, has also turned its offline stores completely into "fitting rooms" and named them as Guideshops, where customers make appointments with "guides" and get one-on-one services. Clothes in all sizes are provided for fitting but cannot be bought in stores. All orders have to be made and finished online. According to its founder, Andy Dunn, customers who had visited the "fitting rooms" would buy 75% more, compared with those who hadn't, and the paramount reason for this was the humanized services and experience they couldn't enjoy in the virtual world online.

Whether a simple online-offline combination can result in efficient sales boosts in all kinds of scenarios still remains to be seen, of course. Suning used to find itself trapped in the dilemma between online and offline business when it first started this model: the online shopping grew slower than expected and the half-year profits saw a 20–30% year-on-year drop.

Since its inception, blockchain technology, as a foundational set of technologies, has provided a robust technical support for various application services at the application layer. As is widely known, the current popular Web3.0 is developing vigorously in various fields. Many star projects have emerged in subsectors such as decentralized finance (DeFi), GameFi, and the Metaverse.

Some companies in China have made commendable attempts in digital marketing for enterprises. An excellent case is the innovative product from Jiaodong Supply Chain Management Service Co., Ltd., the 'NFT-based Digital Marketing Platform—"DM Platform". It is positioned as an "enterprise-level, ready-to-use digital marketing SaaS platform". The product, through its digital marketing platform, assists enterprises by integrating online and offline digital artworks and combining tangible with virtual assets, using these novel marketing techniques to drive consumer upgrades, enhance brands' premium value, strengthen the loyalty of younger customers, and reduce both the cost of customer acquisition and management for businesses.

The "DM Platform" integrates blockchain digital artwork technology, empowering existing business scenarios of enterprises and achieving an organic combination of offline scenes with the digital ecosystem. For instance, enterprises can leverage 3D technology or animation design to present their offline products in digital formats. Customers, when attracted to these virtual products, may develop a purchasing intent and impulse, thereby boosting the sales of the enterprise's physical products. Moreover, these virtual digital products are stored in the customer's virtual wallet, allowing them to access, appreciate, showcase, and even interact with these digital products anytime through an app on their mobile phones. Through the "DM Platform", enterprises can more efficiently showcase their digitalized products and services to customers, enhancing brand recognition and increasing sales. The famous MICHELIN vegetarian restaurant in China, Vege Wonder, successfully used the "DM Platform" to combine its annual marketing campaign with traditional Chinese paintings from Rong Bao Zhai. Customers had the opportunity to purchase digital collections of the masters' paintings online while enjoying the delightful experience of the MICHELIN restaurant's dishes. The campaign received a strong and positive response from customers. This also attests to the importance of blockchain technology in various application service sectors. It is believed that as various scenarios are further explored and applied, blockchain technology will surely provide support in even more industries.

3.4.3 Online Towards Offline

As mentioned, online channels are short in experience, then how can we make them as authentic as offline?

For this, an American game, *Second Life*, gives a good example. In this game, players can construct cities, build their own houses and make furniture, and decide the clothes their avatars wear—all contents in life can be defined according to their preferences so that they can live in a world they like. That's why the game is named as "Second Life". It has more than 36 million registered users and, by the end of 2017, there were still 600,000 active users "living" in the game, making it like a small city.

As the number of users reached a certain degree, interesting things happened: Toyota opened a 4S shop in the game, where avatars could try driving their latest models! Researchers from the University of Hawaii even "built" a city there, and designed traffic lights on roads to collect information on driving behaviors of the avatars for their study in real life. Traffic scholars are also studying in this virtual platform. This is what Virtual Reality (VR), another domain that highly attracts venture capitals in recent years, in addition to AR, can do. VR is an excellent approach for online platforms to learn from offline business and improve user experience, and on the other hand, prove their commercial values.

The Chinese E-commerce company, JingDong (JD), has a branch company named JD Home. It has launched a cloud design platform called "JingDong Designer". By leveraging VR model rooms and Dongdong intelligent design tools, they have constructed a digital and scenario-based system ecology centered around design in the whole chain. The aim is to bridge the gap between consumers and professional service personnel, establish a complete service process, achieve precise matching between products and consumer needs, and ensure the delivery results meet the consumers' expectations. JingDong Designer creates VR showrooms with different styles, using immersive scenario experiences to assist users in their purchase decisions. For consumers who are unsure of what they want, they can also use the AI design tool to generate customized design solutions with just a few clicks.

My own smart service lab made similar R&D attempts in 2012. As shown in Fig. 3.6, on the left and right sides of the first picture were two students of mine, who were, in their respective dormitories, each looking into a Kinect camera of Microsoft X-box, connected to a screen. As they walked in front of the cameras in dormitories, their avatars shopped together in a virtual mall in the screen. They could talk to each other via voice call, to exchange opinions on a product. Usually, when people shop online by phone or computer, they are pretty lonely since they have to look through and pick virtual products alone. But when buying things offline, they'd often go with friends, listen to their opinions or catch up on each other, making offline shopping an interesting social experience. So we tried to simulate the experience and scenario of offline shopping in this way.

The interesting exchange of words among friends in offline shopping promotes consumption significantly. Our study allowed two physically separated real people to shop together on a virtual platform, so that the social experience provided by offline shopping was simulated. The site could be changed as the users wish. If you do not feel like shopping in a mall in Beijing, it can be changed into Galeries Lafayette in Paris.

Then in the second picture in Fig. 3.6, the boy was walking in the virtual mall and saw an iPhone. He could pick it up and rotate for 360° to check all the details. With icons on the right side representing his friends, he just had to throw the "phone" to any one of them, a real iPhone would be on the road towards this friend's home. This

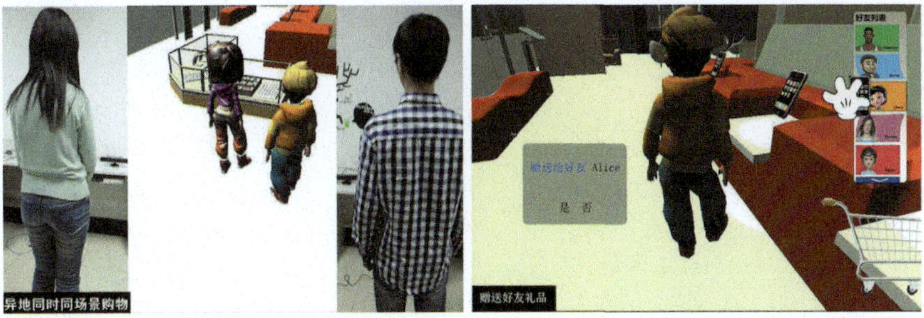

Fig. 3.6 Shopping in a virtual mall

is a simulation of sending a gift to your friend offline. These were quite interesting and pioneering attempts back in 2012. Soon after we presented them in an event for scientific and technological innovation of college students, a product manager of IBM found us and said they wanted to commercialize this idea as soon as possible. He told us that their client, a leader in the household appliance market, was very fond of this design, hoping to use it to enable users to shop around furniture stores in this way online. This example fleshes out how VR helps offer offline-like shopping experience to online customers.

Be it online efforts to approach offline experience, or accessing online resources in offline business, they are both parts of online-offline integration in the broad sense. With all advantages combined, the power would become impressive. The smart retailing department of Tencent has committed to packing resources in seven major business sectors, namely, WeChat Official Accounts, WeChat Pay, WeChat Applets, Tencent Cloud, social advertising, Enterprise WeChat and pan-entertainment IPs, into a "toolkit", to empower traditional retailing. For example, when Carrefour launched its first Le Marche Smart Store in Shanghai, May, 2018, consumers' enthusiasm went far beyond their expectation, and rewarded them a sales performance 40% higher than expected. The credit belonged to the adoption of Tencent's smart retail toolkit, including "face ID payment", "hype through interaction with IPs" and other features. It can be predicted that the profound fusion of social experience and retail practices, as supplemented by fitting AI and technologies of Operations Research into service procedures, will truly lead the brand-new experiences provided by seamless online-offline integration. In view of this, "new retail" has just made its debut.

Reference

Anderson, C. (2015). *The long tail: why the future of business is selling less of more.* CITIC

Chapter 4
The Perspective of Resources

4.1 Making Information An Asset

What are the values of information for services? Obviously, information plays important roles in services by driving their business procedures and supporting data analysis, but the more insightful way is to take information as an asset.

United Parcel Service (UPS) provides a good example in this regard. I used to ask their director in Greater China: "UPS is a benchmark in international delivery and logistics industry though, when you accessed the Chinese market at the beginning, how did you compete with Chinese logistics companies, especially SMEs, to win over the manufacturing clients in China?" What I meant was that SMEs were pretty sensitive to logistics costs, while as an international giant, UPS's lofty stance might not allow it to compete in the same way other contenders did. But this director told me: "I'll give you an example. During our negotiation with a small and medium-sized jewelry maker in Guangdong, we offered to take advantage of the information of hundreds of thousands, even millions, of UPS users to expand overseas market for them, and our supply chain financing department would help solve their capital problem through cross-border supply chain funding. If these work, the costs on logistics will not really matter".

This is thought-provoking. If you and your competitors are bound in the same game, you might end up in a price war; but if not, you may hold the bargaining power in your own hands. What UPS did was typically use its overseas client information as a resource for market development, with the help of its capital advantage, instead of simply competing at the level of logistics and transportation service. This was how they got the upper hand in the arena.

How can we make use of the information assets? It means that we have to always keep in mind how we can develop and use the information we have, especially for value creation.

The famous credit card company American Express sells to retailers, after data masking, abundant card use records of its users. This sounds a bit strange since

L. Li, *The Era of New Services*, Management for Professionals,
https://doi.org/10.1007/978-981-99-9565-3_4

retailers like Walmart should also possess a large amount of data. Why would they buy it from American Express?

As we may imagine, all the data a retailer, for example, Walmart, can get are users' consumption records at Walmart stores. But where did they go after leaving Walmart? Which restaurants did they visit? What films did they watch? Who would have these answers? The credit card company. In the era of Big Data, one thing retailers often do is to create user portraits, which are profiles of users built upon their behaviors and attributes, requiring the support of abundant information. Only credit card companies hold the information about more consumption activities of these users (in China, that may be WeChat and Alipay), so their data is greatly attractive to retailers.

The amount of data does not matter. The key is the type of data and the values they may create.

Recommender systems of e-businesses like Amazon would go through the buying and browsing history of a certain user, select users similar to him or her, adopt a collaborative filtering algorithm in analysis to find out what the similar users are buying and browsing. When this user buys something, the system will immediately find out commodities interesting to similar users and recommend them to the buyer. Amazon is known as the "King of Recommendations" within the industry. As McKinsey & Co points out in a research report on retailers, 35% of what consumers purchase on Amazon comes from its product recommendations.[1] Fortune Magazine also mentions that Amazon's conversion to sales of on-site recommendations could be as high as 60%.[2]

Everyone has been talking about Big Data these years, but what is Big Data capable of? Let's discuss two cases. The first is the ZTE Nubia Z5 Mini mobile phone launched cooperatively by JD and Nubia that made a hit soon and became Nubia's top seller. In 2017, the customer-to-manufacturer (C2M) gaming mobile empowered by JD's Big Data, Nubia Red Magic, became the company's first hot-selling gaming mobile product. When Z18 Mini and Red Magic gaming phone were launched exclusively at JD, on the "Nubia Brand Day" of JD.com in 2018, the sales of several popular models, including Z18 Mini, exceeded RMB 10 million in 10 s, and the daily sales was 12 times higher than the daily average in the past 30 days. Red Magic, in particular, saw a sales of 10,000 units within 37 s, successfully started the booming era of gaming mobiles.

The interesting thing about Red Magic is its specifications, including the chip, screen dimensions, camera resolutions, etc., which were all selected based upon data mining of JD.com. JD studied the mobile phone purchase choices made by its users to find their preferences in phone configuration and devices, then put these configuration and devices together so that the newly developed phone would cater to the preferences of most people.

A similar case is the American TV series, *House of Cards*. Why did it succeed? Its investor Netflix did some research on users' watching choices of existing TV series before the investment and found that a 1990 BBC series named *House of Cards* still

[1] Mckinsey (2013).

[2] Mangalindan (2017).

had a large audience today. Then they went further to find out the favorite directors and actors of the audience, invited them for an adaptation and finally came up with this hit series that has a great vogue in more than 40 countries and hit the highest ratings in all countries and regions that Netflix covers.

What can we learn from these two cases? The charm of Big Data is that we may find out the connections and patterns between users through digging into the flooding data and then design products according to users' preferences. Things developed in this way would win their favor.

But, still, even Big Data "does something but not everything". We have to find out the things Big Data is incapable of.

The inborn deficiency of Big Data is that it cannot "transcend the customers".

What are the data analyzed in Big Data technology? They all happened in the past, showing only the past and present of customers. Why can't it transcend the customers? Because things unknown to customers themselves can never be discovered in Big Data.

Then how can we transcend our customers? There are some solutions provided by design thinking (as discussed in Chap. 5). We have to understand Big Data, but it is by no means a "panacea".

Still, the application of Big Data means significantly to service improvement. Taking casinos in Las Vegas as an example, a dozen years ago, they used coins for slot machines. People put dollar coins or quarters into the slots, pulled the handles and waited for a bundle of coins to tinkle out if a jackpot was hit. The jingle of coins echoed throughout the casinos. However, all the casinos in Vegas changed coins into prepaid cards someday, requiring users to deposit money in their player ID cards and insert the ID cards into slots of the machines when playing. If a jackpot is hit, the slot machine will make a sound effect of coin drop and add to the balance in the player ID card. We might think that coins falling for real provided better gaming experience, so why did they change them into cards?

Picture this. If someone has played the slot machine for a whole afternoon in the casino and lost almost all his money, he may feel upset, angry, even furious enough to leave the place and swear he'd never come back again. Right at this time, the lobby manager comes and, respectfully, tells him: "Hello, my dear sir. It has been a long day, so the hotel is offering you a free coupon for tonight's seafood buffet. Would you like to go upstairs and enjoy yourself?" This man, surprised though, enjoys this unexpected, nice seafood feast for free and forgets his painful loss in the afternoon. What does he do now? He'd go downstairs again and continue gambling. Now we'd understand why all the slot machines use cards. The card system helps the casino monitor in real time the situation of all machines—who is playing which one, winning or losing more, with how much left in his or her card. When the system infers that a player is in great depression or fury, some remedies would be made to cheer him up so that he could continue playing.

Information systems remind us that modern information technology has brought before us chances to know about our customers that we'd never had before. Now, our ways of services should never be restrained to conventional management models. A good master of customers' mental states would help carry out process interventions more timely and effectively.

The Target department store chain in the U.S. is another example. The business department of Target is conducting very comprehensive Big Data analyses, including a pregnancy prediction on female consumers. They can predict whether the females are pregnant or not, even estimate their expected dates of confinement based on the things they buy. Such a prediction is totally based upon their buying behaviors. Target's has gradually expanded the use of these Big Data analysis techniques from expectant mothers to other customer segments and had its sales volume increase from USD 44 billion in 2002 to USD 67 billion in 2010, indicating that service providers' observation and understanding of their customers have stepped into a new era.

UPS serves as a more comprehensive case for us to study information utilization. Their practices can help us sort out some underlying principles in this respect.

Each day, UPS has to deliver about 21.2 million parcels throughout the world, with the figure continuously growing. Of course, this is not an unusual amount in today's China, since many companies are dealing with over 20 million parcels per day, as express delivery develops extremely rapidly here. But if UPS were to spin off the airplanes it owns now and found an airline company, that would be the world's ninth biggest airliner. In addition to the large number of air freighters, UPS also has more than 100,000 trucks. What is more, it owns an air hub, UPS Worldport, that functions as a sorting center with an area as large as 43 football fields. Each day, the 100 mile-long conveyer at UPS Worldport has to deal with 324,000 parcels with one travelling 8 min on it. But the place is run by dozens of employees, for most of the sorting procedures are handled through automatic control.

The following are some interesting practices of UPS that fully embody the thinking of Industrial Engineering. The first one is its Delivery Information Acquisition Devices (DIADs), a kind of handheld terminals used in the delivery industry.

UPS is the world's first delivery company to use handheld terminals. Of course, they did not make the devices themselves, but proposed the design based on demands found in their management process and entrusted the manufacturing to Motorola, so that Motorola was the final producer.

When I studied in the U.S. in 2002, the deliverer who came to my door usually brought a big DIAD, along with an electronic pen for signing. After I signed, the deliverer put the device back into the slot on his truck so that the data was transferred to the headquarters to confirm my receival. The whole process was impressive to me.

Actually, all the tasks and routes of the truck driver throughout the day were fully planned and arranged by that device, including where he started, which parcel to deliver first, and through which route. All were calculated by UPS's supercomputers. I once invited an IT director of UPS Asia Pacific to my class at Tsinghua University. According to him, it is pretty easy to work as a deliverer at UPS All you have to do is to drive the truck and stop it properly. Because all the itineraries are well calculated, and deliverers work easily with the help of their DIADs.

Up to today, handheld terminals, even mobile applications, have become a standard in the industry, used by almost all delivery companies. UPS, as the earliest user, actually designed such devices out of its demands in management, asked Motorola to develop, and utilized them well in service provision. Therefore, when we think about Industrial Engineering from the perspective of service innovation, we have to firstly consider how we can create values. Innovative ideas for management come first, and IT approaches, as actuators and supporters, come second. This points to the relationship between Industrial Engineering and information technology: we should adopt the thinking and methodology of Industrial Engineering to improve operation management in the same way we use IT to actualize and support Industrial Engineering ideas. This also explains why so many UPS executives have an Industrial Engineering background, including Apple's current CEO Tim Cook and the CEO of Walmart.

The latest version of DIAD also derived from the originality of UPS, who launched a new-generation scanner in 2011. A traditional scanner gun is bulky while UPS turned it into a ring that can be worn to the operator's finger. Let's think about it. What are the advantages of these ring scanners, as compared with previous bulky guns? What is the purpose of this design? The answer is that one more hand is freed so that the operator can work with both hands. If working with the scanner gun, he or she has to carry it all the way, take and hold it for scanning, and put it back afterwards. However, the ring scanner enables hands-free operation, so that the operator won't bother to put it away and take out when needed. UPS's optimization has taken each and every move into consideration: Can the staff make one less move? What sort of technology is needed for them to move less? These demands are the determinants that brought about the convenient devices. And this is the logic of leading IT development with Industrial Engineering.

The second interesting practice is in UPS's cooperation with Toshiba Laptop. If you buy a Toshiba laptop in the U.S., it is normal to have it delivered by UPS, since this is the responsibility of a third-party logistics (3PL) provider. If your laptop fails and you have registered for repair, it is also normal to have a UPS staff knocking at your door for pickup. Then what is so interesting? This staff of UPS does not send your laptop back to Toshiba after picking it. Instead, he takes it to UPS's technical center for repair and then gives it back to you. That is interesting. What makes UPS take so much trouble to repair your laptop for Toshiba?

Think about it. If Toshiba Laptop is to run a repair network in the U.S., it has to select several repair facilities, employ technicians and have broken laptops delivered for repair back and forth by UPS deliverers. This is how things work in the conventional model, easy to understand. But the problem is, if Toshiba is doing this all by itself, it has to sustain these facilities and their employees. While, if the work is entrusted to a UPS technical center, their technicians would also be capable of repairing other brands and models of laptops, like Sony and Dell, with some training. Isn't it? In this way, the third-party provider can be transformed into a third-party repairer.

This leads to a more essential issue. What are 3PL providers? That is the initial question. Why don't the companies establish their own logistics networks? The logistics demands of one individual company are not high enough to sustain a complete logistics network, or the costs are too high. The operating principle of 3PL providers is to integrate demands of different companies together into one network so that it is easier to form scale effects and circles, generating high-enough profit margins for logistics providers to operate efficiently. This is the essential reason for the existence of 3PL providers. It also explains why UPS is performing as a third-party repairer. It repairs not only products of Toshiba, but also other brands of laptops. With the repair demands of all brands coming together, UPS, as a third-party repairer, actually functions better than single-branded repair networks.

A similar practice of UPS, also a popular concept in previous years, is fourth-party logistics (4PL). 3PL undertakes transportation, warehousing and other logistics tasks for clients, but what does 4PL do? In fact, 4PL is a business that coordinates and manages the whole logistics system for clients, also what UPS is doing for Harley-Davidson now: the unloading and acceptance of all parts and accessories of Harley-Davidson, its internal logistics, and the distribution and delivery of finished products to retailers and end users are all organized by UPS. This is the connotation of 4PL—logistics management. Logistics providers are more professional than their clients in this regard, so such a model allows manufacturers to leave all logistics tasks to 4PL providers and commit themselves to technological upgrading, process improvement and product design. Therefore, 4PL is a much profound service in a higher realm.

The third interesting practice is route optimization. As mentioned above, UPS has more than 100,000 trucks and each truck driver is equipped with a DIAD that tells him what to deliver, through what route. Their route planning even takes traffic conditions into consideration. UPS employed a team of operations scientists and great powers of its supercomputers, and spent years in development and evolution of complex rout planning algorithms for the sole goal of route optimization (For more details, please see the introduction of UPS ORION for winning the INFORMS Franz Edelman Award of Institute for Operations Research and the Management Sciences). This optimization has miraculously saved more than 30 million mileages for the over 100,000 trucks of UPS. Imagine how much fuel and labor is saved, including wastage of vehicles. All these owe to the advanced computer algorithms. Route optimization has also become a core competence of UPS. It is said that its routing software is now used by over 1000 companies and turned into a successful new business sector by UPS.

Let's do an analysis. UPS kept developing algorithms and software for route optimization out of its demands to lower costs and improve management. Then after setting a benchmark for the industry, it now sells the software UPS designed for others so they can use it together. This leads us back to our subject: we have to firstly have an idea on management improvement, then proactively direct the use and development of new information technology, and finally turn the achievements into a benchmark and even make them into new products.

The optimization of sorting facilities is UPS's fourth interesting practice. As I said, UPS Worldport performs rather efficiently in parcels handling. Here is a detail for you to experience the system design of UPS: Upon leaving the sorting center, each parcel is tagged with a special label, which is an interesting output of the Preload Assist System (PAS). For example, the route code "R101" on the label means that this parcel is to be delivered by the truck responsible for Route 101 and the digits

"23" followed indicate Slot 23 on this truck. This is very worth learning. In normal practice, parcels arriving at their destinations would be piled on the ground altogether; the deliverer has to look hard for those they need. What about UPS's practice? When any parcel enters into the truck, its place is specifically designated by the system.

What is the point of this? For delivery companies, the day time is limited, so the delivery has to be efficient enough. The numbers of customers they serve and destinations they reach are both measured as performance indicators. The route optimization mentioned above saves travel time of trucks, but how about the service time consumed at different destinations? The key here is to hand over parcels to customers as quickly as possible. If the deliverer has to spend a long time looking for parcels at the destination, time is wasted. Therefore, when he gets into the truck for a parcel, the PAS saves him from any thinking and judgment by telling him directly where the parcel is through the DIAD. All he needs to do is to hand it over to the customer.

UPS has used various means to avoid any waste in all links in the day time and rid the system of redundancy through technical guarantee. Therefore, the IT system of UPS, upholding the thinking of Industrial Engineering and lean management that removes waste everywhere, is in the superior stage of information utilization, whereby information services, internally, remove waste and improve efficiency, and externally bring a significant boost to the service level.

4.2 Secrets of Information Transfer

The transfer, spread and exchange of information is one of the most unique symbols of human civilization. The advent of language directly facilitated communication and cooperation among people to a large extent. With the help of linguistic tools, vehicles and forms of information transfer became essentially important. Many services emerged in human society to meet the needs of information transfer. For example, ancient posthouses played a supportive role in the earliest communications transfer system; and the ancient city in Turkey, Ephesus, had doorless public toilets so that, as some say, the toilet-goers could exchange information and gossip easily. Nowadays, services for information transfer have taken up abundant time and resources in people's lives. Many innovative businesses, including Google, Facebook and Tencent, are tools for message transfer and information retrieval. Of course, traditional media like television and newspapers are also serving information transfer.

Then, what options do we have when choosing information transfer approaches? Still taking Ephesus as an example, the type of information service there was the most traditional, namely, gathering people at one place to conduct one-on-one or many-to-many communication. Letters and phone calls are also typical point-to-point services. When one subject in these services needs to transmit some information simultaneously to several people, demands for media like broadcasting come into being, but they are usually one-way services. Television has added images to traditional radio, evolved from monochromes to colored ones, kept improving the color resolution and transformed from 2 to 3D, thanks to technological advance. The general trend of its development is to make the images transferred as authentic as possible. Today's VR technology can immerse people totally in remote scenarios. So the transformation from radio to television is a giant step forward in information transfer services that brings the audience into a more authentic world.

Back to point-to-point information transfer, mails have been electronized into emails; the phone system carried a short messaging service (SMS) first, and then instant messaging thanks to the spread of the Internet. The original text-based instant messaging has evolved into voice and video messages. It can be seen that, point-to-point communications, also, are developing toward the trend of continuously augmented authenticity.

The two approaches of information transfer are both based on connectivity. Information transfer supported by communications and broadcasting facilities keeps offering more authentic experience, as the connectivity grows. Apart from this pattern, we also find some varied practices, such as changing one-way transmission into two-way exchanges. For example, the emergence of *danmu* (bullet chats) gave the program and video viewers a channel to express themselves in real-time for the first time. Of course, such expressions existed in a less effective and efficient way before, but the immediate feedback channel provided by *danmu* is very popular among young people. Bilibili, nicknamed "Website B", has actually built its success on the unique video-watching experience enriched by *danmu* and become a cultural community full of interaction, sharing and re-created contents. By the end of 2022, the number of monthly active users on Website B reached 92.7 million, with an average use time of 96 min per user.

Another variation derived from the expanded connectivity allows us to, for the first time, easily and fully understand social networking services (SNS) and the possibilities to integrate all kinds of social activities and scenarios of human kind with these information transfer services. Social retail is a representative example. Friends of yours posting their latest purchase to personal homepages, or inviting you to join group buying for special discounts on applications like Pinduoduo, these are both online renditions of offline social experience. There are more similar offline social scenarios that can be further exploited to empower providers of information transfer services with significant ways to foster distinguishing services and improve competitiveness.

Of course, one prerequisite for this empowerment is to ensure safe information storage and conduct sufficient analysis and mining over the information stored so as to develop innovative services. The ever-enlarging storage of information sounds like inevitable, but "burned after reading" services provided by some platforms, such as the "snaps" of Snapchat, represent another type of variation pointing at an opposite direction. This unconventional practice tends to release users from mounting worries about privacy infringement when the problem gets only worse in today's background.

It is imaginable that information transfer services in the future may piece together not only scenarios we live in, but also, to some certain degree, our life. If these services were strong enough to piece together someone's life, it would implicate something else. Unprecedented opportunities would be there for us to look into the patterns of human behavior and society at large, as well as choose the objects, contents and quality of social information transfer. In this case, services of friends-making and dating sites may be bound with intelligent analysis in information transfer in a more profound way.

Back to one-to-many information transfer scenarios. Backward information transfer technology in ancient times restricted the transmission of ideas to conversations and books. Today, books are still an efficient way for transmission, though, diverse platforms are giving voices back to normal people so that everyone has the chance to transfer information one-to-many. But this results in a surplus of information supply, so for information transfer platforms, precise matching and marketing, good algorithms and the construction of comprehensive accurate user portfolios become important competences.

In fact, the transfer of information is an issue to be considered by all types of services, for it, on the one hand, can help promote services to the great number of users of information transfer platforms, and on the other hand, can implement service quality control and find opportunities for further service innovation through directing the flow of users' information. Therefore, in service systems of the future, the information contained in a service package will not be limited to simple records and service-supporting processes. They will take more important shares in service experience, create service scenarios we've never seen, and understand users from the perspective of their demands to offer them better services.

4.3 Tapping into Advantages to Expand the Market

In today's service sector, all advantages are opportunities to incubate new markets.

Again, using Amazon as an example, as we know, it started as an e-bookstore, so it had to store a huge amount of information on books, and the print-on-demand service required it to store more e-books and construct a library for Kindle. As the amount of data increasingly grew, Amazon realized that it had acquired an invincible capacity in server cluster management and the storage and computing capacity of its servers were far beyond its own demands. That was when Amazon separated this capacity and developed it into AWS. Now, AWS generates 20–30% of Amazon's total revenues, and is used even by the National Aeronautics and Space Administration (NASA).

What made Amazon, an e-bookstore, a seller, offer cloud service? How did it contribute 20–30% of Amazon's total revenues and become the most profitable business sector of the company? Those were the results of tapping into advantages. It means that a company may have strengthened a certain link in the process of business and management improvement, without even noticing it. When this link is strong enough to provide services beyond the company's requirement, it is time to think about converting its service capacity into some new service product.

We may as well look at a logistics service provider in China, whose name sounds not very familiar, but the value of cargo it delivers is among the first rank in the industry. The company named Jusda is a subsidiary of Foxconn that used to serve

Foxconn only—also the reason for its high cargo value. But Jusda is now a public platform that offers 3PL services. The same thing also happened in JD when it spun off the logistics system it built into a public platform, JD Logistics, which operates independently for development.

Likewise, the 3PL service capacity of Amazon, including the pickup capacity of its warehouses has all exceeded the company's own demands and been, therefore, separately operated to provide independent services. If you want to open a B2C website in the U.S., there is no need to build your own warehouse because you can leave all the goods in an Amazon warehouse and hand your orders over to them, they will finish the pickup and delivery for you. In this way, the capacity of Amazon warehouses is expanded into an independent 3PL service.

Now, think about it carefully: are we holding resources more than what we need, or scarce advantageous management capacity in some links? If so, we have to spin them off and create some new services, so that the advantages can be converted into tangible profits.

Tencent, throughout its growing process, has also made great use of the supreme social advantages of its instant messaging platform, QQ, to expand in all directions and achieved fine effects of "scope economy", successfully turning its social advantages into edges in gaming and other domains.

In addition, reputation, brand, management capacity and other advantages are also resources that can be converted, from the perspective of resources at large. Joyvio, the agribusiness owned by Lenovo Holdings, has set foot in the traditional agricultural industry on the basis of Lenovo Holdings' capital strength, human resources and, especially, abundant management experience in manufacturing. Joyvio has successfully taken up 1/3 of the total kiwifruit output in China, acquired influential liquor and tea brands, including fine farmsteads, chateaus and seafood brands overseas, thus constructing premium upstream resources in a short period of time. This is another type of advantages conversion.

Essentially, the conversion of resource advantages belongs also to the "scope economy". The flexible use of service capacities in this process creates a broad pliable space between absolute resource guarantee and absolute resource sharing. For example, the long-established travel group in Europe, Thomas Cook, not only owns and runs travel agencies and tour groups, but also has its own car rental companies, airlines and resorts, so that these core resources constitute, as supplemented by other resources, a whole service chain surrounding the subject of travel experience, with the way paved for scale expansion.

4.4 Resources Sharing is not a False Proposition

The other direction worth studying is the sharing of resources.

I want to tell you a personal experience of mine: I once took a flight of Royal Dutch Airlines to Amsterdam for a conference and was asked by the flight attendant on the journey: "Would you like Chinese or western food, Sir?" That made me curious

Fig. 4.1 Airline meal of Royal Dutch airlines

about the Chinese cooking level of Royal Dutch, so I ordered one. The food delivered to me was put on a nice plate, sided with bread and salad, looking very tasty. The point was the three big Chinese characters printed on the red food container: 俏江南 (*qiao jiang nan* or "South Beauty", a high-end Chinese restaurant chain), as shown in Fig. 4.1.

That was pretty impressive to me. Why did a Dutch airline serve passengers the packed meals of a Chinese brand? That made sense to me after a second thought. Firstly, what did Royal Dutch get from this? Obviously, it greatly improved the quality of Chinese food offered onboard, since it was difficult for them to cook Chinese cuisine better than South Beauty.

Secondly, how did this benefit South Beauty? This was definitely a valuable brand promotion for them. But why didn't they sell Chinese food to budget airlines? It was out of the concern of client groups. Actually, Royal Dutch could directly screen many premium clients for South Beauty since the two share similar target clients—this is thought-provoking. To put it another way, the groups of people or resources we are in urgent need of may be in the hands of another business. It is time to consider cooperation, if the two of us share a strong relevance.

Lastly, we have to figure out the rationality for South Beauty hidden behind this cooperation. Did they have to spend a lot more money to deliver packed meals to airplanes? Absolutely not. As a catering company, South Beauty had a complete food supply chain. All Royal Dutch needed was a product line for food delivery developed on the basis of what South Beauty already had. In other words, the "scope economy" was diversified in the smartest way in this case.

Similar cases can also be found in people's lives. We'd often find condiments and sauces of Haidilao (a trendy chain of hot pot restaurants) in supermarket counters selling hot spot food and products. The principle here is the same. Haidilao has to deliver all kinds of condiments and sauces to chain stores in all cities, so it can just pack them properly to be sold in supermarkets. Shoppers can easily see them, buy them home for hot pot meals, and be reminded about the dining experience at Haidilao. This small extension of scope barely adds any costs but expands services with the help of a new channel and resources it contains. We may take this as a great idea for resources sharing, and more importantly, with customer experience improved.

WeChat and Dianping have to be studied in the discussion of resources sharing. Why did Tencent choose to invest on Dianping, rather than developing a similar service of its own? Think a bit carefully and you would find: the core resources of Dianping are not its software, website or application. Instead, they are the information of the registered businesses and users' comments and reviews accumulated over many years. These are Dianping's core assets that cannot be acquired in a short time. Therefore, Tencent has made a very smart choice by cooperating with Dianping, rather than repeating its practice. The two have exactly complementary advantages and Tencent can act as a powerful social support for Dianping. The cooperation between them is an important sharing of resources.

What if resources sharing is extended to a larger scope, then? It would evolve into a sharing economy, as represented by Uber, Didi Chuxing and Airbnb. Idle resources and time held by individuals are fully shared and utilized under the management of these platforms, forming the most extensive resource-sharing practices.

Airbnb is a well-known sharing platform of short-term accommodations founded in the U.S. Its booming development struck heavily on the traditional hotel industry, so it was even sued by the Hotel Association of New York City. The model of Airbnb is also used by Chinese platforms like Xiaozhu.com: Vacant rooms and apartments are offered on a platform so that a tourist can easily find a place (usually someone's home) to stay in a strange city and make a payment to the owner.

However, it is noteworthy that these are not simply information matching services, at the core of their design is a bilateral review and credit system. It is a very important feature that distinguishes these platforms from other services for simple information exchange. Short after Airbnb was started in San Francisco, apartments were ransacked by guests renting through the platform. So they developed a two-way review system that allows both property owners and guests to score and comment on each other. If a guest messed the rented place, broke or took something, the negative review posed by the owner might make it difficult for the guest to apply for other accommodations in the future. This credit system even includes insurance and supporting services like cleaning. The completeness of the system ensures mutual trust between all users of the platform so that short stay becomes an important option for tourists.

If the sharing economy at the largest scope is the sharing of idle resources held by individuals, it is predictable that similar models for sharing economy will be developed in healthcare, aged care, transport and other fields. There are still huge spaces to be tapped.

What kind of idle resources do communities possess? For example, the elderly people at home enjoy plentiful spare time. Then what can their time be used for? In a startup project in Beijing called "Back Home for Dinner", young people too busy to cook themselves can register on a platform and choose a "home" of the elderly in their own neighborhood for dinner. The elderly will then spend their spare time cooking for the young and earn little money. This is a great practice that solves the dining problem of young people while building stronger relationships within the neighborhood. On this account, it is possible to set up a new model based on a good platform that organizes idle resources and time well.

For example, an American company for service outsourcing, Directly, is functioning a platform for some users, registered and approved as Directly Experts, to provide outsourced services to other users. In such a way, problems like high staff turnover and inadequacy in skills of temporary service staff that often perplex outsource service providers are well solved. In the meantime, Directly has established a game-like bonus and scoring system, coupled with a flexible support team and AI software, to considerably improve its service capability and level. It is reported that the average weekly income of a Directly Expert is around 200 dollars and the top 5 Experts each earn over 2000 dollars per week. According to the survey on a game platform, which has replaced its former Indian outsource service provider with Directly, the average response time of players' questions dropped from 12 h to 10 min and the customer satisfaction was 10 times higher after the replacement. What's more, 30% of members of the current service team for this game platform have higher education qualifications. It proves that resources sharing platforms of this kind not only ensure the supply of abundant resources through crowdsourcing, but also, more importantly, provide better services to their users.

Indeed, failures cropped up in bike sharing business in China, along with the waste of resources in "bicycle graveyards", encroached sidewalks for pedestrians and other problems caused by them, have raised doubts about the sharing economy. Particularly, Didi Chuxing's social carpooling service, Hitch, was suspended due to safety accidents, and legal online ride-hailing services are trapped in the predicament of safety issues—these are making heavier waves in discussion on the sharing economy. Does the Achilles by the name of sharing economy really have a fragile heel?

Throughout history, new things or newly emerging models always took cities and seized territories with wild powers and impulses (Didi Chuxing used to take 90% share in the market), but the return of reason was also destined once they dominated the realm. Such a return is now observed in three aspects. Firstly, the maintenance of profitability after the ending of the "subsidies war" feasted by vast amounts of capital becomes an issue to be surmounted by all enterprises, challenging their operation level and ability of continuous innovation. Secondly, in the typical platform-based model of sharing economy, companies' ability to serve customers at both ends (drivers and passengers in the case of Didi Chuxing) becomes an ultimate test for them. Their managers have to find out ways to empathize with customers profoundly, instead of attracting them simply by high technology. Thirdly, a path commonly explored in the world is using "scope economy" to rapidly enhance profitability while lowering costs of public facilities owned by the platform (including technical and labor costs). For example, Uber has expanded on the basis of ride sharing to compete in parcel delivery with Uber Rush and in food delivery with Uber Eats. All the three business sectors actually share their resources on the same Uber platform.

Therefore, resources sharing is a more extensive concept than sharing economy. To develop this economy well does not mean to share in the literal meaning. In-depth thinking has to be carried out on the scope of sharing (external and internal), its pain spots (matching and maintenance) and evolvement (joy and leaning).

References

Mangalindan J. P. (2017, July 30). Amazon's recommendation secret. https://fortune.com/2012/07/30/amazons-recommendation-secret/

Mckinsey. (2013). How-retailers-can-keep-up-with-consumers. https://www.mckinsey.com/industries/retail/our-insights/how-retailers-can-keep-up-with-comsumers. 2013-10.

Chapter 5
The Perspective of Needs

As the S-D Logic tells us, the most important purpose of any service is to satisfy people's needs.

How can we probe into customers' needs and demands? How to improve from satisfying customers to surprising them? How can we really engage customers so as to exceed their expectations? These are the questions to be explored in this chapter.

5.1 From Needs to Demands

I proposed the Need-to-demand Model (Fig. 5.1) in a paper in 2015. As service managers, we are often concerned about customers' demands. For example, a customer who had a meal at a restaurant and watched a film in a cinema would be considered having these demands by managers of these facilities.

But why do we dine at restaurants? What is the essence of dining? The essence is that we need to eat. Also, people watch films because we need to relax. Relaxation is an essential need for us. Venture capitalists today often use the term "high-frequency entry" to determine whether a project is investable. Is this project aiming at high frequency needs of potential users or consumers, or needs occurring once a year? Clearly, entries with higher frequencies look more attractive and valuable.

Which one occurs more frequently, needs or demands? Needs, of course. Demands are like dining in a restaurant, which happens once or twice a month; while for eating, people need to have three meals a day. Behavioral research even says that people have to make 227 decisions on eating each day, on average. That is to say, needs happen at higher frequency.

Big Data and other analytical tools in common use are mostly studying demands, have not gone further enough to understand people's needs. So we have to explore deeper to find ways to convert the essential needs of people into demands.

L. Li, *The Era of New Services*, Management for Professionals,
https://doi.org/10.1007/978-981-99-9565-3_5

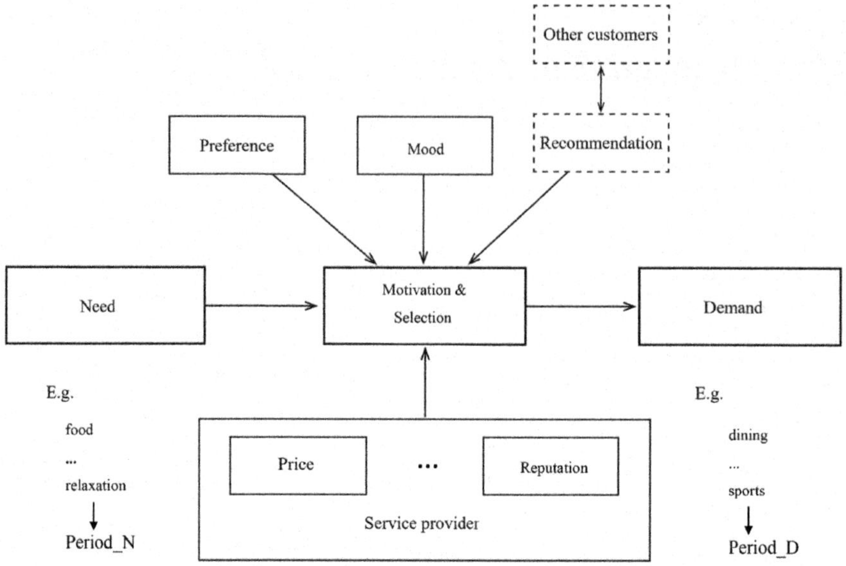

Fig. 5.1 Need-to-demand model

Actions that happen between needs and demands are motives and choices. For instance, we have to have three meals a day, but why do we choose this restaurant over that one? Obviously, we are comparing different service providers, their prices, word-of-mouth communications etc., when making choices.

What kind of motives drive us to enjoy these services? That is related to our preferences—Sichuan cuisine, seafood or others, they are all personal preferences.

Also, choices are related to emotions. This is an interesting but often ignored thing. My lab did a study on convenience stores and found that people buy totally different things in positive or negative moods. Think about this. When would a person buy more junk food, when he feels good or bad? Our experiment told us it is the negative emotions. When we feel bad, we'd think "No, I had to have something to cheer me up". When I am upset or frustrated, I'd give myself a big indulgence by having chips and coke. That is the influence of negative emotions. But when feeling good, people tend to buy healthy stuff. So your emotions at the time would influence your choice and motive.

Lastly, choices may be made due to other customers' recommendations, thanks to social networking. In many cases, instead of having trouble finding a delicious restaurant, we just try the place highly recommended by our friends. Such choices are results of others' recommendations and indicate the influence of social relations on choosing behaviors.

To sum up, all the factors above are influencing the conversion from needs to demands, and data produced in this process is easier to acquire these days. Analysis on these process data can show us clearly what customers need and render customized understandings on specific differences between individuals. In other words, precise matching and supply based on data analysis and intelligent algorithms is becoming an important service competence in today's era.

5.1.1 To Expand "Dimensions of Life"

Buddhists trying to release themselves from samsara and attain nirvana can be seen as seeking a new height of life. The pursuit of immortality in Taoism is a pursuit of the length of life. What are the other two dimensions of life? They are breadth and depth. The former can also be termed as "broadness". Then what is the breadth of life? People may acquire new experiences or inspirations through reading, travelling or observing other people's lives, without prolonging life length. That is the breadth of life.

For instance, there are many people like or unlike us sharing videos of the most wonderful and interesting moments of their life on a popular platform, Douyin (TikTok is the international version of Douyin), so that we may experience with some swipes totally different life that we have no time to enjoy, cannot afford, or even had never heard of before. At the heart of this novelty is a way to broaden life.

Similar experiences used to be acquired through reading. We read histories, biographies, even novels to imagine or explore another way of life. This is a fundamental need of people.

Then what are our needs for the depth of life? They urge groups of people, or larger communities, to explore the principles running behind things, like me, exploring the principles of services. Many promising education and knowledge-sharing platforms at present, for example, online learning app iGet, are services catering for people's needs of "in-depth" exploration, which may satisfy our curiosity.

Both depth and breadth are basic needs of people to enrich our life experience. Of course, a large service domain here is health. In essence, healthcare keeps studying ways to extend people's lives and improve their quality of life, and are, therefore, services for the length of life. Based on the above discussion, the four dimensions of life, namely, height, length, depth and breadth, are all essential needs of humans, so innovations on these dimensions boast strong potential.

5.2 From Satisfying to Surprising

Here is another essential question: service managers want to improve customers' satisfaction, but what is their satisfaction composed of?

To answer this, we have to start with things that concern the customers.

Firstly, the reliability of service. For example, high-speed trains would outperform airplanes in their comparison of reliability.

My most painful experience was that I sat on a plane for 7.5 h when the actual flight from Hangzhou to Nanning took only two hours. Because Hangzhou was hit by a once-in-a-century heavy snow and the whole airport had only two snow blowers, which had to work on the tracks once every half an hour. Therefore, I was delayed again and again. Air flights can be seriously unreliable in extreme weather, especially in winter and summer. This is something that concerns customers seriously, also a competitive edge of high-speed rails.

Secondly, responsiveness. It means, when any problem occurs, can the service provider listen to the customer immediately and provide a solution right away. Responsiveness is of great importance. Many group events happened to airline companies are problems in responsiveness, caused by their ill arrangements of passengers at the time of flight cancellation or delay.

Another example is Haidilao. As we know, Haidilao's core competitiveness is its service quality, but what exactly makes the service good? One key point, also an important difference between the wait staff at Haidilao and other restaurants, is that they have the right to give away free meals to customers. If something happens when we dine at a restaurant, we often tell the waiter to send his manager here, but why? Because we know the waiter does not have much authority to solve the problem for us. But how about in Haidilao? If the customer asks the manager to come, the waiter could confidently say: "No need," and directly free the customer from the payment, then how would the customer feel then? The trouble will be solved before the customer gets angry, who might even feel surprised. This is what we mean by responsiveness. The speed and effect of responses are very important in service.

Thirdly, security of service, referring to freedom from danger or doubt, which is very thought-provoking. In addition to being well guaranteed, the services you provide should also be known and understood by customers. Still with Haidilao as an example, I saw a show window by the staircase from the first floor to the second in a store of theirs, displaying many food ingredients, but on two plates each. For example, there were two plates of cabbage in display, with the one on the left labelled as "overnight leftovers" and the right one "fresh-cut today". The cabbage in the left plate looked wilted while those on the right one were fresh and juicy. I did not understand their point until the dishes were served to our table. All the ingredients looked like the ones put in the right plate, showing to the customers that all the food was fresh cut on the day, with no leftovers used. This is a guarantee of safety to the customers.

Let us turn to KFC or McDonald's who put a paper sheet on each food tray. It is for food safety and ease of cleaning. But special care is taken to the contents of the paper. For example, KFC used to print on the paper sheets: what oil was used to make French fries, where did KFC buy it; what was the cooking temperature of the oil, after how many times of cooking would the oil be wasted, and where did it go after that. All questions were answered in full details to tell the consumers: the oil they used for French fries was of good quality and the food of KFC was healthy to eat. For another example, KFC claims the chickens it offers to Chinese customers were "white-feathered chickens" and printed information about their breeding and nutrition on paper sheets. The purpose is to prove to the customers that their chickens are safe to eat.

Also, KFC has held "kitchen visit" campaigns in many cities, allowing customers to see the appearance, growing environment and process of white-feathered chickens through VR glasses. Henneries behind the glasses all looked serene and beautiful as surrounded by farmland, equipped with supermatic monitoring systems that control the temperature, humidity and supply of food and water indoors. Participants in the kitchen visits were also led by staff members to see the ovens and water filter systems, so that they understood the strict sanitation control at KFC. All of these were to render the security of their services.

The practices of Haidilao and KFC are enlightening in many aspects. For one, service managers have to improve the security of their services. For another, they should make good use of visualizing approaches to let customers know this security. In this regard, railway operators in China are doing great: passengers can see from the promotional videos broadcasted in high-speed trains that rail employees are working hard to maintain the operation of railways and trains, including cleaning up and maintaining safety. Lastly, information like this can actually enhance customers' perception of the security of service.

Fourthly, understanding and knowing the customer. It is very important for service managers to put themselves in the shoes of the customers.

To illustrate with a common scenario on air flight, when a passenger falls asleep with the reading light over his head on, the flight attendant would come and turn the light off for him. This is a typical example of understanding the customer. The passenger turned on the light for reading when he was awake, but now that he is asleep, the light becomes a disturbance. So the flight attendant turns the light off after putting herself into the passenger's position.

We'd also notice that, especially on international flights, if any passenger is asleep during food service, the flight attendant will put a sticky note on the chair back in front of him, telling him to use the service button if he feels like eating after waking up. The flight attendant is thinking in the position of the passenger and decides not to wake him up since no one wants to be disturbed asleep, but still, she uses the sticky note for a reminder so that he will not miss the meal. It shows a great understanding of her customer.

Of course, understanding the customer does not mean that every flight attendant has to always keep in mind the feelings of all passengers. Instead, it has to be designed into standard operating procedures through the deliberation of service designers. If so, the flight attendants will carry out the right procedures specified in their SOP according to the status of passengers. It also means that they are understanding and knowing the customers.

Fifthly, tangibles. The most important thing about service should be the provision of its essential attribute to the customer. For example, the service that a subway passenger wants to enjoy in essence is the physical movement from one station to another. However, the broad aisle, beautiful lightboxes, soothing music and comfortable seating in the process of movement are explicit and tangible experiences that must be noticed by the passenger. These make the tangibles of a service.

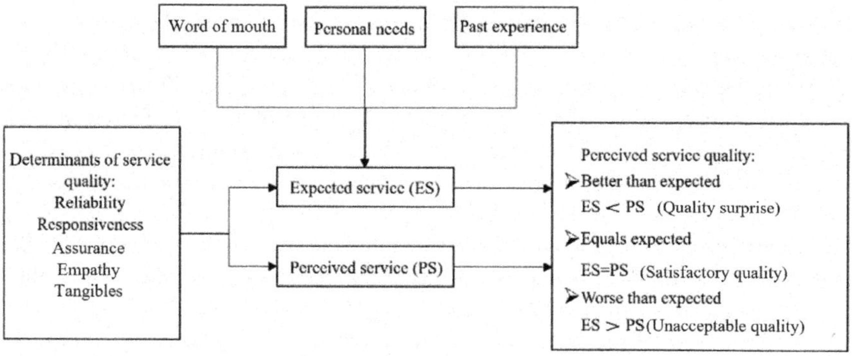

Fig. 5.2 Determinants of perceived service quality. *Source* Parasuraman et al. (1985)

We have to understand that, although services are intangible, their tangibles are important components in customers' minds that bring them distinguishing experiences.

The five factors above are the "five major determinants" of service quality, which need to be accomplished well in our practices.

American marketing scientist A. Parasuraman and his colleagues analyzed the reasons for customers to feel satisfied or unsatisfied in the paper published in *Journal of Marketing* in 1985 (in Fig. 5.2). On the left of the figure are the five determinants introduced above: reliability, responsiveness, security, understanding and knowing the customer, and tangibles. But what makes a customer satisfied or unsatisfied? A golden rule is that every customer would have an expected service, or an expectation of the service, in his mind, while a perceived service, or a perception of the service, is generated when the service is actually provided. His satisfaction or dissatisfaction is the result of the comparison between the expected and perceived qualities of the service.

If the service quality perceived by the customer is better than his expectation, the quality is considered surprising. If the expectation is normal but the actually experienced service turns out to be excellent, the customer would feel surprised. But if the perceived quality is far from his expectation, the service would be a failure.

Therefore, satisfaction and dissatisfaction are not absolute values. They are results of comparison made by the customer between his expected and perceived service qualities. According to the golden rule of perceived service quality, service designers may wish to maximize the perceived quality and minimize the expected quality of customers. However, when the expected service quality hits too low, no customer would come. So the optimum state is not to lower the expected service quality as much as possible, but to make it a bit lower than the perceived one. In this way, customers holding a not-bad expectation would be easily surprised at the optimum state.

As service designers, we have to intentionally manage users' expectations of service while diligently improving their perceptions of the service. That is the direction towards which we should work.

To manage users' service expectations well, we have to understand the sources of these expectations.

The first one is word-of-mouth communications. Expectations on a place go high when it is praised by everyone. This is the result of word-or-mouth communications. It is the best advertising in the service sector and will naturally compose the fundamental expectations of customers. Platforms like Dianping provide more vehicles for word-of-mouth communications, since reviews given by existing customers serve as important references for potential customers to establish an expectation.

The second one is personal needs. Sometimes, a customer's expectations for a service depend on how much he or she needs it. For example, people often find dinners (suppers) provided by restaurants in Beijing delicious. Because, to gather for dinner in a megacity like Beijing, friends have to travel long from different places and arrive at the restaurant at 8 p.m. after suffering heavy traffic jams. They are starved at the time of dinner and would easily find everything tasty. That is the work of personal needs.

The third source is past experience. A customer would expect the service to remain the same as he had it before, basing the expectation during his past experience.

In my revision to Parasuraman's study, I add two factors that influence people's service expectations. First is the price. The price of a service would exert great influence on customers' expectations. If a doctor tells a patient, "you need to pay RMB 2000 yuan to register my service and wait long in queue", the patient may take him as a very good expert (please be careful of "faked experts" who are only high in prices). If another doctor says that his registration costs only 5 yuan, dare you visit him? I think you would doubt his ability. So price is an important influential factor for consumers' expectations of service.

The second one is advertising. It also acts heavily on customers' expectations of service. Here is an example. A startup specializing in online drug retail and delivery advertised its slogan in lift rooms, saying "Ordering anytime around the clock and anywhere downtown, you'd get the drug in 28 minutes." However, I bought twice on their platform and received nothing within 1 h, both times. They promised to deliver in 28 min but took more than 1 h. That would definitely dissatisfy the consumers. If they changed the promise to 1.5 h downtown and fulfilled the delivery in 1 h, consumers might feel surprised.

That reminds me of an interesting television advertisement I watched in the U.S. A blonde, chased by a group of men in black, ran into a skyscraper and came out of the door at the roof deck. She stopped at the edge of the roof, turned around to look at the men following her, calmly. Just as she looked at her watch, the hour hand turned to 9 o'clock and she jumped off the skyscraper to fall exactly into a passing UPS truck, successfully dumped the chasers. Right at this time, the UPS logo appeared on the screen. What did UPS tell us in this advertisement? Sure, UPS services were so punctual that she had known that the truck would pass by at 9 o'clock and put this into her plan for escape. The advertisement was good and funny. But I couldn't help thinking, "UPS is humorous. But that makes it hard for me to take if my UPS delivery is 10 minutes late next time. Because that's not what they promised in the advertisement." So service providers have to be careful with the advertising and promotion of their services. Never promise anything that is too difficult, since it will pile on users' expectations. The best service design is to maintain the optimum state, where the expectation is slightly lower than the perception.

5.3 Engaging "God" in Design

5.3.1 Customers' Needs and Design Thinking

How can we understand users' needs? Please try to empathize with them and engage them in design.

I want to share with you my personal experience when I visited Amsterdam Airport Schiphol in the Netherlands. The airport looked very nice with waiting rooms like stands in a stadium and comfortable lounges equipped with cozy sofas, good lighting and pleasing music, as shown in Fig. 5.3.

The next area shown in Fig. 5.4 represents the specialty of the Netherlands—Delftware in the airport. There are big tea cup-shaped booth seats made by Delftware and a large "tea pot" for visitors to walk through.

Let us look at the details of a table nearby a boarding gate, in Fig. 5.5. The stools around it make it comfortable for passengers to work, and more importantly, a socket is installed in front of each stool. In most Chinese airports, apart from those built lately, people have to find sockets down on a pillar and squat next to it to charge their laptops or phones. Some airports have made improvements by placing the charging ports nearby seats so that passengers can work conveniently. This is a user-friendly design.

Fig. 5.3 Lounge areas at Amsterdam Airport Schiphol

Fig. 5.4 Delftware. *Source* http://bluesky0301.blog.sohu.com/174131063.html

Fig. 5.5 Table and stools at Amsterdam Airport Schiphol

The library of Amsterdam Airport Schiphol, shown in Fig. 5.6, provides books on shelves for passengers to read, along with nice tables, chairs and lamps. There are even iPads for web browsing and email checking.

The place shown in Fig. 5.7 is even more amazing—the Schiphol branch of Rijksmuseum Amsterdam (the national museum of the Netherlands). It is like the Palace Museum has opened a branch in Beijing Capital International Airport. The whole place looks very beautiful, with the second floor exhibiting oil paintings and sculptures, and the first floor selling art souvenirs.

The area in Fig. 5.8 also looks quite interesting, decorated with a sophisticated three-dimensional wooden carrack. The Netherlands is known as "Maritime Coachman" in China, because of its historical success in trade and logistics as well as the developed commerce there. Displayed on the three walls surrounding the carrack are all popular commodities imported and exported in ancient Netherlands. For example, shelves by the wall with a male portrait in the left picture in Fig. 5.8 sell cigars, and the

Fig. 5.6 The library at Amsterdam Airport Schiphol

Fig. 5.7 The Schiphol branch of Rijksmuseum Amsterdam

right shelves are full of chocolates for ladies. These are clearly places in a duty-free store. But passengers shopping here will not feel like buying goods, they are buying history and culture. At this moment, their power of consumption will be significantly boosted.

As I rested on a cozy sofa after visiting so many interesting places, a staff member of the airport came to me, "Would you like to take part in the airport's improvement plan, sir?" I agreed since I am teaching service design and systems engineering at Tsinghua. Then she brought me a large green paper sheet, as you see in Fig. 5.9, and asked me to fill my personal information in the white box on the top left corner. Words in the middle of the paper were "My favorite waiting time" and she gave me a pen, saying "Please write the things you like doing while waiting at the airport. The more you like it, write it closer to the center." So I thought of the things I liked to do in an airport, reading, listening to music, shopping in a duty-free store, having something in a restaurant, or a cup of coffee, and nothing else.

Fig. 5.8 A store at Amsterdam Airport Schiphol

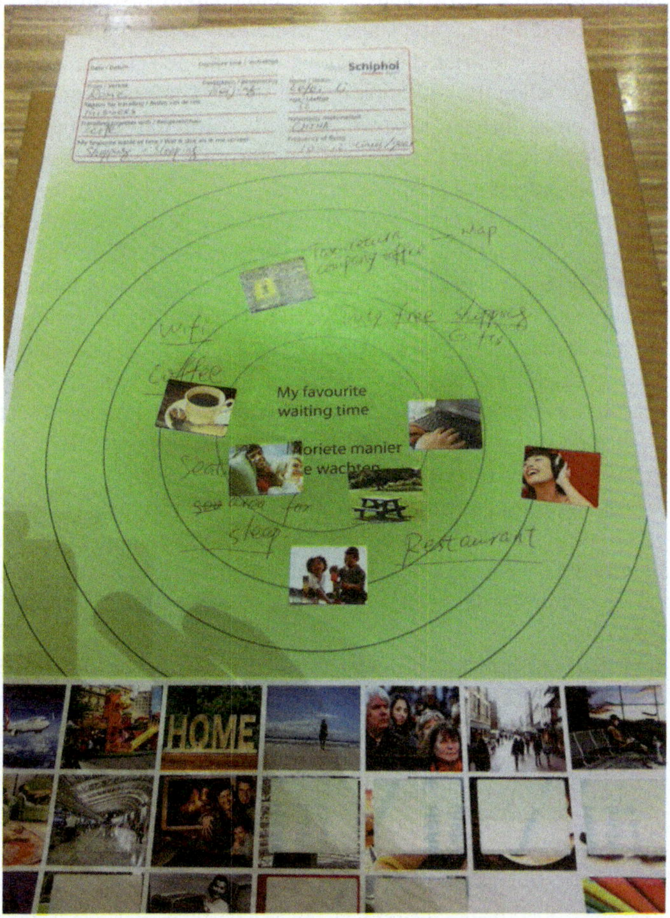

Fig. 5.9 The user questionnaire at Amsterdam Airport Schiphol

Seeing that I couldn't think of anything else, the lady took out three rows of stickers and asked, "Are there anything in these stickers you want to do in the airport, sir?" That got me interested, so I pointed at one of the pictures and said, "This looks like a bench in a park, but you can't build a park in the airport, right?" She gave me an unforgettable answer, "If you think there should be a park in the airport, we can build one." Her words encouraged me, so I covered the paper sheet entirely with all the stickers I found interesting. Then I realized this sheet was actually a questionnaire on demands, the most interesting one I've ever filled.

It was interesting, not because of the graphic representations. Or should I say being interesting was not that important for the questionnaire. As we learned, the inborn deficiency of Big Data is that it cannot transcend the customers, but the greatness of this tool was that it successfully overcame this deficiency.

Please note that there were two stages when I filled this questionnaire. I was given a pen to write by myself in the first stage. I wrote only things I knew that I could do in an airport since I was restricted by my own thinking and couldn't go any further. In the second stage, when the staff took out the stickers, she was encouraging me to think harder and break through my own mentality. More possibilities were offered to motivate me to choose more things that I would like to do in an airport. So this was a great tool to understand people's demands.

I asked her more questions upon realizing the value of this tool, like "Where did you get this tool?" She said it was from her professors, making me more interested, so I asked, "Where did you graduate from?" She said she studied Industrial Design at Delft University of Technology (TU Delft). The Faculty of Industrial Design Engineering at her university is very prestigious and the professors taught students like her to survey users' demands in such a great manner.

My experience at Amsterdam Airport Schiphol unveils an important section in our discussion—design. Why are things around us the way they are? Because they are designed this way. Things to be designed may be as large as a city, a plane, or as small as a toothbrush and toothpaste. They are all results of designing. One of the most heated topics in design in the international community, design thinking, has become a tool and methodology for the whole sector of innovation and entrepreneurship. The following are discussions on the adoption of design thinking in innovations in this interesting section.

There are three core concepts in design thinking, the first of which is the space for business. The service designer has to test the business feasibility of any innovation. The second is the space for technology, referring to the technological feasibility of innovation. The third concept, also the one often ignored by service designers, is the space for people, which emphasizes people's desires. The place where the three spaces converge is actual experience, also the space for innovation. Therefore, the use of the three core concepts of design thinking is to find the convergence of spaces for business, technology and people, so as to define the experience to be created for users. The process of exploring ways to design and transfer such experience is design thinking.

Design thinking helps us analyze the space for people and solve problems related to people from the perspective of design. Tim Brown, who put forward design thinking for innovation and started a firm IDEO, once said, "design thinking in business is based on the designer's sensibility and proper methods." Designers have to be sensitive since they need to take the subjective initiative in design and rely on their keen intuition. Proper methods ensure that people's demands and feasible technologies can be combined to transform feasible business strategies into values for clients and market opportunities. The two are indispensable compositions of design thinking.

Design thinking has been adopted by many large international corporations, such as Apple, Marriott International, Ford, IBM, Samsung and Buick. The Department of Industrial Engineering and Academy of Arts and Design at Tsinghua are collaborating with Stanford, IDEO and other institutions to introduce design thinking into China.

Two classical models of design thinking are illustrated in the following part, with their principles explained. One is the Delft Design Approach, a model and a set of methods proposed by the Faculty of Industrial Design Engineering, TU Delf. The other is the methodology proposed by the famous Stanford d.school (Hasso Plattner Institute of Design).

Generally, product innovation is to develop a new-generation product based on the existing one. In the direct linear thinking approach towards innovation, we will think of all the features needed for the new product based on past experience, and put them in design. But the result of this may be unreasonable, or hard to be accepted in the market.

The Delft Design Approach explores product innovation at three levels: The question of "what" is answered at the bottom level, also the product level. But design has to go higher to the "how" level, the interaction level that studies how the product interacts with people.

After figuring out the interaction between the product and people, we have to find out the reason behind it, by moving up to the "why" level—the background level. Then we would have a clear understanding about details of the existing product, its interaction with people and the exact background of the interaction.

The next step is to think about the interaction we would like to see between the product and people in a future background, since this new interaction will bring forth a new product design. The innovative design of a product has to experience such an upward exploration process that answers questions like how does it interact with people, why is it so, how would the interaction become in future, and finally, back to the question of what would be the new product.

Specifically, the focus is on the attributes of the product at the "what" level. Different customers would focus on different attributes, therefore hold different opinions upon the product, including its appearance, materials and quality. However, the focus is shifted to the way people interact with the product, at the "how" level, and under what circumstances will this product be used and what will it be used for, at the "why" level.

For example, when would we use a car, and for what? When we return to the product level, our focus may go beyond the car itself. Tsinghua University cooperated with Art Center College of Design (U.S.) to hold the Create Change forum under the theme of "Design for a Better Life" in Beijing, June 23, 2018. The chief designer of

Uber's Advanced Programs and Aviation department shared with us Uber's flying car project at the forum. In their design, urban transport will no longer be limited to the ground. Instead, a car can fly from a parking lot in the air and land in another lot. Uber is about to test this product in 2022 and has finished many versions of the initial design. What they are doing is revisiting the question "why do people need transport" and imagining the transport scenarios in the future, which then brings forth the concept of the new product.

Design thinking requires us to return to the reasons to use the product, the scenarios for its use and then the background environment. These are related to the frequently mentioned "5W1H" questions. The "5W1H" tool is commonly used in Industrial Engineering and system thinking, almost applicable to the conception of any project, including the one at work. "5W", namely, what, who, where, when and why, and "1H", how, is telling us that we have to make these clear for anything complicated: what is this thing, who is doing it, at what time and what place, to what end; why and how is the person doing it. This tool is particularly useful in system thinking so it can also be used to explore at different levels in design thinking and find out why people need the product.

In the design thinking model of Stanford d.school, product innovation goes through three stages: understanding, exploring and materializing. The designer has to firstly acquire a good understanding, then make exploration to materialize the conception. The whole process includes six steps: empathize, define, ideate, prototype, test and implement. The first two steps will be explained here.

Firstly, to empathize, this is a psychological term. What does it mean? It's similar to understanding and knowing the customer, requiring us to put ourselves in others' position to feel their pains and needs. Service designers have to observe the users' behaviors, communicate and interact with them, and understand their needs. How important is empathy? I visited d.school a couple of times as a visiting scholar of UC Berkley and one of the founders of design thinking, Professor Larry Leifer said to me, "our lab has been studying innovation for decades and found that, among all the influential factors on innovation, empathy is the only important one." There are so many influential factors, but empathy is the only one important in his mind. This made me confused, even shocked (I knew the meaning of empathy, but had never thought it was that important). He gave me an example right away, saying, "As we talk, I see you carrying a backpack, then I should realize it may hurt your shoulders. So I need to think about designing a better backpack that would make your shoulders comfortable. The process of how this new product comes about is the work of empathy. We have to understand what other people are suffering and form new ideas based on such understanding, to solve their pain spots. This is where innovation starts from." That was why he took empathy as the only important influential factor for innovation. It was very impressive to me.

To empathize with the users means that we have to step into their shoes. "Do unto others as you would have them do unto you." I found a major difference in Chinese and western cultures in my study of Management Science: Chinese people are good at induction and conclusion. Our ancestors reduced their wisdom to incisive mottos to guide people's deeds. "Do unto others as you would have them do unto you" also has its Chinese version. However, we are not good at deduction, or explaining why we have to do so. For example, the old motto tells us to treat others the way we would have them treat us, but does not explain the reason nor provide any methods. We often put a lot of emphasis on "what", but ignore "why" and "how".

What is the use of an empathy map? As you can see in Fig. 5.10, we tried to analyze from the viewpoint of citizens in Beijing with the help of an empathy map when writing the report *City of Taste* for Beijing Municipal Government at the end of 2017. In the middle of the map is a person, the citizen we had to empathize with. The words "think and feel" on top of his head refer to things he encounters and feels; in front of his eyes are things he "sees" and behind are what he "hears"; and "say and do" below refer to his words and behaviors. The map tells us how to step into other people's shoes.

Supposing we have to empathize with passengers to improve services at a train station, the person in Fig. 5.10 would be the passenger. Staff at the train station have to step into his shoes to see what he sees, hear what he hears, find out how he thinks and feels and what he will say and do. The findings are then put into the corresponding columns in the map and discussed by all participants who work at the station. "Troubles" in the lower-left corner of Fig. 5.10 remind us of the pain spots that give users a sense of unease, which are opportunities for innovation. The most important goal of empathy is to find the users' pain spots. In the lower-right corner of the map are the users' "demands", requiring us to explore things they need based on

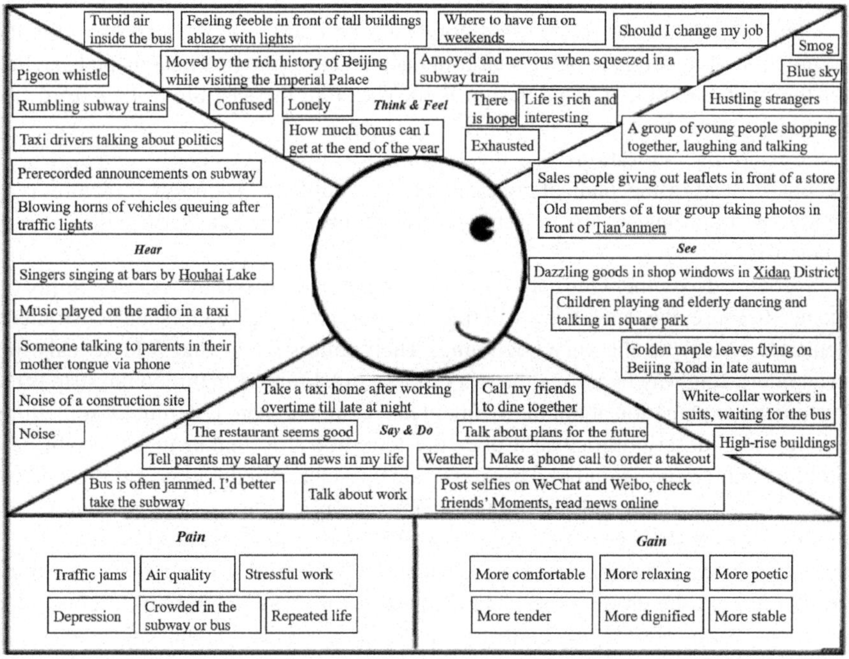

Fig. 5.10 The empathy map of Beijing citizens

the pain spots. What should we provide to users to solve each and every pain spot? The answers would also be our "rewards". Of course, I think a further step can be taken while using this tool. We can move further by telling users what they might need in the future for things not yet painful to them.

My lab is developing a new tool that can perform better than the empathy map. To acquire innovation ability is not simply to learn some model or idea, we have to master these tools, use them to find out what the users are thinking, hearing, seeing and doing, fully understand their pains and confusions, define their actual pain spots, and make innovations accordingly. This is the right way to make innovations satisfying to our users.

Stanford students enjoy intern opportunities to solve practical problems for businesses every year. Professor Leifer told me about a problem they solved for NASA. A perplexing trouble for NASA was that one of their satellites was meters high, therefore very laborious for assembling and testing. It was especially hard for test engineers since they had to wear wire rigs and be hung to the ceiling for work. The students decided to empathize with a test engineer named John, who was responsible for testing satellites for NASA. Of course, to empathize with John meant to analyze his background, such as what kind of person he was, what he saw, heard or thought, things he liked or not, and what his concerns were. They took his position to analyze the problem and made a design that could save him some trouble. At last, with the help of their mentor, students of Stanford came up with a novel satellite structure—the satellite still stood high, but in the shape of a flower bud that could bloom and unfold its "petals". Since petals could lie flat down, the satellite was lowered so that test engineers could operate, assemble and test easily on the ground. Upon the completion of testing, the petals can fold back and turn into the bud-shaped satellite for the final assembling. This design helped shorten the satellite testing from two months into one week.

Overturning innovations like this often are results of designers' empathy with people, instead of mechanical creation of linear thinking. Therefore, empathy is of significant importance. The first thing I'd teach my students in service design is to empathize.

Secondly, to define. Our hard work does not always result in desirable improvements, because we may fail to define the problems and understand customers' demands clearly, at the very beginning. The comic strip in Fig. 5.11 reveals this in an interesting way by telling the story of a swing. Frame 1 in this comic strip is the customer's explanation about the swing in his mind, but there is definitely something wrong in his description since it does not look like a normal swing. It might be a problem in his expression or he has not made up a clear mind. Frame 2 is the product in the project leader's understanding, obviously wrong since it does not swing, and the work of the designer in Frame 3 would hit the customer's head on the tree. In the programmer's design in Frame 4, the swing is simply tied to the tree, with the board lying on the ground, there is no way for it to work. The business consultant describes it as a sofa hanging to the tree in Frame 5, implicating that consultants tend to beautify things. Then how is the project recorded? We see nothing in Frame 6, no idea put into words, not even to mention documents. However, the billing to the

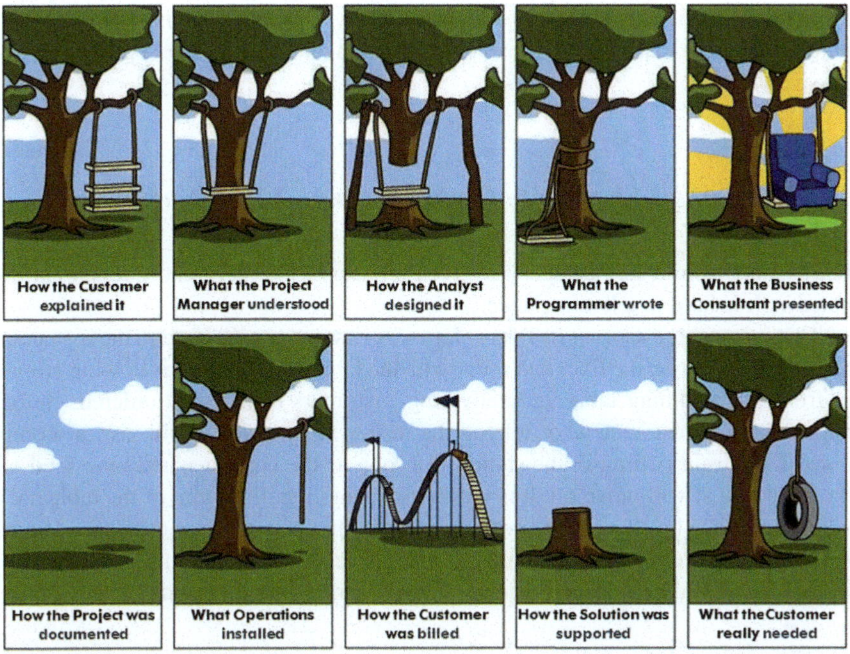

Fig. 5.11 How did a project move on. *Source* https://blogs.perficient.com/2015/07/01/ibm-cognos-tm1-atlassian-jira-client-success/

customer goes on like riding on a roller coaster, requiring the customer to add the budget yesterday, offering a discount today, and changing the offer tomorrow. The thing finally delivered would look just like in Frame 9. But what is the swing that the customer actually needs? As we see in Frame 10, a tire hanging to the tree is satisfying enough.

What are the key features of the design thinking model of Stanford? I'll give you a brief introduction. Firstly, it emphasizes the value of people, starting from empathizing with users to solve their pain spots. Secondly, it requires designers to demonstrate their ideas, rather than just telling stories. The design thinking labs at Stanford provide a great many cardboards and wooden boards for students to prototype their innovative ideas for demonstration. Thirdly, it teaches us to make complex things simple and clear. This is also an important principle in Stanford's design thinking, to look for the direction of design in complexity through process control and repeated iteration.

Of course, design thinking has a profound connotation that can be interpreted in various ways. This book provides only a brief introduction. Please refer to the textbooks and documents of Stanford d.school or IDEO for more information. Design can be very tricky. It takes a long time and many efforts before we set a clear definition and direction, and get an epiphany of the exact thing we want to design. We have to make many iterative generations of prototypes since one demonstration is far from enough. Changes must be made immediately when the customer feels unsatisfied. Please note that your customer must be engaged in the process, proactively or passively.

5.3.2 How Far Should We Go in Customer Engagement

Let us start from a service scenario. Please observe Fig. 5.12 and guess what the place is. It is hard to tell at a glance.

This is a sushi restaurant in Tokyo, Japan. A customer stepping into the restaurant can find a seat as he/she likes and order with the tablet. A conveyor is flowing around in front of the dining table and delivering customers dishes they ordered. Before approaching a customer who ordered the dishes, the conveyor will give a prompt tone, like a train pulling in the station. As soon as the customer takes the food off the conveyor, it will move on. It is worth mentioning that, in front of the table are a white soy sauce bottle, a tissue box and a tap for hot water. Every customer can get hot drinking water from the tap in the front. Please think, what is the design purpose of such a system? What advantages and convenience does it provide?

Fig. 5.12 Scenario in a sushi restaurant

We can say the customers are helping themselves most of the time in this restaurant, so the service system is designed to minimize the engagement of wait staff, thereby improving service efficiency and quality. All the cases included in our discussion are to inspire a system thinking on service: Self-service represents the acme of customer engagement, in the design of which, the service capacity approximates the service demand (with the help of sufficient self-service facilities). Certainly, this kind of self-service with total customer engagement is not applicable to all scenarios. New business models where no customer engagement happens are also emerging.

For example, the rental service provided by traditional real estate agencies is basically an information matching service, requiring tenants or housing owners to undertake furnishing, facilities and daily maintenance by themselves. However, the Chinese rental platform ZIROOM runs in a different business model. It provides uniform furnishing and facilities to apartments and rooms entrusted by their owners, and then rents them to tenants. At the same time, it provides the tenants with full-chain post-rental services, starting from room hunting and moving to cleansing, repairing and other demands that may occur after the tenancy agreement is signed. All the properties at ZIROOM are in move-in condition. The company now manages over 200,000 apartments and rooms in Beijing, Shanghai and Shenzhen and has served more than 500,000 tenants in accumulation. ZIROOM has established the largest online-to-offline (O2O) community of young residences in China. In conclusion, the highest and lowest degrees of customer engagement both contain unique values and charms.

5.3.3 Functions and Beauty

High attention is paid to functions in the development and design process of any complex product because they are expressions of the underlying architecture of a system. A typical complex system should have three types of architectures: The first is its operating architecture, with operating behaviors of the system described in a black box. The second is a logic architecture, also known as functional architecture that describes necessary functions, which support the system as a whole and are rendered into operating behaviors. The function perspective has taken us into the system, turning the black box into a white one, but the realization of these functions is yet to be discussed. The third is the physical architecture of the system, which truly realizes the functions defined by the second architecture in various forms of software, hardware and organizations. Therefore, for a complex system, functions are the key that bridges the overall goal of the system and its actual forms.

The concept of service package is often mentioned in discussion of service systems to illustrate their compositions. A service package includes five elements: supporting facilities, auxiliary items, information, explicit services and implicit services. According to the correspondences between these elements and architectures of a system, supporting facilities, auxiliary items and information belong to the physical structure while explicit and implicit services are functions and behaviors of the system.

Till now, functions still seem to be colorless. They exist just to serve certain purposes. However, these purposes should be extended into real services and product competitions. Like in the mobile phone market, all the phones have camera, call, browser and other functions, but the way they look and feel, including the taste and sense they deliver, are also essential, sometimes more decisive on purchase, in comparison with those explicit functions.

In other words, among all the purposes served by the functions, if we single out those to be rendered through implicit services, a considerable part of them would be closely related to beauty—the kind of beauty that is not restricted to traditional artistic forms like painting and sculpture. It means that if the pursuit of beauty is included in the implicit part of products and services, their functions will no longer stay utilitarian, but be granted with further significance. Functions not generating any direct effectiveness may also be necessary, even a finishing touch that distinguishes the service or product from others.

Ikko Tanaka wrote about a high realm of design in his book *Awakening of Design*, saying that how the design is used can play an essential role to infuse the work with refreshing beauty. It enlightens us that pursuing a higher realm of service design means we should not rest content with commercial success. If the aim is to lead the aesthetic trends with service systems of beauty, our design will be given a tremendous vitality that makes it socially significant by fulfilling its mission in some other sense. When this mission conforms to the trends of the time, commercial success would just be a byproduct.

Brand new practices have to be taken to achieve a profound integration of functions and beauty. For example, the evaluation of startup teams is no longer the work of only investors when they select projects for investment at Silicon Valley. More evaluation teams are joined by designers, indicating that both functions and beauty are items to be evaluated.

Also, taking the composition of Disney's design team as an example, any scene design finished by designers has to be handed over to industrial engineers and team members specializing in other engineering fields for a discussion on realization. That is when beauty is integrated with functions, of course, with compromises and trade-offs made.

I believe that in tomorrow's service design practice, cross-disciplinary team composition, namely, integrated product development teams (IPDT), will become normal in comprehensive development of products and services. Designers of fine artistic attainments will become indispensable in such a team. What's more, the aesthetic cultivation and training of other team members is an important facilitator that helps an integrated team generate unique designs and put them into perfect practice.

In general, functions are still at the core of service system design, but the connotation and denotation of the concept of "function" has to be seriously deliberated. The sense of beauty has to be integrated into all the links in practice, from organizational environment, team composition, methods for development and tools used, to scenarios and sites to be developed. To achieve this, we have to courageously transcend and lead our customers so as to create a genuinely distinctive service system that keeps seizing the initiative in diversified fierce competition.

Reference

Parasuraman, A., Zeithaml, V. A., & Berry, L. L. (1985). A conceptual model of service quality and its implications for future research. *Journal of Marketing 49*, Fall, 48

Chapter 6
The Perspective of Culture

6.1 Looking in the "Satisfaction Mirror"

Willard Marriott, the founder of Marriott International, has a famous saying, "Take care of your people (employees) and they will take care of your customers." It echoes a concept in the service sector—the "Satisfaction Mirror".[1]

The Satisfaction Mirror uses the metaphor of a mirror to illustrate the relationship between satisfactions of customers and employees, as shown in Fig. 6.1. On the left side of the mirror are concerns of the managers, factors that will satisfy customers; while on the other side are factors important for employee satisfaction, which are symmetrical to those on the left. Managers care very much about customer satisfaction, but the Satisfaction Mirror tells us the feelings of the employees on the other side of the mirror are also important. Happy employees make happy customers. So we have to keep in mind to "take care of our employees so that they can take care of our customers".

Haidilao provides benchmarking employee support in this respect. Most of Haidilao's employees are hired through the recommendation of existing wait staff, with no open recruitment conducted. This is very smart. Because waiters and waitresses in the catering industry are actually not well recognized in society. Most people do not see it as a decent job. How can we make these under-recognized employees feel better then?

The recommendation system for recruitment offers a good solution. If an under-recognized man working in the catering industry helps find a job for his family members, he may earn more respect from the family, for himself and his career. Also, the trust put by the company on him in this recommendation is also a recognition. There is an additional advantage for the company to adopt such a system. The new recruit recommended by a senior worker tends to be more reliable, since the senior, with his own reputation involved, will be careful about his recommendation. This

[1] Schneider and Bowen (2007).

L. Li, *The Era of New Services*, Management for Professionals,
https://doi.org/10.1007/978-981-99-9565-3_6

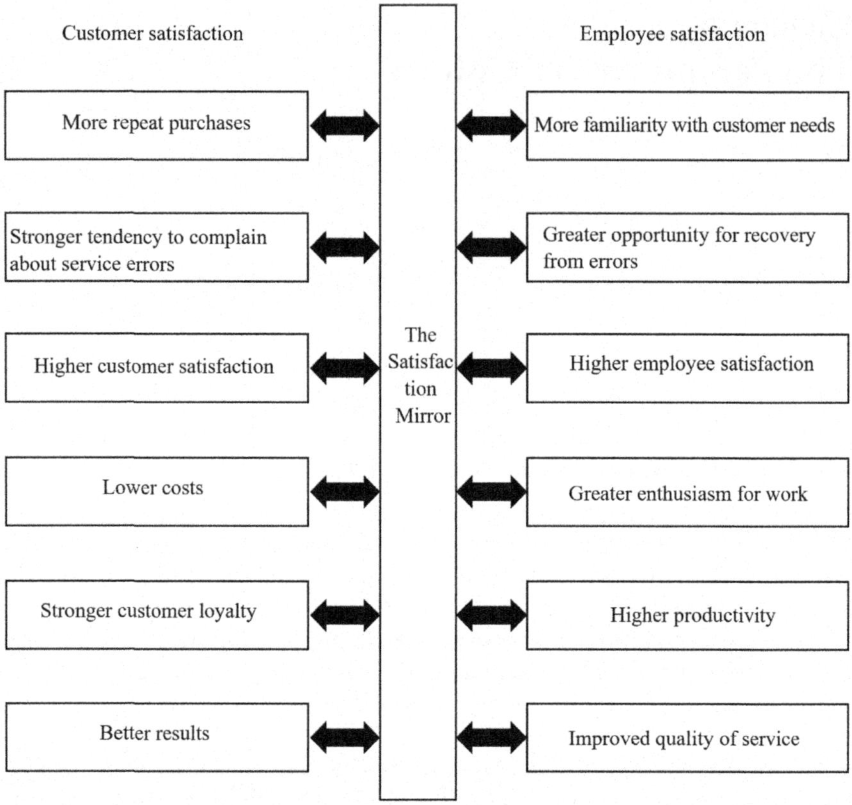

Fig. 6.1 Scheme of the satisfaction mirror

recruitment system is a smart move since one more layer of guarantee has been added with the senior's recommendation.

As for employee benefits, many enterprises have set good examples. For instance, Haidilao accommodates its employees in nice communities in Beijing, instead of packing them into basements or inferior apartments, in the normal way most catering companies treat their workers.

In addition, Haidilao makes another brilliant move by remitting a part of an excellent employee's bonus directly to her parents' bank account. Since filial piety is an important value in Chinese culture, we may imagine the recognition and support she would receive from her parents, as the employee goes home for a family reunion at the Chinese New Year, with these remittances made. Haidilao is earning its employees' respect in this way, seeing that workers in the catering industry are not sufficiently recognized in the society.

Similar practices are often seen in the game industry. In games of King Pro League 2018, proud parents of some players were invited to witness their competition in the

VIP seats. Ways to acquire solid social support are highly recommended practices for employee-oriented service design.

ZTO Express's rewarding policy for excellent employees is also worth learning: the employee takes a part from his bonus and remits, along with an amount added by the company, to his parents. I once attended an annual meeting of ZTO and heard the story shared by a store manager in Hubei Province. The company had taken very good care of him, so he returned this care to his customers. It rained heavily one day when he was trying to develop new customers and expand the market. He held the package in his arms to keep it dry. As you may imagine, the customer was moved, seeing that the deliverer soaked in rain handed her the intact and dry package out of his arms, and became determined about the delivery company of her choice.

A case published in *Harvard Business Review* also shows the importance of caring for employees. In the case, the Qingdao Seaview Garden Hotel provides sincere personalized services to its customers. Once I checked in there with my family. My child and I stayed in one room and my parents stayed in another. We went out for dinner after resting a while in our rooms and leaving luggage there. When we came back, we found a hand-written welcoming note placed in each room by their staff. Words on the notes were different, and customized for guests staying in different rooms. They put a fluffy toy bear in my room, seeing that my child was with me. What about the other room? Their note was: "I see that one of you smokes so I cut some pear slices for you. Wish you good health." A gum was put next to the note, since the room server saw cigarette butts in the ashtray and knew that the guest smoked.

Moreover, all the employees at the hotel greeted us with a sincere smile. I kept wondering why the wait staff were so gratified and passionate at work, until I found a handbook circulated among the staff members—a book of letters of thanks written by employees to the hotel, full of touching stories. For example, there was this residence assistant at the employees' dormitory who was very considerate and keen to help them with whatever they needed. She would buy medicines for those who are sick and bring them fruits. The canteen, too, specially assigned a staffer to observe the condition of each employee. If anyone were found coughing, a tomato salad with caster sugar would soon be given to him. Each and every one of the employees were taken care of sincerely, and enjoyed marvelous support. This is why they returned such sincere and considerate care to their customers.

Accordingly, managers have to consider more about the genuine design of employee benefits. The benefits here are in the broad sense, including recruitment, training and other forms. All the input and efforts made by the company in this respect will turn into "answers" on the other side of the Satisfaction Mirror.

6.2 Interactive Behaviors and Service Innovation

Interaction is one of the most important key words in service innovation. Firstly, it appears in the definition of service: "an interactive process between the service provider and its user that produces economic values". Secondly, interactive behaviors are used in Delft Design Approach to analyze the relationship between product or system and people and explore the reasons behind such relationship, so as to define new possibilities for such interactive relationship or behaviors.

Likewise, interaction plays a subtle but significant role in the service process. As the saying goes, teaching benefits teachers as well as students. The interaction in class teaching benefits all the participants when they observe and debate over the same question from different perspectives, with information exchanged in various ways like verbal and body languages, and facial expressions. Also, interactions between staffers and customers in catering and retail industries benefit the former with a sense of value in the meantime when their customers are satisfied. However, the interactive process in standardized service with reduced contacts between staffers and customers is too simple, requiring staffers to completely follow the SOPs and take no initiative, as a result of which, they may feel less valued, therefore impassionate in service provision.

Therefore, to understand interactive behaviors does not only mean to fully master the essential demands of customers at the stage of service design, but also requires a comprehension over the scenarios when such demands are satisfied. To put it another way, interactions designed for a service system have to answer, with the "5W1H" tool adopted, questions like when and where do the interactions happen, among whom, why and how do they happen. The answers will naturally point to concepts like people, facilities and procedures involved in service vision, as well as implicit and explicit services.

For example, a study published in Journal of Marriage and Family states that the popular use of mobile phones and tablets has resulted in less communication among British family members, even with longer time spent together. They stayed "alone together" for about 136 min per day in 2015, 43% longer than in 2000. Against such a new backdrop of interaction, how can we adapt to the new trends (e.g., restaurants are offering Wi-Fi connection), restore and redirect them towards a better way (e.g., developing activities that encourage the participation of family members) is the question that has to be answered in service innovation.

Indeed, if the service system covers a scope as large as a city, the expansion in scale will involve diversified demands over services. The most important byproduct generated by such a diversity would be growing interactions among people, bringing more potential cooperation, innovations and greater values. Therefore, interaction can be taken as an indicator of efficacy in urban scenarios.

As information transfer develops in methods, technology and service forms, ways for service interaction are more diversified. The selection of participants to be involved in interaction is no longer subject to space constraint. For instance, the form of interaction is exerting great influences on service quality in English language education. More and more TESOL institutes now employ native English speakers as service providers to teach children in need of English study via one-on-one remote interaction. Thanks to this, foreign teachers no longer have to leave their homelands physically to interact with students in China. In other words, Master Xuanzang would not need to go to the West for Buddhist scriptures if he lived in today's era.

It is emphasized in previous discussions on the nature of service that customers participate in the service process as co-producers and the production and consumption of a service happen at the same time. However, the development of online educational platforms seems to have separated the two in education service, thanks to contemporary technological advancement. Different from previous video courses, Massive Open Online Courses (MOOCs) and the latest technological platforms allow users to raise questions to others and receive any feedback timely in the course of learning a lesson. Nevertheless, the absence of real-time interaction restrains users from joining the production as co-producers so that the actual teaching effects of MOOCs lag far behind the effects of face-to-face interaction in traditional educational mode. Therefore, interactivity is still irreplaceable in scenarios with high requirements over the quality of information transfer.

Service robots emerging in recent years feature the preliminary capacity to interact with people, but this surprising capacity also has a disappointing side—the AI technology in support of it is not sophisticated enough to exhibit intelligent behavior indistinguishable from that of a human, as requested by the Turing Test. Nevertheless, the development of voice services led by smart speakers, along with technological advances in IPS and Near Field Communication (NFC), has granted service providers with unprecedented perceptivity to learn customers' needs and sufficient information to understand users' characteristics and preferences, to prepare for better interaction.

The use of IT and intelligent robots in services will bring positive results in two aspects:

First, the service process will be facilitated. Taking the doctor-patient interaction as an example, if the patient's electronic medical records, medical imaging information and physical examination results, maybe precise genetic information in the future, are provided, the doctor won't have to spend time on observing and inquiring the patient, but can move directly to diagnosis or even treatment stage.

Second, the quality, especially precision, of interaction will be significantly improved. Abundant and sufficient user information can help avoid interactive methods that may cause negative feelings in users due to inadequate understanding of them. Some of those methods may break certain taboos of some groups of people or go against their value, including the question often used by wait staff in their interaction with diners, "Do you have to abstain from certain foods?". In the meantime, service providers can diversify their provisions within a certain scope, on the basis of sufficient information and corresponding data analysis. For example, if the historical information tells this customer likes eating fish, algorithms will proactively recommend her special dishes of fish cooked in all different ways. Therefore, information and algorithms, none of them is dispensable. Of course, in addition to generating profits with Big-Data-based user analysis, efforts must be made to ensure that psychological needs of customers, such as to be cared for and respected, are satisfied, with an ideal balance maintained.

The latest Haidilao Robotic Restaurants have soon become sensational throughout China, thus representing a brilliant exploration in this regard. Haidilao has integrated the use of robots and humans perfectly in its design of service interaction and created an amazing atmosphere of novelty. The success is observed in three aspects: Firstly, guests interact with both human and robot waiters in the reception and dining area, while intelligent robot arms and automatic dish pickers are used to improve kitchen efficiency. In the dining area, simple tasks like dish-serving are undertaken by intelligent robots, who deliver dishes to the tables for guests to take and cook in the hot pots by themselves. However, responsive demands and signature services are still fulfilled by human staffers, such as the Noodle Dance performance. On the other hand, robotic arms working backstage to pick dishes and prepare for orders bring a great boost in efficiency. Secondly, joy can be found everywhere. Robot waiters know how to dodge and avoid obstacles, with witty remarks made. The wall before the kitchen is installed with transparent glass that could be switched on and off, allowing guests to see the robotic arms working within, like revealing the "secret veil". Thirdly, the interactive scenarios are designed to be explorable. Ceilings and walls of Haidilao smart restaurants are made of LED displays, which can be switched into different scenarios at the customers' choice, to give them a wonderful dining atmosphere.

In general, interaction is a fundamental component at the core of service, an essential element of service innovation methods, and an important factor of service design. Purely triggering customers' curiosity with innovated interaction methods is far from enough to sustain their vitality, as technology-driven methods of interaction are ever changing. Therefore, service designers have to think in a more systematic way, even base their thinking on knowledge and research in Psychology and Human Ethology.

6.3 Excellent Organizational Culture

Organizational culture is the foundation of excellent services.

Southwest Airlines in the United States is used as an illustration here since it is a good embodiment of principles in the design of service-oriented organizations, therefore worth learning and studying.

What kind of a company is Southwest Airlines? To begin with, statistics in 2018 revealed that Southwest Airlines took the biggest share in the American domestic air passenger transport market (17.8%), with annual operating revenues of $21.9 billion, and kept more than 40 consecutive years of profitability, which was especially hard in the rat race of airline business in the United States. Next, by 2017, Southwest had 54,000 employees and used to rank third in *Fortune*'s list of World's Most Admired Companies, meaning that its employees were very fond of their company. Finally, more than 750 new planes of Southwest are running over 4000 flights among 84 American cities, maintaining a sound development momentum and service level.

Now let's look at the financial performance of Southwest Airlines. The operating revenues of Southwest used to take only one-third of the revenues of American Airlines, but its costs on major expenditure items, including fuel charge, take-off and landing charges, rental fees and wages, were obviously lower than that of American Airlines. So it performed nicely in terms of cash flow, holding $2.2 billion cash at hand, compared with the $120 million of American Airlines. The latter had to apply for bankruptcy protection later on.

What are the reasons for Southwest Airlines' brilliant performance? As its co-founders Rollin King and Herbert Kelleher told us, "If you get your passengers to their destinations when they want to get there, on time, at the lowest possible fares, and make darn sure they have a good time doing it, people will fly your airline". The key words here are "the lowest possible fares", "on time" and "have a good time". This obviously reveals the corporate culture of Southwest Airlines. However, instead of framing this culture and hanging to the wall, they implemented these key words to the letter in all aspects of their strategy and operation, which is quite thought-provoking.

How do they ensure the lowest possible fares for passengers? The first and largest part in the cost structure of air services is costs related to airplanes, including expenditures for airplane purchase, repair and maintenance, fuel charge and take-off and landing charges. The second part is wages and benefits of employees, which are relatively higher than wages for workers in other fields. The third part is air ticket selling costs, spent on various selling channels or agencies.

So the key to ensure the lowest possible fares is to reduce service costs. Here are some "Secrets of Southwest" for your reference:

Let's start from an interesting ratio—75: 110. It means that it takes Southwest 75 people to run an air route, but 110 for other airline companies. The key question is how does Southwest manage the operation with so few people?

Firstly, Southwest has insisted on flying only Boeing 737 since its founding. What advantages does it bring? For sure, repair and maintenance cost a lot less since the company needs only to prepare one set of spare parts under many circumstances. The purchase costs are lowered at the same time. In 2015, when I visited an assembly facility of Boeing at its headquarters, the Boing employee pointed at an airplane production line and introduced it as the line that produced Southwest-customized Boeing 737s. As we can see, the bulk purchase of Southwest would bring them lower prices. What's more, the training costs for pilots and flight attendants are also lower since they only need to learn about only one type of aircraft.

The use of the same type of aircraft has also made Southwest more flexible in service operation. If anything goes wrong on a plane, it can soon be replaced by another plane of the same type, with no need to change or tune the flight crew, since the two planes are identical. The benefits cannot be overstated, for there is an important practice known as "overbooking" in the civil aviation industry. To explain with an example, if I have 100 seats on my plane, I will sell 105 tickets at the booking stage, in case someone would cancel their flights before take-off. Supposing that five tickets are canceled, the rest 100 passengers will make a perfect flight with no empty seats left. This is the ideal situation. Any one empty seat on a flying plane means a waste of carrying capacity, so airline companies adopt overbooking to reduce empty seats.

But what will happen if all the 105 passengers show up at the airport? You can simply transfer them to the next flight and offer some financial compensation. Actually, this is a common practice of all airline companies as supported by a set of accurate algorithms that tell exactly how many tickets can be oversold. This is termed as "yield management" in Management Science.

I encountered an overbooked plane once on a trip from Shanghai to Beijing. I arrived at the airport and saw about 20 people queuing for boarding passes at the counter, when a ground attendant showed up and said, "Sorry, the flight is oversold so there is only one seat left. We will transfer the rest of you to another flight a couple of hours later and compensate 300 yuan to each of you." This put me into great confusion, so I asked, "I understand you'd oversell some flight tickets (my discipline also involves studies on yield management), but why did you sell as many as twenty?" She explained that the airline company had suddenly changed the aircraft, so there were not enough seats.

Please pay attention. This is an important point in airliners' operation management. A temporary change of aircraft will cause abnormal overbooking and result in difficulties in operation (not only growing cost pressure, but also declining customer satisfaction). Now you may understand the advantages Southwest boasts—any plane it changes at any time is completely identical to the previous one.

It is reported that American Airlines used to operate a low-cost subsidiary, People Express, to compete for budget travelers, but the subsidiary soon went bankrupt. Because it forgot to learn the secret of Southwest, but flew with over 60 types of aircraft. The difficulties of dispatching that many types of aircraft must have had something to do with the airliner's bankruptcy, since convenient and efficient operation has been coded into the genes of low-cost carriers. In summary, using a single type of aircraft brings many advantages to the operation, purchase, repair and maintenance, and employee training of airline companies.

Secondly, self-help service is realized in an all-round way. A big portion of Southwest's service procedures are accomplished with the support of its official website and check-in machines in airports. Whenever I was about to take a Southwest flight as I studied in the U.S. in 2002, I could print my boarding pass with a piece of A4 paper at home and head directly to the security check and boarding gate, upon arriving at the airport. Today, we have basically gotten used to boarding with the QR code on the mobile phone, but passengers of Southwest Airlines could print their boarding passes at home as early as more than ten years ago. You may imagine how much labor costs have been saved thanks to the extensive application of self-services like this. Therefore, the all-round self-help service plays an important role in Southwest's service design.

Thirdly, they have an employee-centered corporate culture. Southwest saves many labor costs by running an air route with only 75 employees on average. But all the money saved has been rewarded to its employees, so that they enjoy the best benefits throughout the civil aviation industry. Despite the fact that Southwest is a low-fare budget carrier, the great employee benefits have guaranteed a stable staff team for the company.

The next numerical comparison looks more interesting: 15–20 min for Southwest Airlines versus 45–60 min for its counterparts.

The turnaround time of aircrafts is an important indicator for the operation of airliners. It is the time that passes from landing until taking off for a new flight, when passengers deplane, the cabin crew prepare for the next flight and new passengers get onboard.

Southwest Airlines finishes turnaround in 15–25 min while other airliners have to use 45–60 min. The turnaround time is quite significant since capital-intensive service providers like airline companies (with airplanes being their assets) have to make attempts to lower costs and improve profitability. The shorter turnaround time has enabled Southwest to fly two hours longer per day than its counterparts and thereby earn more profits. This means a higher asset utilization ratio and better scale effects.

Conversely, other airliners must also care a lot about the turnaround time, then why is Southwest so much faster? The credit should be given to its interesting tactics in this respect.

The first tactic is to assign passengers into boarding groups, rather than exact seats, to ensure quick boarding. Normally, a passenger selects or is assigned a seat upon check-in. But Southwest does not provide any assigned seats (this practice is also adopted by some airlines lately), instead, passengers are assigned into three groups, A, B and C. Where should this passenger sit without a seat number? He can actually sit anywhere he likes, just like finding a seat on the bus. If he wants a better position, he has to board earlier to find one; and if two people want to sit next to each other, they, too, have to be quick. When all the passengers want to board the plane as early as possible, guess what will happen at the boarding gate? They all fall in line quickly in front of the gate and cannot wait to get a good seat once the gate is open. The passengers' desire for better seats is used by Southwest to make sure of a quick boarding process. As we may recall our own boarding experience, the most annoying part might be sitting on a plane with most of the passengers and listening to the airport announcer that keeps calling two or three stragglers to get onboard.

The grouped seating practice is not something to be overlooked. As we often encounter this in boarding: passengers are required to board according to their seat numbers. For example, we'd hear from the broadcast "Passengers in Row 30–50, please board on the plane" first, and it would then be the turn of people in Row 10–30, after a while. The airlines' intention of putting passengers in later positions earlier on the plane is to improve the boarding efficiency in case that those in front positions block the aisle with their luggage while being seated. Therefore, it is a usual practice for airline companies to board passengers in later rows first and front rows afterward.

But there is some tiny difference in the practice of some outstanding airlines. They would also ask passengers in later positions to board first, but, instead of mentioning their seats or rows, they just break passengers into groups. For example, the worst seats, like those in Row 30–50, are named as Group A, rows before them are Group B, and then Group C. What is this for? Imagine that you spent the same money on the ticket as others but was assigned a seat in Row 50. That was already an upset. Then the broadcast reminded you again, "passengers sitting in Row 50 can now board the plane," so you had to get on the plane, facing all the passengers already sitting, and move towards the tail of the plane. But what are the effects of the grouping tactic? As a passenger in Group A, even though your seat was still in Row 50, you'd feel somehow better than those in Group B and C. It takes care of the nuance feelings of passengers, and therefore bears an important significance.

In addition, many large airports in foreign countries serve First-Class passengers and Economy-Class passengers at different boarding gates, instead of arranging them in different lines before the same gate. The two non-interfering pathways are also a considerate arrangement that avoid causing negative emotions in Economy-Class passengers with the priority services for those in the First Class. Therefore, being able to pay attention to, care for and even "make use of" the customers' mental states means a high realm in service management.

The second tactic is to use small airports. What helps Southwest Airlines to turn around so quickly? With many airlines scrambling for resources like boarding bridges and pavements at major American airports, Southwest takes the less-taken road by avoiding these major airports. Taking San Francisco as an example, Southwest rarely uses the San Francisco International Airport, but prefers Auckland Airport across the Bay Bridge, which is small but with few competitors. Southwest enjoys a higher priority there and can naturally turn around quickly.

Of course, the most useful time-saving tactic of Southwest is the third one: cross training. One common scene in the airport is that the last passenger getting off the plane will find a team of people waiting to get on. They are public area attendants who have to clean the plane after all passengers are off, so that those for the next flight can board when their job is done.

This is a typical serial system in which all links follow a sequence, A first, B second and C last. The first thing a specialist in program optimization will do is to change the serial system into a concurrent one, which means some links have to be done simultaneously to save time. Then, are there any people free when passengers are getting off? The flight attendants. Normally, they are just standing by the aisle and saying "thank you" to the passengers. However, Southwest attendants have already started cleaning up the plane as passengers walk. After all the passengers get off, the plane will be almost clean and tidy. This representative case of changing a serial system into a concurrent system has greatly shortened the turnaround time.

While the attendants are cleaning, the captain is off the plane, checking the passengers in at the boarding gate. That explains why Southwest needs only 75 people for one flight—many ground positions in common use in the industry are cancelled in Southwest. But are there any troubles behind this practice? Why do I have to check in passengers when captains of other airlines are getting off the plane to have a rest? You see, Southwest captains enjoy higher salaries, compared to captains of other companies. In other words, the logic of Southwest is to lower all possible costs, return a part of them back to passengers through low fares and a part to employees through high benefits. This is the core of its corporate culture, driving Southwest to do all it can to lower costs. Cross training is an important reason for its quick turnaround. Less crew members are needed when employees are strongly motivated to work by the superb benefits.

The last factor that supports Southwest to sustain the lowest possible fares is e-tickets and self-help boarding. Southwest has removed travel agencies and ticket brokers from its ticket selling process since very early, with almost all the tickets booked on its official website. As someone calculated, the cost of selling one ticket through an agency or a broker is 10 dollars, but it costs only 50 cents to sell an e-ticket online. Remember, Southwest does all it can to lower costs.

Checked baggage is another example—Southwest does not provide checked baggage service for free. What are the benefits of this? Clearly, when passengers bring less baggage, backstage staff of the airliner shoulders less burden, the airplane carries less weight, thus consuming less fuel.

What is more, Southwest provides no free food on the plane. In our own experience, airline meals are often bad, described as "chicken ribs" in Chinese. Since you have paid for the meal by buying the air ticket, "if you eat it, it may hurt your stomach; if not, it may hurt your wallet", making it tasteless as food but a pity to be discarded, just like "a chicken rib". Now that not every passenger needs the food and they would probably be dissatisfied by them, Southwest eliminates airline meals from the mandatory list, but in the meanwhile, offers more delicious paid food to passengers in real need.

This is a kind of "separation strategy" (it will be explained in detail in the session of service innovation principles) that singles out and removes some mandatory items since not everyone needs them, and adds paid premium services to people in need. Southwest has replaced its coffee with Starbucks drinks very early, but passengers have to pay for them. Also, the sandwiches on Southwest planes taste very good, but need to be paid extra. This is an important logic in Southwest's operation.

We will discuss the second key word "on time" now, which is the foremost pain spot in the civil aviation industry.

As we all know, being "on time" is especially hard to ensure in aviation and Southwest Airlines' coping strategy is to fly point-to-point and use small airports. What does point-to-point mean? The airline network in the U.S. follows the hub-and-spoke distribution model, in which hub airports in major cities like Los Angeles on the west coast and Chicago in the eastern and middle region, act as the centroids, with Airbus A380 and other large aircrafts flying in between, and are also linked to medium- and small-sized cities and some second-tier cities by regional jets. A typical benefit of such an aviation network is economic efficiency. Large aircrafts flying between centroid cities, which aggregate the transport demands of medium- and small-sized cities, give a full play to scale effects by carrying more passengers and making frequent round trips, thereby ensuring a sound economic efficiency for the whole network. However, the hub-and-spoke network has an inherent deficiency as seen from the viewpoint of service providers, since time consumption becomes a great problem for passengers. Due to the need for frequent transfers, extreme weather can easily cause problems in transfers and detain passengers at the airport.

Now that passengers do not like transferring that much, Southwest has found a unique solution by offering point-to-point routes. They connect two second-tier cities or a second-tier city and a centroid city at the far end with a direct route to save a great many transfers and delays, bringing a boost to the service quality. What prevented other airline companies from following suit? It is actually risky to directly connect second-tier cities—the shortage of passengers may result in operating losses.

Whatsoever, the Boeing 737 used by Southwest is a narrow-body aircraft that carries less passengers, therefore an ideal solution to the problem of insufficient ridership. If the passengers on a certain route cannot even fill up a 737, there must be problems with the market, making it worthless to run this route. The successful niche markets maintained through point-to-point routes are exactly the reason for Southwest to transcend others in punctuality.

The third key words are "have a good time". We barely see a "sense of humor" in the recruitment requirements of airlines, apart from Southwest Airlines. They are literally saying, if you are not humorous enough, do not apply for this job.

It is based on a profound truth in Management Science: not anyone can be trained to do anything, you have to select suitable talents according to the needs of certain posts.

My personal experience of the sense of humor of Southwest employees started impressing me remarkably once I boarded their plane. Different from the pretty stewardess and handsome stewards we see on most Chinese airlines, the one who greeted us at Southwest was a senior lady. And the old seats in the cabin, looking like bus chairs in the 1980s, were a bit disappointing. But throughout the 1.5 h flight, the lady attendant kept talking to the passengers through the public address system, about the weather, her feelings or anything else that kept the passengers awake and excited. The atmosphere was fantastic thanks to this humorous senior lady. A captain of Southwest even said this to his passengers in the announcement upon landing in New York, "I'm happy to tell you that we've successfully landed at Toronto International Airport" and, as all the passengers were shocked, added, "Just kidding. It's New York City we're landing in."

You see, Southwest's sense of humor is not only required in recruitment, but also well demonstrated in operation.

The DING! application is another embodiment of Southwest's sense of humor. In a television advertisement, a big family is celebrating the birthday of the grandfather when his daughter holds a big birthday cake full of candles in her hands and walks from the kitchen to the living room. The whole scene is sweet and joyous, with everyone singing the birthday song for the grandfather. But all of a sudden, the daughter, upon hearing a "ding" sound, throws off the cake and rushes to her room to click the tiny airfoil-shaped button flashing at the bottom right corner of the computer—Southwest has sent her messages of special fares departing from her city! That application is DING!

DING! is serving more than 2 million Southwest users, signifying an important marketing innovation in the aviation industry, in my mind. When would people look for air ticket information, even today? We'd normally check airfares with a clear plan in mind to travel for a conference or holiday. But Southwest will present its special fares to you, regardless of whether you have that plan or not. Please note that their messages are, different from the spam messages we often receive, customized based on subscribers' personal preferences and closely related to their local cities or interested destinations.

These push messages mark an important innovation—demands can be stimulated into being. The proactive interaction between DING! and its subscribers with customized recommendations provided is rendered to the audience through a funny advertisement, which is also a part of the joyous experience created by Southwest Airlines.

Many low cost carriers soon followed the examples of Southwest to reduce their costs but merely descended to copycats. Ryanair in Ireland used to come up with an eccentric idea—changing all toilets on their airplanes into coin-operated ones, which was too controversial to be put into practice. That is not a smart move. If they'd really done it, I reckon, they wouldn't be able to sell any drink on the plane. A service is a comprehensive experience, so the kernel should always be users' experience.

Southwest Airlines' corporate culture is closely related to their service design principles, so what we have to learn from them is how they have perfectly utilized the key words of the corporate culture into all aspects of their strategies and operation.

Besides, motivation is also important. How can we ensure that employees are in perfect tune with the company? Salary and benefits are obviously an important aspect, and I want to introduce another incentive method with the case of a Chinese telecommunications business. Years ago, this company had a grand remuneration and incentive plan designed for it by a consultancy. Under the plan named Lead to Cash (LTC), managers asked all departments to specify and report the time needed for return on cash for each project and then evaluated their performance based on the reports. However, managers soon realized that such an incentive system was extremely unfit for the R&D department since employees were misdirected to pay attention only to short-term behaviors in fundamental R&D projects as the time for cash return had become their biggest concern, in spite of the fact that fundamental R&D was full of uncertainty and always took long-term efforts. So managers stopped implementing the LTC plan in that department right away and put them under independent evaluation.

The work environment also reveals the organizational culture to a degree. Different work scenarios require different work environments. For example, for labor-intensive service factories focusing on efficiency improvement, the environment design should take layout, balance of assembly lines, even application of full-automatic systems into consideration, whereas a large number of design companies have to offer their designers an open environment for them to fully play their imagination and freely communicate. Therefore, the design of work environment within a service system is equally important since it guarantees employees' devotion and efficiency at work. An ingeniously designed workplace can even boost their moral and organizational identity.

Reference

Schneider, B., & Bowen, D. E. (2007). *Winning the service game*. The Commercial Press.

Part III
Principles and Methods of Service Design and Innovation

Chapter 7
Principles of Service Design and Innovation

Design explores the needs of more people while arts explore the boundary. According to the design experience of Disneyland in early days, at the core of its design were scriptwriters, those who wrote the stories; it was then the turn of designers to decide the presentation of characters and scenes; and finally, industrial engineers were responsible for rendering the design into reality through engineering practices. As sci-fi films inspired many technical innovations, Bezos got his inspiration for Amazon Echo from the talking computer on *Star Trek* spaceships. Therefore, by essence, if we count all the writers of all types of literary works as designers, the future is designed by them. Of course, scientists and engineers also play their parts in the actualization of design through exploring relevant principles and practical techniques. Service innovation also requires us to follow the lead of certain originative design thinking, instead of simply understanding users' preferences.

Certainly, while taking the leading role, the design thinking contains a profound understanding of constant in-depth needs and trends, including those related to beauty and human nature. For example, our life gets increasingly convenient as it is infiltrated by more smart home appliances. There might even be phoneless service scenarios in the future, because of displays and speech acquisition devices everywhere. However, is it possible that such a ubiquitous and ultimate convenience would trigger another kind of panic? We probably would pine for permittivity—wishing to go back to the unintelligent, not-modern and non-digital purely natural place where things started from.

This is why designs on a higher level would be bidirectional, which, instead of transcending or totally denying the past, think across time from past to present, till future, and see into the big picture. In this chapter, the thinking of service design is analyzed in three aspects: original experience, redesign and diversification.

L. Li, *The Era of New Services*, Management for Professionals,
https://doi.org/10.1007/978-981-99-9565-3_7

7.1 Original Experience

Humans, in their continuous transformation of nature, tend to desire keenly to return to aboriginality or explore their origin as driven by the perceived risks of various technical processes and industrial systems, as well as their attachment, even guilty conscience, to nature. Service experience targeting at such desires is defined as "original experience", which has six major models, as shown in Fig. 7.1.

7.1.1 Place of Origin

We'll start with an example. The Chinese cantaloupe Hami melon got the name from its place of origin, Hami City in Xinjiang, and is one of the specialties of Xinjiang. The Hami government has launched a "777" Project to help increase the income of local people. Hami melons are picked from melon patches in the morning of Double-Seventh Festival (Chinese Valentine's Day, on the seventh day of the seventh lunar month), loaded to Boeing 737s and delivered to customers within 7 h. It takes less than 7 h for the melons to travel from farmland to dinner tables. What is the key to this interesting project? Let us have a close look into the project. Firstly, the melons are customized, with each one subscribed by a customer when it is still a seedling and assigned a serial number. Customers may observe their subscribed seedlings through cameras installed in the melon patches. Ripen fruits would be picked on Double-Seventh Festival and delivered to them in 7 h.

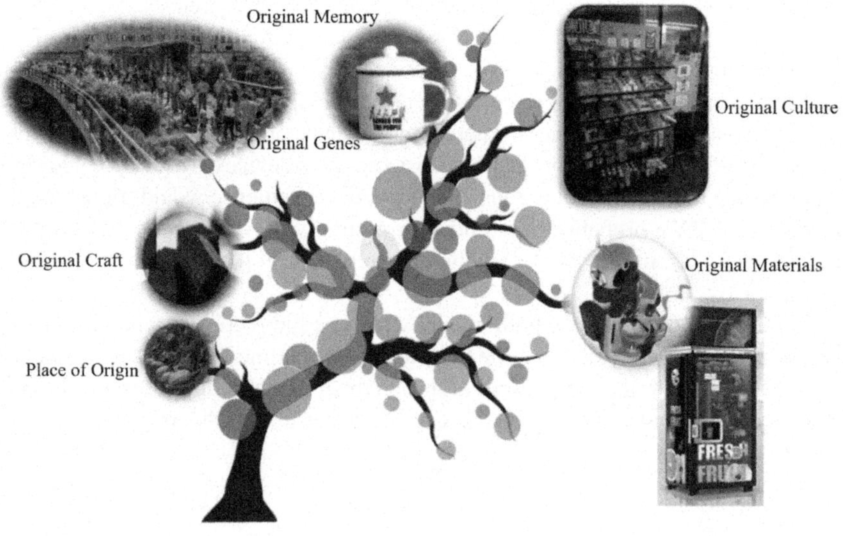

Fig. 7.1 Six models of original experience

How do these melons sell? The normal price of Hami melons is RMB 20/500 g, but these customized melons are tagged as high as RMB 98/500 g, and are often soon sold out. It is said that even local people cannot taste the best Hami melons in their own city, since they are all "for customization". What motivates the farmers to grow these melons? We can make a calculation: Previous revenues of one *mu* (equivalent to 6.67 acre) ranked between RMB 2500–3000, but the average revenues for customized Hami melons are now RMB 6000 per *mu*. Of course, farmers are getting enthusiastic about this project.

There is an idea deeply rooted in people's minds about food: those produced in places of origin are more authentic and worth higher prices. Another approach is to take the customers to the places of origin for them to pick the fruits themselves, which is adopted by many picking gardens in the development of local tourism. "From farmland to dinner tables" and "picking tours" are both embodiments of the place-of-origin thinking.

7.1.2 Original Culture

In the original culture model, people are duplicating and recalling the good old days. For example, an exquisite tea table in a tea room may stand for the Chinese tea culture that dates back to ancient times but is still far-reaching today.

Modern people are willing to visit tea houses, to read, drink, chat and quiet themselves down in the intense Zen atmosphere. The growing number of vending machines in offices is another example of original culture. As we see in Fig. 7.2, they are pretty normal in our life now.

These vending machines need no security measures. All you have to do is to pick the thing you want and scan the QR code for payment. Such a scenario reminds us of the primitive state when honesty prevailed, as "people could leave their doors unlocked at night and lost articles were always returned". It is said that people still buy and sell like this in some remote mountainous villages: Farmers leave their vegetables by the trail for customers to choose and buy, and all they need to do is to collect the money put beside after finishing a day's work. The lovely permittivity also reminds us that the long-standing rich culture of the Chinese nation may very likely be transformed into a "pure and fresh" experience vastly welcomed in the modern service sector.

7.1.3 Original Craft

The very first filling and cleansing machines of Tsingdao Beer in Fig. 7.3 seem to show us the originality of the brand. The first Tsingdao Beers were brewed by German crafts and machines, and history has smelted the passing time into quality. Shown in the figure is the state of the original craft. This model is also used by

Fig. 7.2 Vending machines in offices

many enterprises emphasizing ancient crafts, old stories and long-standing legacies. Consumers today are increasingly curious about the crafts and techniques of products, so these scenarios can convince them better about the products' authenticity.

Fig. 7.3 Earliest filling and cleansing machines of Tsingdao Beer

7.1.4 Original Memory

Does the mug printed "serve the people" in Fig. 7.4 look genial to you? Products like it have formed a special category that arouses people's memory of the bygone era.

Super Wenheyou in Changsha City is one in this category. It made to the hot searches list on Weibo during the Labor Day holiday in 2020 for having 16,000 waiting tables that queued for 12 h. At the entrance of the largest Wenheyou crayfish restaurant in Asia are broken staircases and brick walls that, like a time tunnel, take visitors back to the streets and lanes of the old Changsha City back in the 1970s. Streets, lamps, stores, diners, windows and decorations, the complex is full of timeworn and vintage details, like an age-old but lively community in the city. Not only are locals lured to find the "original Changsha" that lives in their memory, but also tourists from all over the country are attracted to view the unique streetscape of old Changsha and taste the authentic crayfish dishes. Original memories like this can trigger strong consuming impulses in people (Fig. 7.5).

As Don Norman writes in his book *The Design of Everyday Things*, "A favorite object is a symbol, setting up a positive frame of mind, a reminder of pleasant memories, or sometimes an expression of one's self". Because of this, features of a time are related to the memory shared by a group of people who can become extensive objects of design. For instance, the Arctic Ocean Orange Soda suddenly went viral years ago. It had almost disappeared in the market before becoming trendy again among the post-80s (the Chinese generation born in the 1980s) who used to

Fig. 7.4 The mug in the memory of Chinese born in the 1970s and 1980s

Fig. 7.5 Super Wenheyou—the retro-style miniature of old Changsha. *Source* https://www.sohu.com/a/285310342_505162

drink this soda since their childhood. Original memories can cause strong impulses for consumption.

Ellen Langer, an eminent professor of Psychology, conducted an experiment with the elderly by reproducing the life they had 20 years ago. According to the experiment results, the "counterclockwise" experience had given the subjects younger and healthier mental and physical states. It is another proof that positive psychological reflection can exert a strong impact on people. The original memory model, in its essence, is making use of the power of psychological reflections.

7.1.5 Original Genes

In spite of the long evolution history of human kind, the vast changes in society have outpaced the evolution of our bodies in recent centuries. As a result, the unseen side of human genes keeps reminding us of the pleasure brought by "aboriginality", since the lifestyles we used to take were completely overthrown by industrial civilization.

For example, a green forest feels refreshing and pleasant; great mountains and seas broaden our minds. These are inscribed in our genes because our primitive ancestors lived in such an environment. Also, the sound of a mountain, a stream or insects makes it easier for us to fall asleep, as they are all original sounds of nature.

Figure 7.6 is the High Line Park in New York City, created on a former light rail section between buildings in the city. In view of citizens' complaints about traffic noise and wearing of the facilities, the government transformed the rail spur into a greenway surrounded by plants and flowers, rendering pedestrians a sense of

Fig. 7.6 The high line in New York. *Source* https://zinco-greenroof.com/references/high-line-park-new-york-city

permittivity which caters well to the affinity with nature encrypted in human genes. It tells that service designers have to explore this model in their innovative attempts, to please and gratify customers at the genetic level.

7.1.6 Original Materials

We often see such a machine in shopping malls today, behind the transparent case of which are fresh oranges to be ordered and squeezed instantly into fresh juice. Many people prefer such fresh-squeezed juice over packed orange juice in supermarkets, for it shows us the original (raw) materials and the way they are made into juice in a reassuring way.

Practitioners in the service sector have to think about ways to bring consumers closer to the original status of products. Vice versa, if a customer has no idea about the place of origin, quality, security control measures over food processing and the logistics process of the orange juice she finds in a supermarket, questions will crop up in her mind, indicating perceived risks about the product.

However, if consumers can see the original materials right where they are and witness the production process, they will be more assured and at ease. Under such a circumstance, the original experience is defined by its "original distance" from the core resources within the service package. For example, bottled juice bought from a vending machine has to go through two production links—production of oranges and production of orange juice, two logistics links—one for oranges and one for juice, and the storage link and the shelving link at the retail end, so its original distance is six. While for instant juice vending machines like Vingoo, their products experience only two invisible links—the production and logistics of oranges, so the original distance of two constructs a significant competitive edge that considerably

Fig. 7.7 Popsicles with visible fruit slices

lowers the perceived risks among consumers. This is also the essential principle of the original material model. Popsicles in Fig. 7.7 are another example, where consumers can see the strawberry slices in popsicles with their eyes, thereby convinced about the real materials used in the products.

Comprehensively speaking, the thinking of original experience stands for customers' underlying needs for sensory experience. As the CEO of Hennessy, Bernard Peillon, said, people desire to know about the makers of the vintage wine, its place of origin, its culture and crafts. These represent the return of techniques, crafts, spirit and taste.

7.2 Redesign

According to a Japanese designer Kenya Hara, redesign is the process to "make known things unknown". In my mind, this principle is equally important to service design.

A new service may just be a "redesign" of some common and familiar model. Of course, a new service can also be a redesign based on the long-term, focused, in-depth deliberation over a certain industry. As China's leading online examination service provider, Exam Star initially entered the corporate training examination sector, offering online examination services for employees. During the COVID-19 pandemic, due to the prevention and control policies, Exam Star identified a new demand for formal online examinations, with a primary focus on the essential scenarios of recruitment exams and certification tests. In 2020, Exam Star launched an online AI proctoring solution and continued to roll out several industry-innovative AI technologies such as "AI Recognition of Candidate's Sitting Posture" and "AI Proctoring Teacher". Starting from 2020, this segment saw a revenue increase of over 150% for two consecutive years, with the average transaction value increasing tenfold compared to the corporate examination segment. The cumulative number of candidates taking these formal online examinations surpassed one million.

Therefore, the core logic of redesign is "do not take the status quo for granted, do not stay trapped by the familiar". We will discuss the directions for redesign from the following aspects: senses, reflection, design and art.

7.2.1 Expand from Five Senses to More Perceptions

The Buddhist *Heart Sutra* preaches "eyes, ears, nose and tongue" and "feeling, thought, choice and consciousness". The former belong to the five senses of people, and the latter are components in the progressive course from behavior to attitude and then belief, from the perspective of Social Psychology. In the view of service and customers, sensory organs like "eyes, ears, nose and tongue" can be considered as acquisition tools of service experience. The acquired information is then processed by the brain to form certain beliefs and transformed into behaviors through "feeling, thought, choice and consciousness".

The Information Architecture of humans proposed by Kenya Hara is an extension of the five senses in a way. He claims that all our sensory organs are apparatus to collect memories that will then converge into materials for the architecture of information in our brain. This reminds us to think about ways to sufficiently collect and analyze information, to acquire information on service through not five but all senses in innovative service designs. It actually coincides with the commonly used tool in design thinking, empathy map, which is mainly composed of things the users think, see, hear, say and do that are then concluded into their pain spots and needs.

As reminded by these methods, our discussion should be focused on the full use of five, even all, senses in information acquisition. Taking the retail sector as an example, purchases in the traditional mode are made according to planned checklists, though unplanned purchases do happen sometimes. But, anyway, people have to travel to fairs or supermarkets for the purchase and return to their living scenarios to consume the bought commodities. The transformation brought by e-commerce is that consumers can stay where they are and buy things on PCs or mobile phones. The development of equipment has freed the legs of consumers since a few finger moves are enough for e-shopping. The way they move fingers is also changing, from clicking a mouse in front of a fixed computer to swiping over the phone screen. Amazon Echo even allows them to buy things by voice while staying in their rooms or any place covered by a smart speaker. Changes to information acquiring measures in this process result in an explicit trend—people are getting lazier. However, if considered from the biophysical view, people are continuously optimizing their lifestyles to reduce energy consumption, which are self-conscientious practice towards leaning operation at a high level.

Norman mentions three components of product design in *The Design of Everyday Things*, namely usability, aesthetics and practicability. They each correspond to people's demands at different levels, with emotions at a higher level. Therefore, service designers have to tell stories, express the pursuit of beauty and deliver aesthetic values in their design. Successful associative designs combining different senses in previous art projects have demonstrated that, through such association, the aesthetic perception is enriched from one to several dimensions, stimulating people to reflect beyond their behaviors and receive unique pleasure. For example, the keyboard of perfume scents exhibited at Mori Art Museum in Fig. 7.8, Tokyo combines music and scents in the design, so that senses of hearing and smell are associated. In the design of the programs paper of the Nagano Winter Olympic Games, Kenya Hara puts concave letters on the white cover to resemble the footprints on snowfield, associating sight and touch, as shown in Fig. 7.9.

The "Expand from Five Senses to More Perceptions" redesign principle is also applied to the experience economy.

In recent years, the rise of classical Chinese style has permeated various service sectors in China. "PALACE", a dining brand inspired by ancient Chinese palace culture, precisely targets the "modern consumers", predominantly the young generation. By crafting a service model that integrates culture and dining, it offers customers

Fig. 7.8 "Keyboard of perfume scents" exhibited at Mori Art Museum, Tokyo

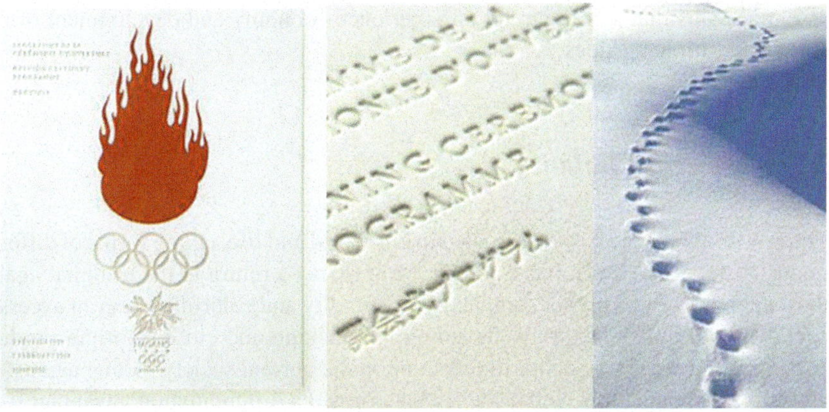

Fig. 7.9 Programs paper of the Opening and Closing Ceremonies of the Nagano Winter Olympic Games. *Source* Hara (2006)

an immersive experience blending elements of Hanfu culture (Ancient Chinese clothing), theatrical performances, imperial dining culture, and courtly etiquettes. The meticulous and lifelike sets, services, and rituals make customers feel as if they've been invited to an imperial banquet. Additionally, they have the option to enhance their experience by dressing up in Hanfu, allowing them to feel the culture from the inside out. This not only elevates the dining cultural experience but also meets the personalized needs of today's consumers to a great extent.

Another case is The *Meet Again* series of performances, a major live-action show brand in China, often set against the backdrop of natural landscapes in southern Chinese tourist cities. *Meet Pingyao Again* is an exception. It's the first project of the *Meet Again* series in northern China. Pingyao doesn't possess remarkable landscapes, and its long winter is too cold, making it unsuitable for outdoor performances set against a backdrop of nature. The show *Meet Pingyao Again* breaks the conventional theater performance model of a fixed stage and audience seating. It features four performance scenes. In the first three scenes, the audience does not have fixed seating. Instead, they follow the storyline and actors, moving from one performance space to another. They are truly immersed in the show, interacting directly with the actors and experiencing realistic scene settings.

This is an innovative performance service model. The core idea is to expand the "scene" to include the audience, offering them a 360° audio-visual experience, enhancing the impact of the storyline on them. In July 2023, the Department of Industry Development of the Ministry of Culture and Tourism of the People's Republic of China released 20 demonstration cases of national-level immersive cultural and tourism new business models. *Meet Pingyao Again* was honored as the leading immersive performance.

Due to the limited cognitive load of the human brain, the transformation from five to all senses cannot easily produce linearly increasing effects. But these attempts are redesign approaches that immerse users profoundly and inspire reflections, and also essential paths that suit the trend of experience economy and development of new scenarios with IoT values.

7.2.2 Power of Balance

The power of balance has long existed in our world and life, taking forms of different trends at the micro level. For example, Muji marks a return to the minimal against the tendency towards higher complexity, profundity and colorfulness, even excessive packaging and manufacturing. Its simplified packing and close-to-origin products stimulate people of rationality to reflect upon the current society. Going against the mainstream though, this new tendency has formed a differentiation advantage.

Another redesign in services is reflected in the marketing model. Every service industry has its own established marketing methods that have been used over the years. Take gyms as an example: prepaid is a common sales model where customers need to purchase 'annual memberships' or 'multi-visit guest pass' to continue working out. The biggest challenge for traditional gyms is customer retention. Many gym-goers choose not to renew their memberships once they expire, mainly because of a subpar customer experience or unsatisfactory results.

SUPERMONKEY is a new fitness brand established in China, targeting its customer base towards the 25–40 age group of working professionals. To enhance the customer experience, SUPERMONKEY reflected upon this traditional marketing model, employed peer-recommendation marketing for promotion, adopted a model that does away with annual memberships, opting instead for a pay-per-session approach. If customers are unsatisfied with their experience, they can simply choose not to attend subsequent sessions. This payment method not only reduces the financial burden on customers but also elevates their overall experience.

SUPERMONKEY's innovative operating model can be summarized as shifting from "selling to more customers" to "selling more to customers". Their courses place a stronger emphasis on results. During the customer experience phase, they offer a wider range of choices based on the customer's preferences and actual conditions, recommending more effective courses. To enhance the customer experience, SUPERMONKEY even introduced a professional curriculum system. The courses are entirely designed from the customer's perspective, satisfying their various needs for "calorie burn, body building, stress relief, and posture improvement".

As of 2022, SUPERMONKEY, which has been established for only 8 years, has over 260 studios in 8 cities across China, more than 2000 SUPERTEAMs, over 1.3 million fitness customers, and offers up to 100 different kinds of courses.

Established in 2013, the Chinese hotel brand ATOUR was amongst the pioneers to introduce the concept of a "Chinese experience" in its design and service concept. Its approach transcends the traditional hospitality framework by creating a "fourth space" that ingeniously fuses elements of home, office, and social occasions. Venturing beyond conventional business hotel perceptions, ATOUR integrates popular youth-centric spots like bookstores, coffee shops, and photography exhibitions, leading to the launch of music-themed hotels, basketball-themed hotels, and literature-themed hotels.

In terms of service design, ATOUR crafts exceptional services tailored to the travel and lifestyle characteristics of mid-scale and upscale business travelers. This again challenges the conventions set by traditional business hotels. For example, to cater to guests traveling on early morning or late-night flights, ATOUR offers breakfast service as early as 5 a.m. and provides a self-service breakfast packing option, with the added convenience of take-away options. Late-night porridge offerings extend until the wee hours. Returning from evening social engagements, business travelers can order "hangover tea" through the ATOUR app. Additionally, female guests who are fond of yoga can reserve yoga equipment via the app, with yoga mats and small speakers placed in their rooms.

In terms of hotel interior design, ATOUR reduces costs in areas with lower customer perceptibility, such as heavy fixtures like marble. However, they prioritize and excel in areas with high guest interaction, such as pillows, teacups, mattresses, and sanitary ware.

This innovative approach to service design results in an exceptional customer experience. According to an independent survey conducted by Brandwisdom, since 2017, ATOUR's overall customer satisfaction has consistently ranked first among the six major mainstream mid-scale and upscale hotel chains.

Along with the progress of urbanization is the ever stronger call for a return to nature made by people living in the forests of concrete and stones. They all hope to get close to mountains, rivers, the sea or farms in their spare time, demonstrating a desire for "original experience", which is the balance on a higher level that, while driving mankind to change and innovate, urges them to reflect and return to nature. People are pushed by a certain force existing in the past, the present and future to keep swinging like a pendulum and, ultimately, achieve diversity at a higher level. It guides people to think towards such a direction in service design: Changes are driven by a constant rule—all things are subject to constant movements and changes, namely, changes are the only constancy.

Back to service innovation, an excellent service designer has to find his or her own direction and boundary between changes and constancy, and strike a balance. To think about it in the viewpoint of engineering, some dimensions may be converted into measurable indexes, such as personality. For example, personality at the ultimate is the expression of artists, but its value declines in designer brands that cater for certain groups of people with weakened personality—still, these groups are the minority. Personality at the bottom level would be even weaker, to satisfy people's fundamental needs with popular commodities, which focus more on functions and serve more diverse and extensive groups of people.

Therefore, we can define an index named "personality density" based on the three forms above. When the personality density of a certain product hits the ultimate level, it is one of its kind for an only client, represented by some masterpieces in painting and sculpture. A reasonable distribution of personality density can associate us with the scales and characteristics of groups of people that we have to contact with. Behind such associations are suitable production modes for different groups of people.

7.2.3 World of Design and World of Art

The essential role of design is often emphasized in discussions of service innovation. The founder of Tsutaya Books, Muneaki Masuda even asserts in his book *Capital of Knowledge* that enterprises in the future belong to designers. There are two types of designers we know of, those who design architecture and those who design product appearance, while designers of book covers and apparel look more like artists. When discussing complicated equipment like mechanical devices, their designers often appear in our mind as senior engineers or technicians. However, service designers seem more like the former type, so we have to discuss a bit about the relationship between design and art.

In terms of the purpose of expression, artists are concerned more about the exploration of boundaries and the pursuit of ultimacy, while designers care more about the majority of people, since their works are products performing certain functions in our life.

Thoughts of designers are close to the concept of "universal love" in Mohism at a certain degree, for they have to keep the majority in their mind, and explore, on their behalf, a better way of life as well as products and services needed for such life. In that sense, designers can be defined as artisans well versed in art. But this does not mean that their artistic accomplishments are inferior to those of artists, with Ukiyo-e serving as a good example.

As a folk art in Japan, Ukiyo-e was extensively painted on wrapping papers used for porcelains exported to Europe, and thus exerted important influences on famous painters like Vincent van Gogh. Ukiyo-e elements are seen in their paintings, such as in Fig. 7.10.

Certainly, the high requirements over artistic accomplishment posed by this type of design also put certain limits over designers' work, especially when the scenarios never stop changing. As a result, two tendencies are observed in their exploration.

The first is that designers are making efforts to develop and improve themselves. For example, some emerging designers attempt to adopt cutting-edge technology, like flexible display and AR, to define latest products and services in brand-new ways.

The other is that more extensive groups of people are taught to think like designers, which is the popular design thinking in present days. Behavioral research and observation on innovative activities are conducted to distill the process of design into procedures, methods and tools, enabling normal innovative teams to think like designers. With this thinking, they would be able to dig into the real concerns of customers, explore the interactive manners and underlying principles, make correct judgment

Fig. 7.10 *Père Tanguy* by Vincent van Gogh. *Source* van Gogh (1887–1888)

over users' pain spots and the overall tends, and build new solutions over seemingly chaotic but actually ordered tests and iteration, even construct feasible service systems.

The second tendency actually lowers the threshold of design to engage everyone in design activities. It echoes Wang Yangming's Mental Outlook System since Wang held that "everyone can become a sage" and "be cultivated in practice" so as to make "the unity of knowledge and action". The tendency is ingenious because it not only encourages practice, but also provides procedures, methods and tools to guide people to practice reasonably and effectively. These principles and logic are also advocated and promoted in the field of service system design.

Back to the subject of design and art, despite its development direction, design, in its essence, is a cause the same as art that explores and constructs a better life and a better society. In view of this, the organic fusion of the two would be far more valuable than dividing them vastly.

A common but simple fusion of design and art in practice is adding artworks that suit the value and philosophy of the service system to beautify the design. Better service designs in the surrounding can also make these artworks better conduits for aesthetic cultivation of the whole society. Traditional channels for art services confined in art galleries can now be overturned to share with more people and render them the value of beauty for life.

7.3 Diversification

Diversification means to offer customers enriched and integrated wonderful experience with service supply that goes beyond the traditional scope. The multiple enjoyment brought at one stroke would feel unprecedented, yet, like the way it should be. Tsutaya Bookstores in Japan, as shown in Fig. 7.11, integrate products of the same subject into diverse combinations (of books, DVDs, music and objects) that include a vast range of items from delicate tea sets to exuberant plants, and from timeworn vintage cars to plain but lofty furniture, making it hard for people to tell the foil from the protagonist: are the commodities setting off the books, or the books telling stories about the commodities? Such a kind of experience coincides with the style of Ikea who displays furniture in well-decorated study rooms and bedrooms to help consumers relate the products to scenarios they'd be used in.

The Chinese national treasure-class painting, *Along the River during the Qingming Festival*, is a depiction of life and the cityscape of Bianjing during the Northern Song. A diverse city is presented vividly by all kinds of figures and business forms in the painting. The use of AR technology in exhibition makes the scene truer to life, bringing viewers across time to experience the prosperous ancient city.

The principle of "letting a hundred flowers bloom and a hundred schools of thought contend" is an important policy for Chinese government to improve its cultural construction through diversification. Let us turn to the view of System Science. A famous writer, Kevin Kelly, writes in *Out of Control* about an interesting ecological experiment carried out by American scientists for more than ten years. They found

Fig. 7.11 A Tsukaya bookstore

a prairie with lush grass, brushes and small animals in the U.S., and turned it into bare land for their experiment to rebuild and restore the local ecology. However, all their attempts failed. After discovering that nothing could survive if only a few kinds of trees and grass were planted, ecologists added more species to the experiment, including all kinds of grass, plants, small animals and insects, and achieved gratifying results. As we see, a homogeneous system tends to be fragile. So the advocacy for diversified designs is supported by scientific principles—diversified ecosystems are worth trying.

Can we construct some interesting ecosystems when designing service systems? The Ring of Taste in Fig. 7.12 is proposed on the basis of the philosophies included in Norman's *The Design of Everyday Things.*

In the middle of Fig. 7.12 is the taste of a person. A better aesthetic sense would bring positive feelings, which result in positive emotions that influence the person's choices. As he or she chooses more beautiful things, the aesthetic sense is conversely defined or enhanced. So it is actually a loop surrounding taste.

Never underestimate design, for it breeds the morality of a society. I often use the Iceberg Model for illustration, as in Fig. 7.13. How do we look at the role of

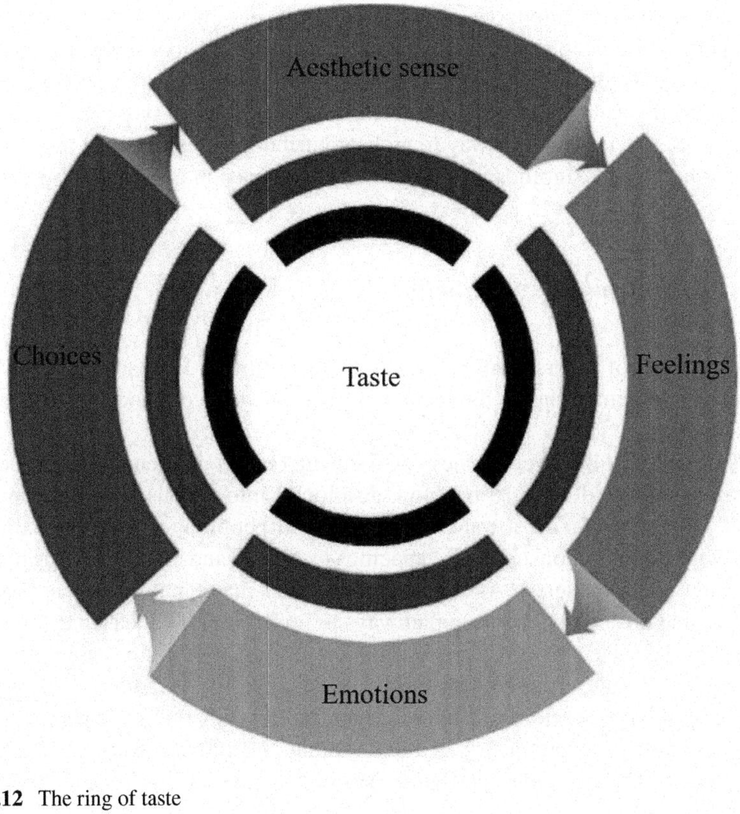

Fig. 7.12 The ring of taste

Fig. 7.13 The iceberg model

products and system design? In my opinion, the design of products and services aiming at visible and useful entities in our life are the part of the iceberg we see above the sea level, but the bigger and more influential part below are tastes and morals. When our customers enjoy the tasteful products and services we provide, we are already influencing their tastes and morals, subtly yet progressively.

Likewise, the task emphasized in China's top-level policy—to always satisfy the aspirations of the people to live a better life—is also the goal that we can see. As in the Iceberg Model in Fig. 7.13, above the water is the goal we see, whereas its essence lies beneath. As a better life brings happiness, well designed systems for products and services are our way to make contributions and positive influences on society, which is the significant role and historical mission undertaken by design.

7.3.1 The Growing "Minorities"

The other form of diversification targets at "minorities". We can understand it as unique services emerging in the diversified overall service market that have three characteristics.

Firstly, they put life over business by focusing on certain themes. The Niceliving application launched in 2016 has now developed into a household consumption-themed community facing towards the minority of people in pursuit of quality life. People with different consumption capacities exchange and explore on this platform for a better aesthetic sense. At the same time, their matchmaking service between designers and customers opens up pathways to implement the ideas that come up in discussion in people's lives. Lifestyle takes the leading role in this case.

Secondly, they turn transactions into social contacts by upgrading customer stickiness. Stickiness to services of traditional brands depends on users' personal experience, including the satisfaction of their explicit and implicit demands. But niche brands serving the minorities tend to build closer social relations between their users and the service providers, on the premise of satisfying users' basic demands. Consequently, the provision of services is totally personalized so that stickiness to service is greatly enhanced, with the help of the providers' "authority" of knowledge in related segmentation. The increasing popularity of customized tours and private coaches are fine examples.

Thirdly, they support prices with values, so that scale becomes insignificant. Services for minority groups of people would naturally abandon the scale effect, but pursue a higher quality for its stead, with clearer focus and stronger stickiness. At this time, customers will put values over prices in their consideration, turning to pursuing "uniqueness" rather than "cost performance". For instance, as a craftsmen-targeted social networking application, iDongjia upholds cultural and artistic inheritance as its vision, offers various business forms like "partnering", "crowdsourcing" and "kiln gambling", and establishes direct links between a large amount of niche brands, even independent craftsmen, and customers. The tasteful experience used to belong only to art galleries and antique shops are available at users' fingertips, making the application extremely popular.

Shanghai, one of China's commercial hubs, has always been at the forefront of commercial innovation and development. Numerous commercial districts are spread across Shanghai, evolving from traditional single-purpose retail spaces to multifunctional spaces that integrate 'brand display, commercial retail, salon events, and art exhibitions', offering a more dimensional experiential scene. In some of Shanghai's older neighborhoods, such as the Taojiang Road area, within the span of less than 1.6 km across three streets, you'll find four new high-end retail stores: LMDS World, Chapter, hAo Market, and 3RLABS. They can be said to represent the Taojiang Road area, and even the commercial districts of Shanghai. These commercial districts have added more vibrancy to the city's commercial landscape and tirelessly promote more experiences to consumers, introducing a more diverse range of lifestyles.

References

Hara, K. (2006). *Designing design*, Shandong People's Publishing House
van Gogh, V. (1887–1888). *Père Tanguy*. The Musée Rodin

Chapter 8
Classical Tools for Service Innovation

8.1 Differentiation-Based Competitive Strategies

8.1.1 Differentiation is an Essential Need

Differentiation plays a unique role as one of the three major strategies for service competition. Viewed as a strategy in service providers' eyes, though, what is the differentiation in consumers' minds? I deem it an essential need of people and the core driver for branding.

Differentiation has found its vehicles ever since the concepts of exchange of commodities and personal properties emerged. The most intuitive representation was that people in different stratums wanted to show their identities and status through differentiated wares, decorations, buildings, etc. Those possessing more social resources in certain stratums had even stronger desires for label-like objects that stood for their identities. Therefore, ancient arts were closely related to preferences and collections of royal members and aristocrats, the most delicate wares and architectures always had things to do with the privileged few.

As society changes, similar fashions, customs and designs were brought to the common folk through exchanges and imitations, thus became tokens shared by all. Demands of this type can be boiled down to mankind's exploration for the significance of life—people are attempting to construct their own uniqueness upon external substances. In a service package, such demands have to be satisfied by implicit services.

There is another kind of differentiation that stands opposite to standardized services, which find it difficult for providers to take care of personal characteristics of all individuals they serve. For example, a cinema cannot vary the volume to suit different acoustic systems of each person, whereas differentiation gives service providers an approach to satisfy personalized characteristics or desires of customers in some standardized services. Such a satisfaction has to be based on supportive facilities, overall information innovations and novel service modes.

L. Li, *The Era of New Services*, Management for Professionals,
https://doi.org/10.1007/978-981-99-9565-3_8

The current development of IoT, Big Data and other technologies has, coupled with upgraded demands of consumer groups, made differentiation the most important one among the three service competition strategies. Apart from the two kinds of services mentioned above, namely, to showcase identity and serve implicit needs, and to solve problems and demands difficult to handle in standardized services, differentiated services are also provided in another kind without changing the service system—precise matching. It means to create many kinds of service options in the service system and offer them precisely to corresponding consumers based on active and passive acquisition of their preferences.

Of course, the differentiation strategy in the broadest sense is to carry overthrowing or progressive innovations in service supply or components of the service package, to bring consumers unprecedented experience. All strategies of this kind are differentiated ones.

Heterogeneity is always a focus in discussions about service attributes, meaning that the final results of any service vary from people and time, from perspectives of both consumers and service providers. It poses great challenges to service management.

In face of the heterogeneity, the only key principle service providers have to follow is fairness, because everyone wants to be treated fairly. So if we take the question back to consumers' essential need, fairness is a constraint over related issues and the space defined by constraints posed by fairness in different aspects is the feasible zone of a service. Precisely differentiated treatments to different customers within the feasible zone are the optimal solutions that service providers may find for each and every one of their customers.

Indeed, differentiations without a sophisticated design may violate the principle of fairness. Discrimination in big data that is often seen in tourist or e-commerce websites lately is a typical example of violating fairness with differentiating practices. Obviously, these differentiations originated from profit-making for companies, instead of benefiting consumers.

8.1.2 Methods and Trends of Differentiated Competition

The book *Service Management: Operations, Strategy, Information Technology*[1] concludes the five approaches towards a differentiation strategy: making the intangible tangible, customizing the standard product, reducing perceived risk, giving attention to personnel training and controlling quality, which are each introduced below.

[1] Fitzsimmons and Fitzsimmons (2019).

8.1.2.1 Making the Intangible Tangible

Services are intangible by nature. How can we turn the invisible and untouchable services into tangibles?

To illustrate with an example, toiletry items, slippers and towels we use at a hotel often bear its logo and are free to take. When we use them again at home, the logos would remind us of the pleasant experience we had at the hotel, making the intangible experience or services tangible.

This approach is also adopted by Chinese Railways High-speed (CRH). I used to get a drink and snack food on a high-speed train from Shanghai to Beijing and the sentence on the paper food bag was brilliant: "Though hundreds of miles away, Beijing or Shanghai is within a day's reach." You can see it in Fig. 8.1, obviously the CRH version of Li Bai's line, "Though hundreds of miles away, Jiangling is within a day's reach". What did it tell the passengers? Clearly, the train is fast enough to travel between Beijing and Shanghai in a single day. Rendering intangible ideas like the brilliant sentence I encountered into words on a tangible package or a tangible product is not only effective, but also interesting.

Many famous brands are also using this approach. Like in a Starbucks store, all queuing customers must pass by a shelf loaded with attractive cups in different shapes but all with the logo of the store. A customer may easily add a nice cup to her purchase and the next time she drinks coffee or tea with it, she'd see the logo of that store. The intangible service is made tangible frequently in such a way.

Services are often intangible. But if providers can design some things that are repeatedly used in customers' work and life in relation to these services, the good

Fig. 8.1 Though hundreds of miles away, Beijing or Shanghai is within a day's reach

experience they received before would keep reminding them about the service providers and attract them to frequently use these services.

8.1.2.2 Customizing the Standard Product

Standardization is always efficient in service cost control. Fast food benchmarks like McDonald's have standardized all aspects of their business, from procedures, store layout to tools used. But if the same standards are followed by all fast food restaurants, they would be trapped in homogeneous competition and fail to sustain attractions to customers. So differentiation drives us to think of possibilities for customization in standardized service models.

Here are two examples. The first is drive-in cinemas, where the audience watch films in their own automobiles. Film-watching is a very standard experience, since all you can do is to find your seat in the screening room, sit down and watch. Where do these drive-in cinemas come from? What are their advantages?

For one, the audience in a traditional cinema cannot adjust the volume. This is a very important pain spot. They could only put on earphones or cover their ears with hands if finding the place too noisy. But in a drive-in cinema, people listen through their car radio system so they can turn the volume up or down freely, even turn it off. For two, phone calls can also be made in automobiles, with no interference on others. Also, they can have any food they want, without troubling others. Drive-in cinemas offer audience with privacy, personalized features and adjustability that cannot be found in traditional cinemas. These customizing practices will, for sure, attract its own consumers in an important market segment.

The customization of standard products is used more commonly in the catering industry. For example, Subway and Burger King, being fast food brands though, are offering abundant choices for customers to personalize their orders. They can choose to double the meat in a hamburger or add one more kind of vegetable.

The second example is an interesting experience I once had in a noodle restaurant in Tokyo. Customers were asked to choose from grade 1 to grade 7 for the saltiness and spiciness, so that the noodle was personalized for them. So to customize standard products means to add some customizing elements to a standard practice, so as to satisfy a customer's unique demand.

8.1.2.3 Reducing Perceived Risk

Two American mechanists who had worked for Volvo for over twenty years saw some room for improvement in the services of Volvo 4S stores, so they started Village Volvo to provide repair and maintenance services for Volvo automobiles. Different from other 4S stores, the customer has to make appointments beforehand, then discuss with the mechanist to make a diagnosis for the vehicle, which is then recorded in the Custom Care Vehicle Dossier (VVCD), an e-file of the vehicle. It seems like the procedures of visiting a doctor and the differentiated competitive approach adopted by Village Volvo is extremely interesting. If the service provider still offers human-like services when facing an inhuman object, such as an automobile, a handbag or a mobile phone, the customer would be highly satisfied.

The customer must be satisfied seeing that the mechanist is treating the vehicle in the way a doctor treats a patient. So service providers have to make serious considerations for the objects they serve. It is easy to treat human objects warmly and considerately, but if it is a lifeless article, how to show the customers your care and passion? In Village Volvo, the replaced parts are put in a clean box to be checked by the customer. This practice is important. What do most 4S stores do? The customer leaving his vehicle at the store would receive a phone call from the mechanist, claiming that some other part has been found broken and a replacement is suggested. He is calling to ask what kind of part the customer wants, a local or imported one? At this time, the customer would mutter: is the part really broken, do I must replace it, or is the new part an authentic one? These are all perceived risks. The asymmetric information held by the customer and the professional is raising a doubt in the customer's mind—am I being cheated? Village Volvo reduces these perceived risks by putting the replaced parts in a clean box, showing them to the customer during pickup and explaining the exact problems of the parts, as all service providers have to try all they can to convince customers about their reliability and risk-free services. What's more, vehicles are always kept clean in the process of repair and maintenance at Village Volvo, with a test drive made after the repair. Also, the comfortable waiting rooms add extra points. The last but most interesting thing is that Village Volvo would train its customers, teach them how to drive Volvo vehicles better to reduce the need for repair. A repairer is teaching its customers to repair less, isn't this a paradox? Please note that they are at a higher realm of delivering value to the customers. They have taken the initiative to put themselves in the position of customers and deliver the values to them. People so treated would understand that the mechanists are saving money and creating values for them, therefore becoming very loyal customers. So this practice is at a higher realm, requiring service providers to figure out ways to show customers that they are working for customers' benefit. I once had a nice experience in a Volkswagen 4S store, when I sat on a cozy sofa in their spacious waiting room and saw through the big French casement window that my car was elevated by a car lift for repair. All operations of the mechanists could be seen clearly, as you see in Fig. 8.2. That reduced the perceived risks in me.

8.1.2.4 Giving Attention to Personnel Training

The attention paid to personnel training is an important differentiator between good and bad service companies. At 5 p.m. on February 28, 2008, all 7,100 Starbucks stores in the United States were closed, but for what? They were retraining the baristas to make better espresso beverages.

Closing 7100 stores altogether simply for internal training could cause a big loss to Starbucks. It is worth mentioning that each store put an announcement on the door after closing, smartly stating: "We're always striving for perfection and look forward

Fig. 8.2 The tactic to reduce perceived risks adopted by a 4S store

to serving you a truly exceptional espresso beverage. So we're taking time and full devotion to perfect our art." Whereas most stores would say "The store is closed for training, sorry for your inconvenience."

What can service providers learn from Starbucks in this case? Training is a way to improve employees' competence and confidence, while Starbucks shifted the focus to customers by rendering them this message: They are taking "full devotion to perfect their art" out of the "strive for perfection". Starbucks' survey right on the next day of the retraining showed that consumers mostly said that their coffee tasted better!

Was it the instant effects brought by the retraining? Probably not. Indeed, the internal survey on Starbucks baristas did say that they felt more confident when making coffee. But this was something within the expectation. The announcement they made to the customers must have been influential since customers had seen the attention Starbucks paid to personnel training, which would definitely improve the baristas' coffee making skills. Therefore, service companies may as well share information about their internal training with customers, to make them more confident about the companies' strengths.

8.1.2.5 Controlling Quality

The company with best quality control would be the winner in the service arena, for it is an important approach towards differentiation.

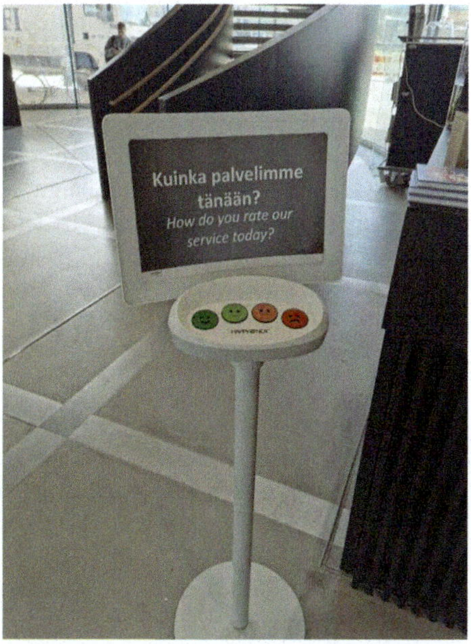

Fig. 8.3 A customer service rating device

Customer service rating devices like the one in Fig. 8.3 often appear in our life. It is a very useful method. I used to visit a bank very often and found the service in the lobby very good, so I'd rate "excellent" every time. But when I went there for a foreign exchange business one day, the lobby manager said it had to be handled on the second floor. So I went upstairs and waited for half a minute, no one received me, even though officers at all the four accounts were serving nobody. I couldn't help wondering why the service qualities were so different on the two floors, and soon found that they didn't have the service rating device on the second floor.

Can we conclude that this device is the panacea for service quality control? Absolutely not. What is the role of such a device? It gives customers a channel to express their feelings and make feedback on services they receive. A tool like this restricts employees from behaving badly in service provision because customers hold a direct feedback channel and their comments would influence employees' performance appraisal.

However, restrictions do not result in optimal services directly. I think the best services have to come from the Satisfaction Mirror—customers will not enjoy first-level services, until employees are motivated enough to perform their work well. So the control of service quality is a very delicate work that can never be finished by some simple tools or methods.

The five approaches above are traditional differentiation strategies in competition. From the rapidly changing service innovations, we can find three latest trends in this competition: delivering values to customers, morality and responsibility, and design of details.

8.1.2.6 Delivering Value to Customers

Village Volvo's practice of teaching customers to drive Volvo automobiles better is delivering value to its customers, and Coca-Cola's sales promotion is another example of this kind. But according to some American scholars, the sales promotion of Coca-Cola, as a marketing campaign, actually led to over-consumption of Coke, and was harmful to people's health. To deliver value to customers requires businesses to take customers' point of view in promotional links, rather than simply trying to sell more products. It means a higher realm which can obviously win the customers' loyalty.

8.1.2.7 Morality and Responsibility

Sound morality and responsibility is becoming a competitive edge for companies. For example, can they do something for environmental protection and sustainability? Walmart set up a designated social responsibility office to transform the power supply of all its warehouses and most stores in California into solar power, and provide support for many cleansing projects. These efforts have significantly improved Walmart's corporate image among the public.

The photo in Fig. 8.4 was taken in a hotel I used to stay in Rotterdam, the Netherlands. The card hung by the towel rack says, "Here, your towels plant trees." This is very clever, since if the towel is not used, the hotel won't need to wash it, with one more bit done for sustainability. And I didn't use that towel the whole stay. Here, we see a new trend, in which people are reminded about sustainability all the time. It is also a way for businesses to perform their social responsibility.

And we should ponder on Fig. 8.5. It shows the common mailboxes in the Netherlands. What is unique is that you can see a short mailbox beside the tall one. Whom is it for?

Actually, the short mailbox is for children and the disabled sitting in wheelchairs. To install one more mailbox obviously adds to the cost and lowers efficiency, but if our focus is on the whole society and social fairness, we shouldn't care too much about costs and efficiency. So this marks the next stage in urban construction and service innovation: human-centered services and barrier-free facilities. It reflects a responsibility that exceeds the contemporary time. Service designers' attention paid to vulnerable groups also reflects their social responsibilities.

8.1.2.8 Design of Details

The key to winning over the competition in future is to focus more on details. I took a photo of the coffee I had on Royal Dutch Airlines, as shown in Fig. 8.6. What are the details in it?

Firstly, the coffee cup. The paper cup was printed with patterns of tulip, kissing boy and girl, and windmill. They are all symbols of the Netherlands. So a simple cup

Fig. 8.4 An environmental-friendly hotel

Fig. 8.5 Mailboxes with human-centered design. *Source* https://you.ctrip.com/travels/youyouctripstar100023/1658274.html

Fig. 8.6 Design of details from Royal Dutch Airlines

was enough to tell others it was a Royal Dutch flight. Do not underestimate this cup for it was tapping into a profound culture and information.

Then we may look at the small plastic bag containing sugar, creamer and stirring stick. Most airline companies offer coffee in one of the two ways: The first is to pour the passenger a cup of black coffee, then hand over sugar, creamer and a stirring stick. The other is more direct, pouring sugar, cream and coffee altogether into a cup and delivering to the customer.

Why do I have to mention the small bag of Royal Dutch? There are two advantages to putting sugar, creamer and the stirring stick in a plastic bag. One is that attendants can deliver more quickly and easily. As for the other, the passenger has to stir his coffee with the stick, so if it has been held by someone else, a perceived risk is generated, making it hard to take for people with higher hygienic requirements. Now you understand how details work.

Let us now turn to a Dutch supermarket. As Fig. 8.7 shows, these shelves sell macaroni. Please pay attention to the picture above the shelves, for this is the key that stimulates consumers' desire to purchase. Because consumers are not sure about the final dish they will see on the dinner table with a glance at the packed goods on the shelves, this picture tells them vividly the delicious macaroni they'd be able to cook with these products. Once their taste buds are fully stimulated, buying becomes only natural.

The next photo in Fig. 8.8 is the trash bin in a McDonald's in Rome, Italy. What is special about it? In McDonald's in foreign countries, consumers have to dump the leftovers in the trash bin by themselves and put the tray on its top, after finishing eating. The normal trash bins in most McDonald's having to be opened by hand,

Fig. 8.7 Design of details: a picture above the spaghetti shelves

sometimes staining customers' hands. Customers caring more about sanitation may be worried about this.

However, bins in this McDonald's restaurant are completely automatic that open by themselves when someone is approaching. Once the sensor detects that the trash has been dumped, the cover would automatically close, with no contact to customers' hands throughout the process. As we often say that technology has to serve value creation, what kind of value is created here?

The restaurant installed full-automatic trash bins to avert a concern of customers upon realizing that they may worry about the health risks caused by hand touch with the trash bins. This is the value created, also a way to reduce perceived risks from another perspective.

8.2 Service Encounters: Economic Efficiency, Effectiveness and Communicative Skills

Service encounter is a link of vital importance in service management, also the biggest risk point and opportunity point for service quality assurance. According to a study made by James A. Fitzsimmons, each service encounter is a chance to satisfy or dissatisfy the customer. Therefore, the design of the process and system of service encounter is a crucial part in service design.

Fig. 8.8 Design of details: a trash bin in a McDonald's in Rome, Italy

In the broad range of possibilities for service encounters are various forms of encounters at different contact degrees. At lower degrees are encounters like mass messaging and mass mailing, or advertisements sent by letters which were often seen in the U.S. earlier. Telemarketing and similar encounters are more direct. Of course, the most direct forms are still one-on-one face-to-face service encounters.

We can study these forms of service encounter from two dimensions, their economy and effects (with the latter indicated by the conversion rate). From the perspective of economy, of course, widely distributed messages and mails at lower encounter degrees generally cost less. In other words, it costs less to push information to a single customer in these ways. However, a fatal problem for them is the worst encounter effects.

One-on-one face-to-face communication will certainly result in the most sufficient encounters and maximum conversion rates. Other forms fall in between these two poles. Despite the better effectiveness, a one-on-one encounter means that the service provider and the customer have to meet each other in person, thereby generating traffic cost and time cost. So this is the least economic form of communication.

In the American film *The Pursuit of Happyness*, the protagonist, a stockbroker played by Will Smith, started from contacting people on a name list by telephone, as in Fig. 8.9, to select certain potential buyers, and then tried all that he could to encounter them one-on-one to make successful conversion. It shows that different forms of service encounters can be combined in practice, even following a certain order.

Fig. 8.9 The protagonist is contacting potential clients by telephone in *The Pursuit of Happyness*

Sure, effective communication is crucial to improve the encounter effects in any form of encounter. Professor Philip G. Zimbardo points out in *The Psychology of Attitude Change and Social Influence* that, according to social psychological studies on the construction of influence, the essential work we have to do to influence people's attitudes and change their behaviors is to persuade.

The process of persuasion includes two steps: step one, to transfer the information; and step two, to urge people to change their attitude on the basis of understanding. Therefore, the quality of information transfer becomes the crux of the problem in service encounters.

Taking a far-reaching service, retailing, as an example, the purpose of product design, packaging and marketing are all to transfer a message that this product is of high quality, and make consumers choose it in purchase. This is the key task for many sectors, like product design, graphic design and package design.

With all these elements considered as supportive information for service encounters, such encounters would go far beyond interpersonal communication, but be endowed with the responsibility to render the design philosophy, process and even underlying principles of the service to the customers in proper manners, which are neither too complex nor too simple with something missed, so as to assist customers in their understanding. Of course, to facilitate their understanding, designers have to stand in the customers' shoes in the first place and provide understandable information pertinent to customers' pain spots.

As the information consumers can access has already been determined, the human factor in service encounters becomes more vital. Since communicative skills of people are not the core contents of the book, we would focus more on the essential principles of these encounters and communication.

To take the commonly used phrase "wholehearted service" that describes the experience of a wonderful service encounter as an example, the first thing about being "wholehearted" is to empathize in service design, to sharply perceive customers' pain spots and desires—these have been fully discussed in previous chapters.

The second is to explore deeply into customers' perceived risks. When choosing a service, a customer often wants to know more about it to "reassure" him- or herself.

The process, security and invisible backstage of the service may all become perceived risks if something disturbing is found. Service providers have to make use of all tangible and intangible methods, even infrastructures and words of employees to reduce their perceived risks.

The third essential principle for service encounter is to deliver value to customers, also an important trend in the differentiated competition of services. In other words, service providers have to make their consumers feel like that it is not a company working for its own profits, but a considerate individual or consultant taking their side, solving their problems and protecting their interest.

There was a saying in ancient China: "all businessmen give tips" (unlike the modern version of "all businessmen are profiteers"). It was because in ancient transactions when a buyer paid for a hodful of rice, the seller would always add more to the hod to make a pointed little rice mountain with a "tip". That was the businessmen's way of showing their generosity and sincerity—they wanted the customers to get more, representing a delivery of value to customers.

Another example is Best Buy, the online retailer that rallied from the verge of bankruptcy. Their door-to-door service staffers have completely abandoned the identity and image as sales persons, while transformed themselves into smart home consultants, as you can see in Fig. 8.10. As they enjoy yearly salaries at Best Buy but charge no fee for door-to-door services, the staffers are more willing to join customers at their homes and in real application scenarios to analyze and solve problems for customers. Undoubtedly, this is a smarter form of encountering.

Technology should play a better supportive role in service encounters, as cutting-edge technologies like AI, IoT and Big Data are developing rapidly today. Pure technology, be it a voice assistant or a service robot, cannot compare with a human in

Fig. 8.10 A best buy home consultant is offering door-to-door service to customers. *Source* https://corporate.bestbuy.com/in-home-advisor-program-brings-best-buyexperts-to-you/

terms of the transfer and expression of emotions. What they should do is to empower the frontline staffers with the huge amount of information, to help them make better judgments and solve problems for consumers more effectively.

Therefore, service encounters will remain, by essence, an activity mainly carried out by people, but with their service competences strengthened by machines and intelligent technologies in the long future. There is a large space for service innovation attempts in this human–machine combination.

Reference

Bordoloi, S., Fitzsimmons, J. A., & Fitzsimmons, M. J. (2019). *Service management: operations, strategy, information technology*. McGraw-Hill.

Chapter 9
SERVINO Methods

Service innovation refers to the behavior of reorganizing the resources of a company (including capital, equipment, personnel, etc.) with the help of internal and external technical conditions, so as to launch a new service or improve the efficiency of an existing service. It is a service-oriented innovative activity ranging from business models to operation management, intangible experience to tangible products and original design to continuous improvement.

The SERVINO Methods proposed here are a complete set of problem-solving tools for service innovation that combine the innovative tools of design thinking, Systems Engineering and other theories, on the basis of the traditional Theory of Inventive Problem Solving (TRIZ) methods. Its core thinking and applications are introduced in this chapter.

9.1 SERVINO System and Its Problem-Solving Process

Once information on service objects' emotions, preferences and social activities are acquired, the service providers have fully mastered the new demands to be addressed by service innovation. The core issue to be solved by the SERVINO Methods is the conversion of demands into better services, while maintaining the traceability and verifiability of these demands throughout the process.

Many useful methods and tools have been found for some links in service innovation design, based on previous studies. But they are far from enough. Firstly, the specific methods are too dispersed to form a system that has to support the whole service innovation process. Secondly, many methods focus more on the thought-provoking process and are short of quantitative tools and standard procedures. As a result, the quality of innovative attempts depends totally on the designers' personal capability. Lastly, existing methods tend to ignore the new opportunities brought by the rapid development of Big Data technology. As data mining studies exploring

L. Li, *The Era of New Services*, Management for Professionals,
https://doi.org/10.1007/978-981-99-9565-3_9

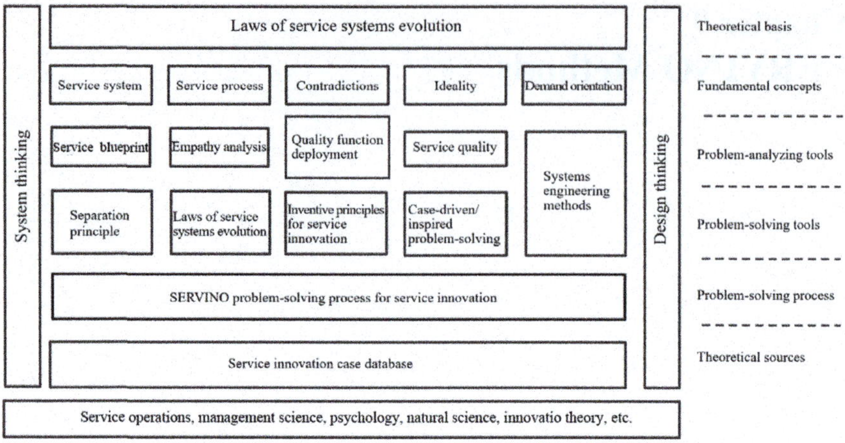

Fig. 9.1 The service innovation theoretical system

the huge amount of service innovation cases may automatically generate some parts of the innovation plan for service design, these case- and data-based supplementary tools for innovation construct one of the most important trends in service innovation in the new era.

Therefore, a Service Innovation Theoretical System is proposed here (as shown in Fig. 9.1) based on the TRIZ methods and system, Stanford's design thinking approach, systems engineering development process and other existing theories and studies. The theoretical system contains not only macro theoretical basis and fundamental concepts, but also analytical and solving tools for specific problems following a certain problem-solving process. What's more, the continuously improving service innovation case database can support the iteration of the theoretical system as well as the development of service design. Important concepts and tools of the system are illustrated in this chapter.

As seen in the Service Innovation Theoretical System, the SERVINO problem-solving process aims directly at service innovation practices and projects, and Fig. 9.2 is the illustration of the detailed process. This problem-solving process is an algorithm that functions similarly to the Algorithm of Inventive Problems Solving (ARIZ) in TRIZ system. SERVINO is a complete problem-solving process constructed on the basis of design thinking and systems engineering development process, with theoretical methods and steps provided to solve service innovation problems. Starting from the mission of a service system, the process dissects the whole system in a top-down manner to make a detailed model, while ensuring that the innovative direction is in consistence with clients' demands. Appropriate tools are selected throughout the problem-solving process to perform evaluation and verification in key steps, so as to make an optimal choice of the innovation plan. Specifically, the SERVINO process consists of four stages.

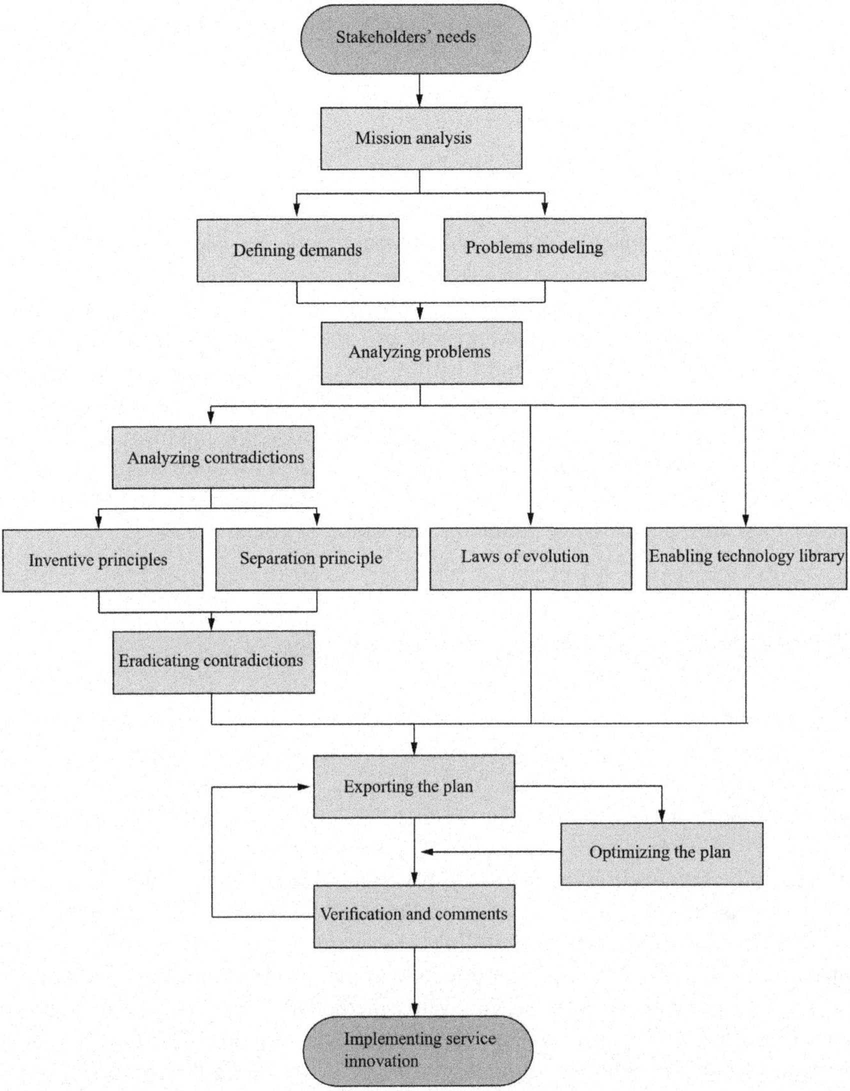

Fig. 9.2 The SERVINO problem-solving process

9.2 Exploring the Overall System

Overall "inputs" of the system to be designed are figured out through identifying stakeholders, analyzing the mission and defining demands, during which needs and demands of clients as well as demands of the system are analyzed to provide general guidance for problem focus in the next stage, and to ensure that the innovation plan is playing its role at the system level to satisfy customers' demands and serve the ultimate mission of the system.

9.3 Focusing on Problems in Design

The two steps contained in this stage, problems modeling and problems analysis, move the focus from the macro system to specific micro problems. Today's service system is often the "system of systems (SoS)", namely, the innovation of such a system has to start from a sub-system at the top, then identify the coupling relations among all sub-systems below, and finally focus on specific sub-systems and sub-problems, with the recursive relations between the general system and interested sub-systems well maintained throughout the application of service innovation problem-solving tools in the later stage. Parameters closely related to clients' demands should be analyzed and acquired at the sub-system level, so that problems can be concretely understood and specific entry points for innovation be found.

9.4 Inspiring and Driving Innovation

Various innovation-inspiring methods are adopted to construct the innovation plan in this stage that leads towards the results of problem analysis. The major methods used to inspire innovation include contradictions analysis, laws of evolution and the enabling technology library. In the first type of method, essential elements of the matrix of contradictions in the TRIZ system are borrowed, to the maximum degree, to be creatively integrated with parameters with service attribute, management attribute and psychological attribute. Physical and systematic contradictions are detected from the problems, and all links afterwards are hooked up and follow the inventive principles and separation principle in the export of the service innovation plan. Compared with the "precise" innovative method of the matrix of contradictions, laws of evolution emphasizes more about the universal innovative rules in service systems, while the enabling technology library is a structural assortment on the basis of acquiring abundant service innovation cases that constructs an assemblage of innovative methods used in actual service systems, especially the technological innovation plans in the new era, to shift current problems towards innovation. The last two methods boast significant guiding significance even for complex systems with hard-to-define contradictions and parameters. The SERVINO process has made all attempts to integrate these methods so that they may be used as service tools to make up for shortages of the innovative method of the matrix of contradictions.

9.5 Verifying and Implementing the Plan

After finishing abstract innovations based on problem-modeling and problem-solving tools, the algorithm in the last stage works to transform the abstract innovation plan into concrete reality. Characteristics of the actual service system have to be considered in this stage, so experts or employees familiar with this system have to do some "translation" work. In the meantime, verifications have to be made on technological and business feasibilities of all plans, so as to choose the optimal innovation plan for implementation.

In addition to providing guidance with theories and methods, the SERVINO problem-solving process also uses the Big Data technology in the Internet age to assist innovation. Data mining and statistical analysis carried out based on the innovation database can help conclude successful cases of service innovation to guide problem analysis and inspire innovation plans, as well as help innovative personnel make practical plans.

Please note that the SERVINO problem-solving process is a set of practical steps for general service innovations. Researchers and practitioners do not have to follow each and every step in their design, as some steps, in particular, may require the organization to invest hugely in research and development, and stereotyped or rigid adoption of the process may demoralize the innovators. Therefore, it is suggested here that the users of the process should "tailor" it for their innovation, which means characteristics of their own service systems and the actual stages of their innovation practices should be considered to ensure an optional use of the system. For example, if clients' pain spots have already been clearly identified, the time and energy spent on focusing on problems can be saved and taken to analyze the parameters and solve the detected contradictions. The following sections are a demonstration of the important concepts and tools in the process and their application in a case.

9.6 Encouraging Service Experience: Starting from Observations

According to principles of design thinking, the space for innovation lies in the provision of a brand new experience based on service designers' understanding of business and technological feasibilities, as well as the needs and desires of people. The origin for all the three aspects is also the first step in Stanford's design thinking model—to empathize.

Empathy requires more observation, as a co-founder of Muji, Ikko Tanaka once said, "Observation is the starting point of design." Of course, the observation of a specific scenario or a specific group of people is target-oriented, focusing on a special service scenario. Design observations in a larger scope have to involve the working and living habits of service designers, and should be enlarged as much as possible to cover the world, human civilization and cultures in it.

Observations like this can help service designers detect all kinds of problems and solutions. They happen not only in the innovative design of services, but also in the process of service quality management. For example, the walk-through test often used in service management is a direct observation of the performance of the whole service system, especially the service encounter process, from customers' perspective.

On the other hand, innovators carrying out service innovation studies should also be observed to find their "epiphanies" and distribution of energy throughout the research process, which may serve as supportive evidence for their innovative results. Therefore, it is fair to say that observations are ubiquitous in service design and management. It occurs in the conception stage, service design process, and the implementation and operation of the service. What's more, the observers may be designers, managers, operators and even customers.

Big Data and IoT have enabled service designers to identify both positive and negative emotions of their customers while receiving the services, according to users' records made in service process, such as click path on a website or walking route in hospital or other scenarios, or even the latest affective computing technique of AI. Clients' emotions have become an important indicator that can be measured and improved in the service system. In other words, emotions have become a resource. Along with the fast development of 5G technology and new infrastructures, unprecedented opportunities for innovation are granted for innovators to observe their clients at various stages of service.

Therefore, service observation should also be taken, like service system analysis, as an input to all links of service design and management. As for implementations at the backend, the real-time observation and thinking capacity is creating unprecedented opportunities for service providers to make interferences based on customers' reactions in service process.

Back to service experience. Innovative applications of new-style service observations in the full lifecycle of the service system are broadening the conceptual scope of service experience. Now, it not only means customers' experience in the service system, but also covers the service designers' ability to experience and perceive in activities related or unrelated to their service design. In a word, to design novel service experience on the basis of experiencing the service might become a fashion, even form a new industry, with Dianping as a representative example. This platform is constructing new service experience for a larger client base on the foundation of the service experience of existing clients.

In their innovation process, service designers have to explore the most real demands and pain spots of their users through observation, since users' pressing needs are the input data for service innovative activities.

We may borrow Stanford's Empathy Map to better understand users. At the beginning of an innovative activity, the IPDT consisted of designers, innovators, domain experts and senior practitioners of the service system should make an empathy analysis together with a blank Empathy Map.

Each participant has to imagine him- or herself as a specific user in a certain scenario of this service system, write the empathized results on notes and stick them to the map. Our practice before tells us that this method has three advantages:

First, the composition of an IPDT makes it possible to collect the wisdom and inspirations from all perspectives and domains, with even more triggered when all the ideas are put into an Empathy Map.

Second, the Empathy Map can facilitate the implementation and actualization of service innovative activities in later stages. Innovation often means reform while reform always meets resistance. The Empathy Map can be used to show personnel of different departments the origin of the innovations, to persuade them to carry out such innovations later.

Finally, empathy allows people to dig into users' demands as thoroughly as possible. When each team member plays the role of a different user and imagines a different scenario, the demands found may be surprisingly rewarding. For example, in an empathy analysis I did with my students on a shopping street, a student imagined herself as an office lady who sat in a taxi and was caught in a traffic jam on a rainy summer day, while another imagined as a young single programmer who had just worked for two years and whose interest was in wellness and health. Concrete character descriptions like these can precisely define the target user groups and their special demands and give designers inspirations. Figure 9.3 is an Empathy Map of the "last-mile" delivery service.

As a demand mining method, the Empathy Map helps designers to shift their identities and perspectives as early as in the starting stage of innovation. It posts higher requirements on designers' deliberation, and also needs to be supplemented by objective demand surveys, such as traditional questionnaires, or emerging tools like affective computing, analysis of user comments and eye-tracking technology.

9.7 "Know Yourself": Decomposing the Service System

In comparison with a manufacturing system, a service system includes complex interactive relations. In the aspect of interaction with customers, a manufacturing system only "meets" its users at the tail of all production links while a service system may be related to its consumers throughout the whole process. Besides, based on our discussion, the five types of resources, namely, space, time, material, human and information, may appear simultaneously in one service system. As important components of the system, these resources are also major objects to be considered in innovative design and should be separated as much as possible when decomposing the system.

Taking hotel service as an example, the service system would definitely encounter with the customers in various steps of check-in, luggage handling, inquiry at the reception, billing and check-out, and they may all exert influences on the service quality.

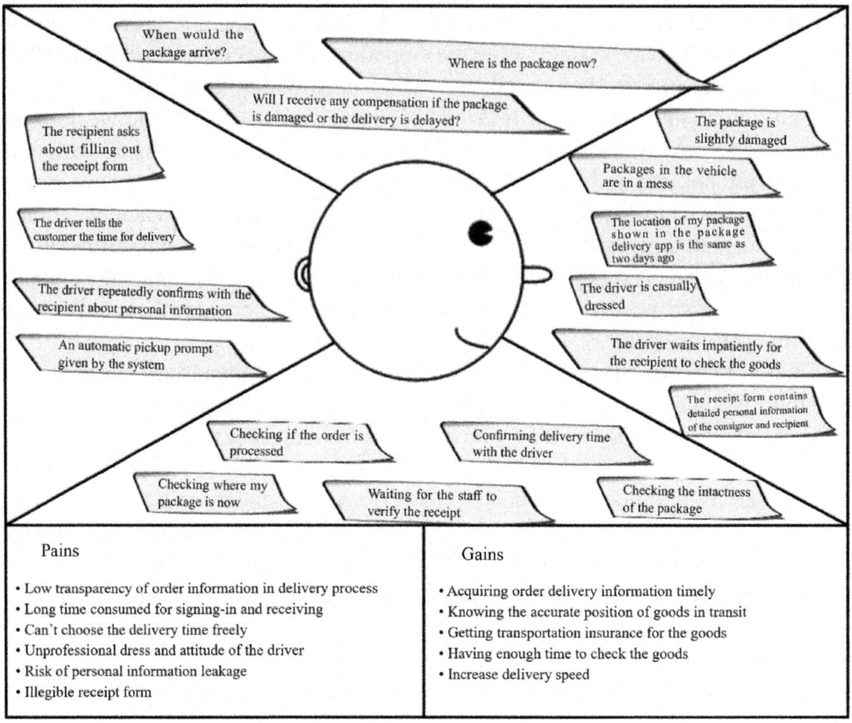

Fig. 9.3 Empathy map of the "last-mile" delivery service

To improve the service effects of the whole system and innovate service process and models, the composition of the service system and complex coupling relations within it have to be considered, with modelling and analysis carried out. Among the many modeling tools applicable for service systems that cut both ways, I suggest innovators to use the Service Blueprint for system modeling.

Firstly proposed by Lynn Shostack, Service Blueprint is a technique that demonstrates the service-receiving process of customers and interactions within the service system with diagrams based on two-dimensional depictions of behaviors of customers and employees, service encounters, service scenarios and other information in the service process. It is often used in service design and problem detection in service operation.

We can take a Service Blueprint Diagram as a customized flow chart of the service system that covers all the functions and links in the service delivery process. Meanwhile, with information delivery process and service encounter process combined in the diagram, a Service Blueprint can help the model-builders find problems and understand the system more effectively. Scholars keep revising this technique by introducing new concepts like line of interaction, line of visibility and line of internal interaction, so that the analysis of procedures of customer interaction procedures and internal coordination has become simpler and clearer. Ideally, the modeling of the

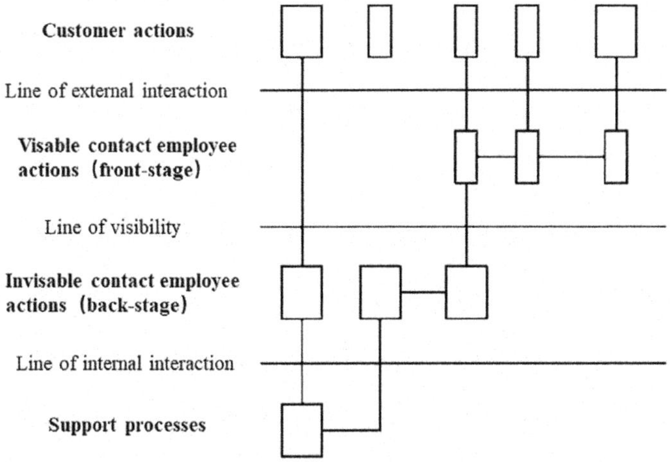

Fig. 9.4 The organization of a service blueprint

service system would help us identify all the components of the system and their correlations.

A Service Blueprint is composed of four parts: customer actions, frontstage employee actions, backstage employee actions and support processes, with a horizontal line going through each two neighboring parts indicating their interactive relationships, as in Fig. 9.4.

Customer actions take place when customers are considered as a part of the service delivery and evaluation processes; frontstage employee actions are steps taken by employees in their interaction with customers; backstage employee actions are steps in support of frontstage employee activities; and support processes cover all the internal services, steps and interactions happening in the service delivery process to support the contact employees.

The line of external interaction delineates the border where customers meet with the service system, and on the upper side of this line, customers are enjoying the experience offered by the delivered service. Cross points of the line of external interaction and vertical lines in the figure stand for contact points and experiential focus of customers in their encounters with the service system, also the direct sources for their perceptions of the service (and important objects of users' observation).

The line of visibility separates frontstage and backstage employee actions. We can understand it as the service window in a restaurant that physically connects the kitchen and dining space. The horizontal line between backstage employee actions and support processes is the line of internal interaction that separates contact employees from backstage supportive activities and technologies, since service encounters do not only occur in interpersonal interaction, non-personal factors would also exert important influence on customer satisfaction.

A comprehensive use of methods like walk-through test and user interview may help us add more customer focus points, employee decision-making points, waiting

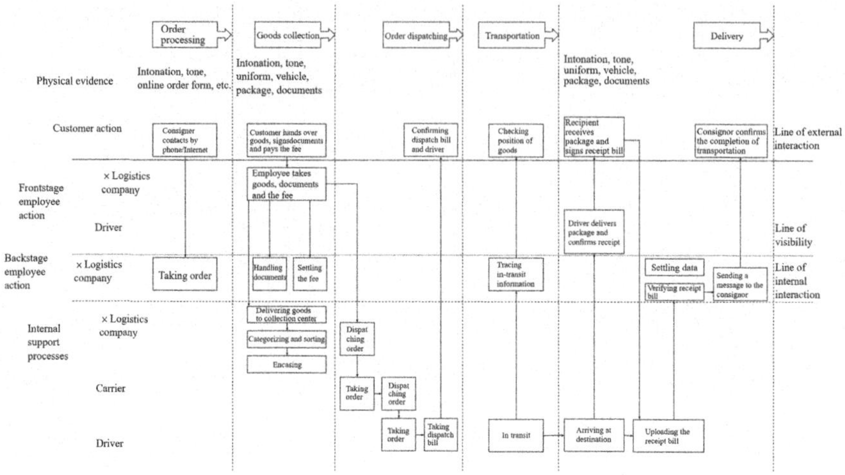

Fig. 9.5 Service Blueprint of the delivery service system of a company

time for resource supply, information flow and other key information to the blueprint, so as to locate common fail points in service and make comparative analysis on their relative importance.

Contact points construct the foundation for customers' perceived quality of the services. Therefore, the identification of these points plays an important role for companies to find their shortages, propose plans for service innovation and, thereby, improve service quality and customer satisfaction. As a client-oriented modeling tool to visualize a system, the Service Blueprint has to be drawn on the basis of real procedures of the service system, with more attention given to key contact points in the service process. Compared to traditional system modeling tools like UML and SysML, Service Blueprints greatly reduce the system modelling difficulty for non-professionals, and suit the characteristics of service systems better, making them easier to be promoted and applied in service innovation processes.

Figure 9.5 is the Service Blueprint of a company's delivery service system.

9.7.1 *Case Analysis: Shangpu Home Design*

In this case, Service Blueprint Diagrams are used to guide home design. The Shangpu Design Studio in Beijing advocates for home systems designed from the perspective of service that perfectly suit the homeowners living habits, namely, the experiential home design service system. So they conclude articles to be stored and organized into seven categories based on living data of their users, as shown in Table 9.1. Information of users' personal life and behavior flow are then collected to define areas for storage and organization, draw a general experience-based blueprint and a quantified experience-based blueprint of home scenarios so as to customize the interior design in a holistic manner.

Shangpu would first collect user information to profoundly understand the living habits of individuals and the family, to master their storage and organization habits, motion lines and aesthetic preferences. Then, specific storage and organization demands of the users will be considered to define storage areas and carry a detailed quantified survey on user behaviors. Next, users would be requested to make quantified descriptions of certain scenarios, rating them in four degrees from "very pleasant" to "uncomfortable", which would serve as pain spots and references for design. Shangpu would also add some highlights and surprise points into the design, to realize emotion-based customization, as seen in Fig. 9.6. Finally, repeated communication is to be made with users to optimize the final Service Blueprint and complete the overall interior design and design of details, as in Table 9.2 and Fig. 9.7.

9.8 Problem Analysis: Bridging Demands and Supply

Observing users is a way to dig into their demands and make profound descriptions for the demand side of the service system, while system modeling is an in-depth structuring of the supply side through analysis of resources in the service system. The next thing to do is to bridge demands and supply through a connection.

This process, as seen from the perspective of operation optimization, starts from defining optimal objectives through demands analysis, to constructing the feasible solution space on the basis of system modeling, and ends in service innovation, during which an optimal objective mapping is found in the feasible solution space. To achieve these objectives, Quality Function Deployment (QFD) is creatively adopted in the final step of the SERVINO Methods so as to quantify the contradictions in the service system and shift the focus of a complex service innovation process to sub-problems that may bring utmost improvement to service quality. This approach not only ensures systematic service innovation practice, but also makes sure that the innovative objects are specific and innovative plans implementable.

QFD is a method developed in Japan to help transform demands into requirements over products. Multilayer deductive analyses are conducted over the demands of stakeholders to transform them into design requirements, features of parts and accessories, technological requirements and manufacturing requirements of products. The method has been revised and developed by American scholars and is now extensively used worldwide.

After decades of development, QFD has been broadly applied in many fields, extending from product design and manufacturing to management and service sectors. For example, my team and I used to apply it in the product design of a railway freight transport reform project, to transform the needs of stakeholders into design and technological requirements of the products. As in service innovation activities,

Table 9.1 Categorization of home storage system

Category of articles			Articles stored	Storage area						
				Hallway	Living room and study room	Bedroom	Bathroom	Kitchen	Cloakroom	Storage room
Food	Food	Staple and subsidiary food	Rice, flour, millet, fragrant rice, black bean, soybean, green bean					★		
		Seasoning	White sugar, black sugar, soy sauce, dark soy sauce, vinegar, sesame oil, cooking oil, chili sauce, sweet soybean sauce, ketchup, Sichuan pepper, aniseed, baking soda, cooking liquor, five-spice powder					★		

(continued)

Table 9.1 (continued)

Category of articles			Articles stored	Storage area						
				Hallway	Living room and study room	Bedroom	Bathroom	Kitchen	Cloakroom	Storage room
Bedding and clothing	Clothing	Clothes	Down coat, coat, jacket, trousers, shorts, skirt, underwear, undershirt, long johns, wind coat, jewelry, tie, scarf, gloves			★			★	
		Shoes	High heels, sneakers, leather shoes, boots, children's shoes	★					★	
		Travel accessories	Suitcase, shopping bag	★						

(continued)

Table 9.1 (continued)

Category of articles			Articles stored	Storage area						
				Hallway	Living room and study room	Bedroom	Bathroom	Kitchen	Cloakroom	Storage room
	Beddings		Bed sheet, coverlet, pillow slip, quilt, mattress, pillow, woolen blanket, flannelette blanket, back cushion, thin quilt, bed brush			★			★	
Sanitation	Daily use chemicals		Soap, shampoo, hair conditioner, shower gel, toilet soap, facial cleanser, facial mask, toner, lotion, perfume, razor, comb, hair dryer				★			

(continued)

Table 9.1 (continued)

Category of articles			Articles stored	Storage area						
				Hallway	Living room and study room	Bedroom	Bathroom	Kitchen	Cloakroom	Storage room
			Towel, bath towel, massage towel, plastic box, storage box				★			
Healthcare	Healthcare products		Medical kit, gauze, woundplast. bandage, clinical thermometer, manometer, alcohol, cotton ball, tweezers, scissors, antipyretics, dissolved medicine, ointment			★				

(continued)

Table 9.1 (continued)

Category of articles			Articles stored	Storage area						
				Hallway	Living room and study room	Bedroom	Bathroom	Kitchen	Cloakroom	Storage room
			Donkey-hide gelatin, edible bird's nest, calcium tablet, ginseng, vitamins. Sanqi tablet					★		
	Maternal and infant supplies		Milk powder, bellyband, town wear, cloak, cape, bib, feeding bottle							
RecrEation Andsports	Stationery and sporting articles		Book, novel, magazine, notebook, graphics tablet, stapler, blue, pen container, folder							

(continued)

Table 9.1 (continued)

Category of articles			Articles stored	Storage area						
				Hallway	Living room and study room	Bedroom	Bathroom	Kitchen	Cloakroom	Storage room
			Table lamp, tableware, photo album, artwork, ceramic, antique		★					
Tools	Kitchenware		Bowl, dish, pot, fruit bowl, pan, casserole, steamer, rice cooker, kettle, thermos jug, egg steamer, knife, slice, spoon					★		

(continued)

Table 9.1 (continued)

Category of articles			Articles stored	Storage area						
				Hallway	Living room and study room	Bedroom	Bathroom	Kitchen	Cloakroom	Storage room
			Oven, microwave oven, steam box, dishwasher, disinfection cabinet, storage bag, plastic wrap, oven mitt, dishwashing liquid, steel wool, scouring pad, linen					★		

(continued)

Table 9.1 (continued)

Category of articles	Articles stored	Storage area						
		Hallway	Living room and study room	Bedroom	Bathroom	Kitchen	Cloakroom	Storage room
Cleaning products	Rubber gloves, duster cloth, toilet brush, broom, tissue, cotton swab, toilet roll, detergent, softener, disinfectant, toilet detergent					★		
	Mop. wash basin, foot bucket				★	★		

(continued)

Table 9.1 (continued)

Category of articles			Articles stored	Storage area						
				Hallway	Living room and study room	Bedroom	Bathroom	Kitchen	Cloakroom	Storage room
	Home tools		Tissue box, desk trash can. electric bug killer, electric mosquito repellent, fan, fire extinguisher, extension cod, electric iron, clothes hanger, tool kit, vacuum cleaner	★						
			Humidifier, air purifier, formaldehyde meter, air quality monitor		★	★				

(continued)

Table 9.1 (continued)

Category of articles			Articles stored	Storage area						
				Hallway	Living room and study room	Bedroom	Bathroom	Kitchen	Cloakroom	Storage room
	Safety tools		Safe box			★				
Others	Sundries		Umbrella, cape, baby carriage, bicycles, walking stick, wheel chair, baby chair							

Home Storage System—A
The system is applicable to regular apartments and villas in cities, excluding public rental housing
The articles to be stored fall into seven categories: food, bedding and clothing, sanitation and healthcare, recreation and sports, tools and others—categories of everyday consumer goods
The storage principles are unit-based storage and behavior flow storage. The former means to categorize articles according to their major service units; the latter is the storage form based on individual behavior characteristics
Source Shangpu design studio

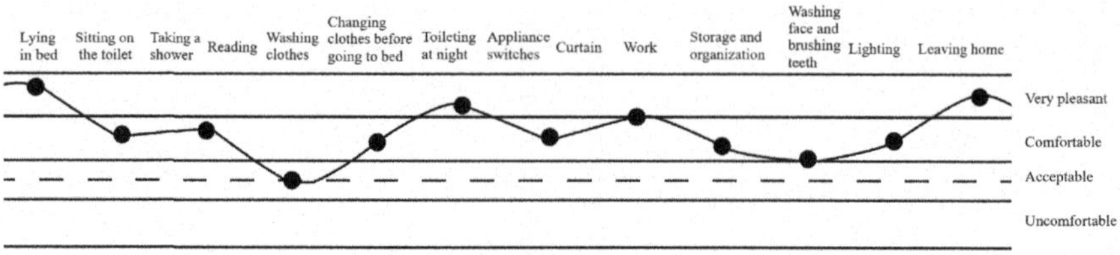

Fig. 9.6 Final quantified design of home experience. *Source* Shangpu design studio

QFD can be used to quantify the relationship between customers' demands and innovation objects (plan), identify essential measures that can contribute mostly to satisfy customers' demands, and then provide pertinent guidance to service innovators.

QFD helps product designers to master the main contradictions (physical contradictions and system contradictions) easily, make stabilizing and optimizing designs to develop satisfying service products. A commonly used tool of QFD, "house of quality", is a quality matrix that relates users' demands to the corresponding technological requirements, so that three important questions can be answered for service innovators: What are the greatest demands and expectations placed over the service system? What components of the service system are needed to realize these demands and expectations? What does the ideal service system after innovation look like?

The design we made for the railway freight transport project is offered as an example in Fig. 9.8. A complete house of quality should include the following parts:

Left wall: Demands of stakeholders (also known as "the voice of customer") and their weights.

Ceiling: Technical measures are proposed and quality features are specified for the freight transport products, in order to satisfy the stakeholders' demands. The results are filled in the ceiling.

Room: The interrelation matrix used to record the interrelations between stakeholders' demands and technical measures; if the interrelation is closer, the value is greater.

Floor: Indicators and importance degrees of the technical measures.

Roof: The correlation matrix used to evaluate the correlations among technical measures, because of possible interactions existing between different measures. For example, some technical measures may be mutually strengthening while some may offset each other. The influence of such interactive factors has to be considered when selecting technical measures and their indicators.

We put the demands and troubles of users identified with the help of an Empathy Map into the left wall of this house of quality, along with their weights concluded from a survey and focus group interviews.

On the other hand, the Service Blueprint was used to identify the key components of the service system and their coupling relations, which were then filled in the ceiling and roof of the house of quality. Scores given by experts were filled in the

Table 9.2 Quantified blueprint of home experience

	Lying in bed	Sitting on the toilet	Taking a shower	Reading	Washing clothes	Changing clothes before going to bed	Toileting at night
Scenario description	Lie back in bed, feel soft and comfortable in glare-free warm light; charge mobile phone easily; independent controllable readier lamp	Open the toilet lid easily and cleanly, sit on the warm self-flushing toilet; sensor light turns on at night; toilet roll is on the users' left and trash can on the right; read magazines on the toilet	Warm floor; nonslip easy-to-use toiletries; quick-heated water	Controllable light, glare-free and un-interfered space for books	Wash clothes noiselessly in living room and bed room	Laundry basket and place to put/ hang clothes are needed	Soft light with no influence on others, easy-to-operate switch, not dazzling at night
Article description	Back cushion (for laying back with open vision but no glare) 3000 K spotlight; Night stand, automatic charger, bed runner (socks often have bacteria) open-type high-leg night stand for tissue box and trash can	Smart voice-activated toilet, touchless flushing, sensor light, magazine stand, sensor trash bin	Nonslip mat, toiletries holder, fan heater	Independent reading lamp, with color temperature higher than 3000 K	Anti-vibration washing machine	Removable basket	Bed side sensor lamp, with double-control switch installed on bedside floor
Material/ equipment		TOTO smart toilet	Matt black metal rack	…	…	…	…

	Appliance switches	Curtain	Work	Storage and organization	Washing face and brushing teeth	Lightening	Leaving home
Scenario description	Intelligent air-conditioner works in sleep mode at night to lower noise and improve sleep quality	Intelligent curtain connected to alarm clock to automatically open in the morning and close night	Can charge laptop And mobile phone; independent light source desktop width no shorter than 0.5m	Storage place for carry-on bags and valuables different storage organization for different people, areas ad categories	Listen to music and news while brushing teeth; don't have to use toothpaste, tooth brush, shampoo, toner or toilet soap	Glare-free neutral color temperature, independent and one-touch controllable lightening	Double Control or above switch to close all appliances together
Article description	Intelligent air-conditioner	Electric curtain	Seven-hole socket and USB connector on the wall, foldable office table, concise table lamp	Bedside, easy to use	Smart vanity mirror, toilet soap and soap put in front of the wash basin; toothpaste, toothbrush, shampoos, and towel can be hung to wallet if space is limited	Switches to adjust luminance and color temperature	Master appliances switches
Material/ equipment	…	…	…	…	…	…	…

Source Shangpu design studio

Fig. 9.7 Case of experience-based home design service system. *Source* Shangpu design studio

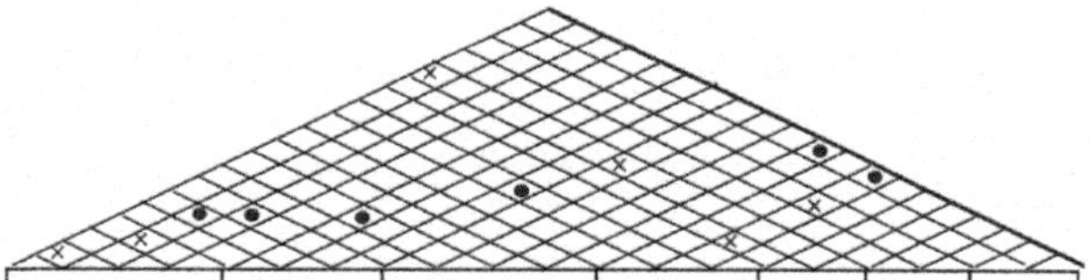

		Driver				Application			Backstage database				Deliverer			Vehicle		Receipt		SMS	
Demand	Weight	Simpleness of work	Information feedback speed	Information accuracy	Driving safety	Convenience of use	Data update speed	Information transparency	Data update speed	Data completeness	Data accuracy	Convenience of use	Service attitude	Receiving speed	Work efficiency	Safety & reliability	Cleanliness	Convenience of use	Information completeness	Information accuracy	Time efficiency
I want to have the driver's information	3							3		1									1		
I want to check the position of my package at any time	2	3	9	1		1			9												9
I want to get my package ASAP	5	3			3		1						3								
I want to contact the driver at any time	3		9																		
I hope the deliverer is properly dressed	1																3				
I hope the deliverer is in good attitude	3												9								
I want to choose the time for delivery	2										3										
I hope my package is intact	4				3											9					
I want to have my personal information well protected	4							3				3		3					3		
I want to fully check the items	5													9					3	1	
I hope the receipt procedure is short and easy	2											1		9	1			3			
	Score	21	45	1	27	2	5	21	18	3	6	14	42	75	2	36	3	6	30	5	18
	Ranking	7	2	20	6	18	14	7	9	16	12	11	3	1	18	4	16	12	5	15	9

Fig. 9.8 An example of house of quality

interrelation matrix in the room to indicate a positive or negative correlation, with the final score of each system component (feature) calculated.

Based on the structure of the house of quality, scores and indicators in it revealed their priorities in the improvement of the service system, because the score of each component feature was traceable to its origin, which was the observation on users, and pointed to a demand of users. It ensured that all the following service innovation activities were driven by users' demands, which is the foundation of successful innovation.

The house of quality can precisely locate physical contradictions and system contradictions in the service system. A physical contradiction means that two opposite expectations are placed on the same parameter. For example, users want to have larger mobile phones that are easy to operate and legible for reading, but they also hope phones are small and convenient to carry (clamshell phones and slide phones before, and latest folding phones are all working at this contradiction). For another example, customers at a restaurant sometimes want to have a waiter nearby to serve them always; but sometimes, they would hope he could leave them alone for them to dine without being interrupted.

A system contradiction occurs when the improvement of a parameter would cause another to deteriorate. For example, to make a tank more bulletproof, the armor has to be thicker, but that would slow down its movement. Service innovation activities should also be based upon physical and system contradictions.

The first thing we have to do with the house of quality is to locate the points for service improvement. The receiving speed in Fig. 9.8 is a good example: two different demands of users—"I want to fully check the items" and "I hope the receipt procedure is short and easy"—were driving service innovation into two opposite directions, presenting a physical contradiction. Also for the parameter of another component in the Figure, "information feedback speed", if the feedback on real-time delivery process is facilitated, the correlation reflected in the roof would cause an increase in the workload of the driver and deliverer, resulting in a system contradiction.

Constructing a quality matrix in the house of quality can not only clearly visualize all the links and procedures, but also deal with a large amount of information. The house of quality applied in service innovation activities can combine inputs at both demand and supply sides, identify specific physical and system contradictions and make it easier to carry out standard innovative actions according to the transferred TRIZ inventive principles. Accordingly, physical contradictions are to be solved with the separation principle, and system ones with inventive principles.

9.9 How to "Invent" Services?

9.9.1 Separation Principle in Service

As a principle of universal guiding significance for innovation, the separation principle has long been extensively used in many innovative design processes, without being noticed by innovators. For example, we used to undertake the innovative design of an online hospital, for which the client's requirement was to design an online hospital product featuring chronic disease management aiming particularly at Parkinsonism. An important problem of the client's platform we found through mission and demand analysis and other activities was that senior citizens had difficulties in using smart phones and applications. Most patients suffering from Parkinsonism and other chronic diseases, the target users of the platform, were middle-aged and aged people who tended to be unfamiliar with the use of smart phones, which, however, as the important terminals of an online hospital, were almost inevitable in the service process. Therefore, we proposed a commission mode, through which family members of the elderly could operate on behalf of the old patients. We simultaneously developed a linked application for patients' family members so that they could make an appointment with the doctor, initiate a tele-consultation, buy and pay for medicines, etc., while the patients needed only to touch one button to access into the tele-consultation and tell the doctor about their conditions, including drug use. This proposal was, by its essence, a separation of the application users' operation procedures and information exchange procedures. In a traditional application like a news platform, the operator and beneficiary of the software functions are the same person—the user receives the software service (news and information acquisition) through logging in, selecting, typing and searching (operation). The operation and information exchange are in a unified process, conducted by the same subject. But in our online hospital system, all the complicated operations on the smart phone were carried out by younger family members and the elder patients had only to participate in information exchanges (telling the doctor their conditions and listening to the doctor's treatment plan and advice).

The separation principle normally includes four measures, separation of space, separation of time, separation of conditions and system-level separation. For example, the parking lot of a scenic spot is often a distance away from the entrance so as to ease the congestion, this is a separation of space. For another, IKEA furniture takes different forms in different processes of transaction, as a separation of time: displayed as a complete product in IKEA store, disassembled into boards and parts to be delivered to the buyer, and reassembled at the buyer's home. Many video websites are making profits through providing no-advertising service for paid subscribers, which is a utilization of separation of conditions.

9.9.2 Inventive Principles for Service Innovation

If the separation principle is the main solution to physical contradictions, inventive principles for service innovation are powerful tools to solve system contradictions. The 40 technical inventive principles in TRIZ approach are transferred to the domain of service invention, and each re-illustrated with a case in the service sector.

For example, Jay Walker, the founder of online travel agency Priceline.com, advocates that accommodation prices should be set by the users and therefore has established a client-pricing system, in which customers can name their price for a certain commodity or service and leave it for a bidding by suppliers (e.g., hotels). It is, on the one hand, creating a new market based on the perishability of services; and, on the other hand, making use of the reverse thinking principle ("the other way round") to transform the way "customers choosing a hotel based on prices" into "hotels competing for customers with a consideration of their profits and losses".

For another example, TRIZ principle 10: preliminary action, is performing the required change of an object or system before it is needed, or prearranging an object or system so that it comes into action from the most convenient place and without losing delivery time. It can be told from the definition that this principle has been widely applied in service systems, such as the popular "preposition warehouses" in logistics service systems or the practice in the hospitality industry of putting the bill into the guestroom the night before check-out—they both echo with TRIZ principle 10.

Designers can either directly choose from and use the nearly 40 inventive principles for service innovation, or make use of the contradiction matrix, which is more of stylized innovative procedures that can reduce the designers' workload. Specifically, we have firstly redesigned the contradiction matrix to selectively retain and transfer 39 technical parameters from the traditional TRIZ parameters, and provided supplementary definitions to 15 important parameters. For example, the original parameter 29 "manufacturing precision", indicating the extent to which the actual characteristics of the system or object match the specified or required characteristics, is further defined as the gap between service delivery and service standard (the third gap in the Gap Model of Service Quality).

After transferring and supplementing the service parameters, we have made a two-dimensional matrix of the interrelations between deterioration and improvement of these parameters, so that designers can choose appropriate inventive principles for service innovation from the matrix according to their identified service parameters (system contradictions). Then, industrial experts and senior professionals can make a brainstorm to "translate" the abstract principles into a concrete innovation plan, which has to go through simulation, verification and earnings estimate to ensure its effectiveness in operation.

9.9.3 More Methods to Inspire Innovation

In addition to the separation principle and inventive principles for service innovation, we have proposed, as inspired by the laws of technical systems evolution, laws of evolution that suit service systems better. These laws of service systems evolution can serve as a reference for the development of any new service system to help designers expand the way of thinking, find a sound direction for innovation and thus shorten the time used for development. The eight laws of technical systems evolution have been transferred and revised into following ones: the law of the completeness of the service system, the law of shortening value conductivity of the system, the law of harmonizing the rhythms of parts of the system, the law of increasing the degree of ideality of the system, the law of uneven development of parts of a system resulting in system contradictions, the law of transition to a super-system, the law of transition from macro to micro level, and the law of increasing the system flexibility. Taking the law of shortening value conductivity of the system as an example, it represents the direction of service systems evolution in the engineering field and requires the shortening of the length of energy within a system. In the service sector, Carrefour is adopting the direct supply mode to shorten its path of value conductivity. What Carrefour has been doing is removing the delivery links undertaken by dealers in its supply chain, bringing a considerable reduction to inventory costs, and ensuring effective exchange of demand and supply information while reducing stock-out rate and improving service efficiency.

To better leverage the Internet and data mining technology, we used the algorithms of SERVOINO problem-solving process as main logic in the development of a web-based software (in Fig. 9.9), which has integrated all major tools in problem-solving processes of service innovation to function as a relatively complete solution. The retrieval mode that relates innovative theories to problem-solving algorithms through structured assortment of data, based on the service innovation case database and the enabling technology library integrated in the software, allows users to put the newly-acquired knowledge into immediate practice, inspires their thinking in service development and makes it convenient to verify the feasibility of any innovation plan. As the service innovation case database is under ongoing construction, many service innovation tools of the software, including the contradiction matrix, will keep being itinerated and improved.

Fig. 9.9 A screenshot of the SERVINO software

Chapter 10
Parallel Services

It is known that the customer is king, but how much do we, the service providers, know about our "king"? The intrinsic attributes of services (intangibility, heterogeneity, perishability, etc.) have made service management extremely challenging, but the core of all the challenges is people. Without incorporating behaviors, characteristics and motives of people into service management, we'd never successfully "put people first", nor achieve excellence in service.

Today, Service Science studies have produced a set of research achievements through combining the characteristics of services with manufacturing-based management theories and practices. However, the systematic integration of human factor at levels of strategy, tactics and operation is still a very attractive and challenging issue.

Here, a parallel service management framework is proposed for complex service systems, based on Professor Fei-Yue Wang's Parallel Control and Management Mechanism. Firstly, a model is built for a service system, taking it as a typical complex system, so as to construct an artificial service system; secondly, a large number of computing experiments are conducted to support decision-making of the service system at various levels; and, finally, the artificial and the real service systems are executed in a parallel manner so as to implement parallel management over the real services.

The key foundation to construct a parallel service system is to build models of the customers, which include three essential parts, the service demand cycle model, the service channel choice model and the parallel learning and optimization model. Typical potential applications for a parallel service system include analysis of service channel evolution, micromarketing of services, intelligent service recommendation, and so on. Generally, a parallel service system boasts the following advantages:

First, it combines behavioral science, environmental impact (social and natural environment) and other factors into service management, enriching the connotation of Service Science.

L. Li, *The Era of New Services*, Management for Professionals,
https://doi.org/10.1007/978-981-99-9565-3_10

Second, it provides evaluation and support to service decision-making through the artificial service system based on computing experiments, enhancing the scientificity of service management decisions.

Third, the parallel execution in artificial and real service systems supports smart and personalized service innovations, on the basis of deepening the understanding of customers' demands.

10.1 Parallel Services

Figure 10.1 shows the basic framework of parallel service management, in which, the real service system on the left includes three components: the actual service system, customers and environment, while on the right is the artificial service system that not only simulates the real service system, but also analyzes and understands clients with the help of Big Data as well as studies the environment through IoT and social computing. The ultimate goal of parallel service management is to provide decision-making support to the actual service system through a parallel execution in the artificial service system.

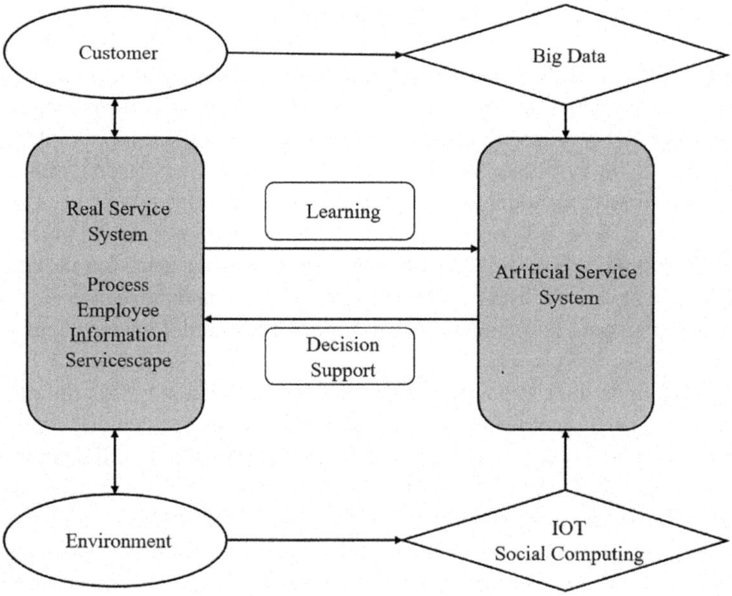

Fig. 10.1 The basic framework of parallel service management

10.1.1 Uniqueness of Parallel Service Management

In current practices, service providers can only acquire data when clients use their services, meaning that their understanding of clients depends highly on transaction data. However, parallel service management takes data from different sources into consideration, not only data of clicks, cameras and locations, but also social networking data, concerning both existing clients who have bought or are buying the services, and potential clients with similar demands.

Although top-notch businesses have adopted ambush marketing and other tactics in certain campaigns to promote sales, the dynamic tracking of changes in (social and natural) environment for service improvement is still beyond the capacity of most service providers. The parallel service management approach holds that the same client may have different perceptions of services in different environments. Therefore, service providers considering the impacts of the environment on clients' behaviors are able to make a better use of the artificial service system to provide smart decision-making support to the real service system.

10.1.2 The Three-Scale Model of Parallel Service Management

Parallel service management is flexible at different scales, as shown in Fig. 10.2. Traditional complex adaptive systems focus on macro emergent behaviors caused by interactions between intelligent agents and the environment, while the model built for service systems through parallel service management includes three layers, individuals, groups and the public. As the scale expands layer by layer, the complexity of the organizational structure grows, causing studies to focus more on interrelations and interactions among people, with the complexity of thinking/motive/preference ignored.

The three-scale model of parallel service management is an integration of the most advanced achievements of cognitive and behavioral sciences, social networking and group studies.

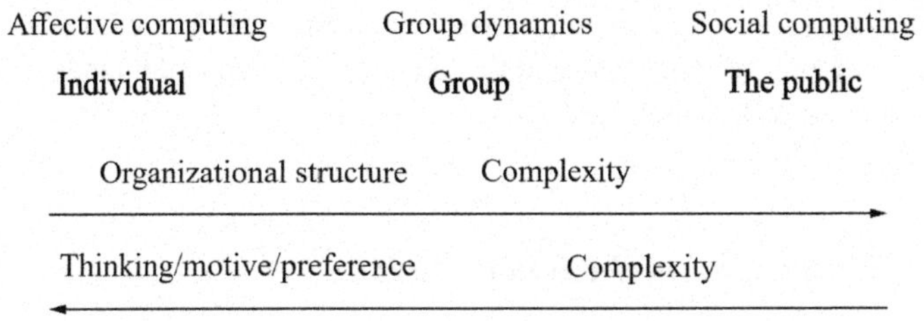

Fig. 10.2 The three-scale model of parallel service management

At the individual level, affective computing and other techniques are used to simulate in detail the behaviors of clients and employees. Key elements at this level are individual thinking, motives and preferences, which are related to people's characteristics, affections, demands and beliefs.

At the group level, group dynamics and related techniques are adopted to construct an understanding of the unique behaviors of certain groups. For example, is a group satisfied with the services or not, and how does the group choose services?

The study at the public level is similar to social networking analysis—using social computing technology to observe and describe complex social behaviors.

Discussions on customer satisfaction in current service management studies and practices only vary the research methods and study individual clients, paying no attention to the differences between different group clients. Therefore, the group level and the public level are included in this model.

The structure of communication and relations within a group may all influence the overall service satisfaction of the group. A broadened group may ultimately cover the whole public, and public satisfaction is another essential issue to be explored. Taking public services as an example, the public welfare is actually an issue of service satisfaction of the broadest group of people.

10.2 Services Empowered by AI Technology

To support the computing experiments and parallel execution in parallel service management, the design of the artificial service system has to include three components: the service demand cycle model, the service channel choice model and the parallel learning and optimization model.

10.2.1 Service Demand Cycle Model

Analyses on clients' demands carried out in service practices are usually based on actualized service data (e.g., retail terminal data in the retail sector). But they are under certain limitations: the unsatisfied demands and demands not actualized because of unobserved needs are ignored. So the service demand cycle model is proposed in the artificial service system to present the cyclicity of clients' demands in stochastic model and generate demands data.

10.2.2 Service Channel Choice Model

The service channel choice theory followed by service providers is of vital importance. While the Utility Theory is the dominant theory that lays the foundation for channel choice modeling research, the selection of a service provider is much more complex than selecting a product. For example, clients of Fab.com are reported to get their satisfaction from curiosity and joy, instead of favorable prices or quality products. Therefore, the Gap Model of Service Quality is used here to compare users' expected and perceived qualities, and combined with Utility Models to construct the final service channel choice model.

10.2.3 Parallel Learning and Optimization Model

Parallel execution requires the artificial service system to carry the capability to learn real-time from the actual service system, posing a great challenge to current machine learning algorithms, not to mention the observation of clients and environment and the extended processing of information. Concerning the present computing power, semi-real-time approach or concurrent processing may be a feasible solution.

Providing decision-making support to the actual service system is the fundamental task of the artificial service system. We have put forward an intelligent agents-based double-layer optimization model on the basis of our previous experience and the effectiveness of applying the model to optimize urban transport services has been proved by computing experiments. The artificial service system at the lower layer of the double-layer optimization model can be used to predict customer responses (e.g., passenger flows in urban transport), with the heuristic algorithm adopted at upper layer to find better solutions to service problems (e.g., bus frequency in urban public transport). The double-layer structure makes it easy to integrate different techniques of Operations Science at the upper layer and use the artificial system as the evaluation function, bringing significant flexibility and potential to the parallel service management framework.

The Chinese logistics company, SF Technology, integrates artificial intelligence into practical business scenarios, linking each business process. Through the accumulation of business experience and technological innovation, it further enhance the interconnectivity of information across the entire logistics chain. SF utilizes artificial intelligence technologies such as machine learning, computer vision, operations research, and global optimization to achieve logistics system state perception, real-time analysis, scientific decision-making, and precise execution of the logistics system, constructing the "intelligent brain" of the SF logistics system. SF's AI Argus provides basic data for its transportation network, including vehicle loading rates, vehicle dispatch, capacity monitoring and energy efficiency of site personnel. It offers real-time feedback to optimize capacity. The platform's video analysis capability can detect and identify rough handling, thereby significantly lowering the chances of parcels getting damaged or misplaced.

10.3 The "Parallel" Age of Service Management

10.3.1 Service Channel Evolution Analysis

A pattern of service evolution can be found in most service industries, with service innovation as a milestone on the evolutionary path. The possibility of building service innovation predictions or evaluations upon service evolution analyses is a matter worth being discussed.

Taking the retail sector as an example, supermarket magnate Walmart opened its first store in the 1960s, followed with the emergence of warehouse clubs, while online retailers came into being in the 1990s, with Amazon as a typical example. But the timeline constructs only one dimension in evolution.

The other important dimension is market share. Online retailing in China grew from 1.5% in 2006 to 19.6% in 2017,[1] driven by the development of major factors like price competitiveness and convenience. Theoretically, if these factors are included in the clients' choice process, we should be able to reproduce the evolution of retail service channels. Also, computing experiments can be made to estimate the potential development paths for innovative trends like O2O.

10.3.2 Micromarketing of Services

One way of carrying out parallel service management is to directly develop intelligent services embedded with parallel service management. Its unique advantage is that service designers can better understand the clients and environment as the foundation they rely on includes information and knowledge sources provided by Big Data, IoT and other technologies.

The development of intelligent services embedded with parallel service management is similar to the Microsoft gaming platform Xbox One which recognizes different members of the family through a Kinect camera and recommends different films to them. With the help of embedded parallel service management, service suppliers can recommend suitable services for each user according to the results of computing experiments.

Under certain circumstances, suppliers' service recommendations based on embedded parallel service management may even go beyond clients' expectations. For example, a catering service provider can take advantage of the embedded parallel service management to recommend low-carbohydrate diet to clients in need of healthy food, even suggest a serial of ideal dining places for them.

---

[1] E-Commerce Research Institute, Data Monitoring and Warning Report of 2017 Chinese Online Retail Market [R], (2018–6–13).

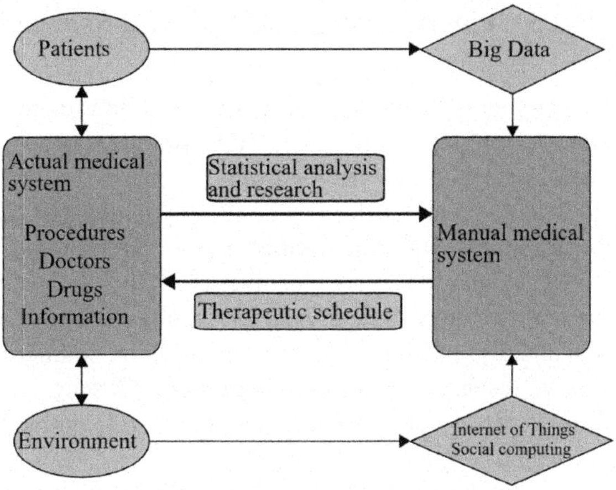

Fig. 10.3 Parallel service framework of the precision medical system

10.3.3 Intelligent Services

A precision medical system is used here as an illustration. A large database has been established in the system to focus on physical signs of individual patients and tailor a personalized therapeutic schedule for each of them, so as to guide and improve the actual treatment. Figure 10.3 is the parallel service framework of this precision medical system.

In spite of the various treatment means for cancers nowadays, the way to achieve the best therapeutic effects is to make scientific schedules according to exact conditions of individual patients. Thanks to technologies like gene sequencing and target detection of cancer-targeted drugs, precision medicine is able to make a precise match of patient's information and drug information, so that a personalized treatment of cancer is realized, with the drug efficacy improved, best therapeutic effects achieved and expenses reduced.

10.3.4 A Case Study

Improved waiting experience and enhanced perceived service quality in a railway station may help increase the number of passengers, on the premise that an ordered passage is guaranteed. As the layout of the station exerts heavy influence on passengers' perception of services, we did a computing experiment at Chengdu East High-speed Rail Station to improve the layout there based on passengers' decision-making process and, as a result, effectively increased the number of passengers visiting stores in the station.

10.3.5 Constructing the Artificial Service System

Questionnaires were used to analyze the interrelations between attributes of stores and attributes of passengers as well as their decision-making process on entering into a store or not. The stores were divided into two types based on the analytical results: set A includes stores that can be seen by passengers, and set B includes stores within the acceptable walking distance in passengers' mind.

The simulation system generated 13 stores and their respective attributes based on the real situation and questionnaire analysis. The system also generated 500, 1000, 800 and 500 passengers at eastern, western, southern and northern entrances of the station, respectively, for each hour. Each passenger was given 4 attributes, available time, mode, train type and ticket entrance, to define his or her initial probability of entering a certain store.

As shown in Fig. 10.4, set A updates once every second as the passenger moves from the station entrance to the ticket entrance. As he arrives at the ticket entrance, both set A and set B have finished updating and the passenger shall decide whether to step into a store or not.

According to the analysis, passengers may pass by two areas on their way from station entrance to ticket entrance: the space between stores and the ticket entrance—area A and the space between two rows of ticket entrances—area B. We added two screen walls (indicated by the grey bold lines in Fig. 10.5) to adjust the layout of the station in the simulation system. In the adjusted layout, the ticket check flow line connecting eastern and southern entrances is improved so that area B is used only for static queues in front of ticket entrances, with the horizontal human traffic reduced and check-in order guaranteed. In the meantime, the dynamic route surrounding area

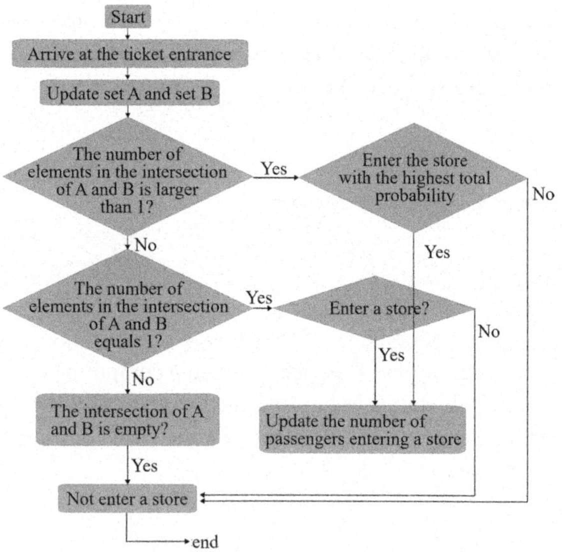

Fig. 10.4 The decision-making process of a passenger as an intelligent agent

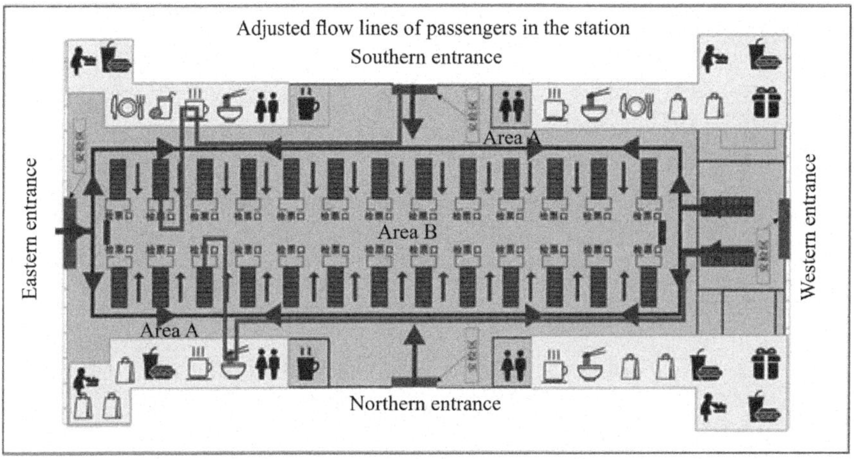

Fig. 10.5 The adjusted layout of Chengdu east high-speed railway station

A performs more business functions to increase the store-entering probabilities of passengers on their way towards the ticket entrance and boost effective purchasing power.

10.3.6 Actual System Implementation

Records were kept on the number of passengers entering into stores between 8.00 a.m. and 9.00 a.m. before and after the adjustment of the simulated layout, as in Fig. 10.6.

According to Fig. 10.6, the number of passengers entering into stores after the adjustment shows a significant increase over the pre-adjustment level.

As shown in Fig. 10.7, the entry rate of stores also performs better after the adjustment. The entry rate stabilizes at around 21% after the simulated preheating process (0–1800 s), 24% higher than the pre-adjustment level.

The same method was then used to adjust the station layout in practice and the results showed that the number of store-entering passengers grew by about 20% after the adjustment, as compared with the number before the adjustment, generally consistent to the predictions made by the artificial service system.

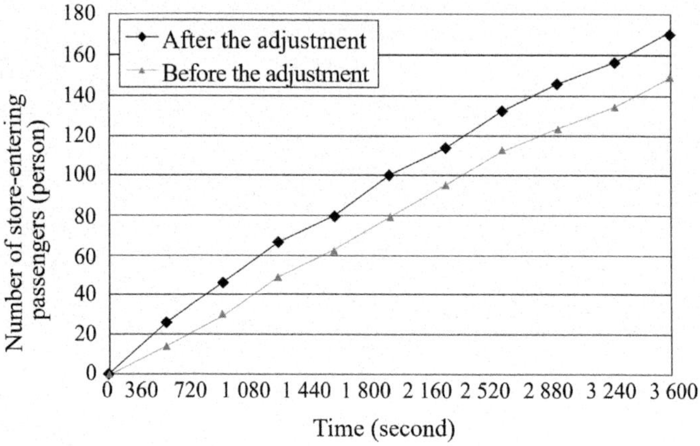

Fig. 10.6 Statistics of store-entering passengers before and after the adjustment

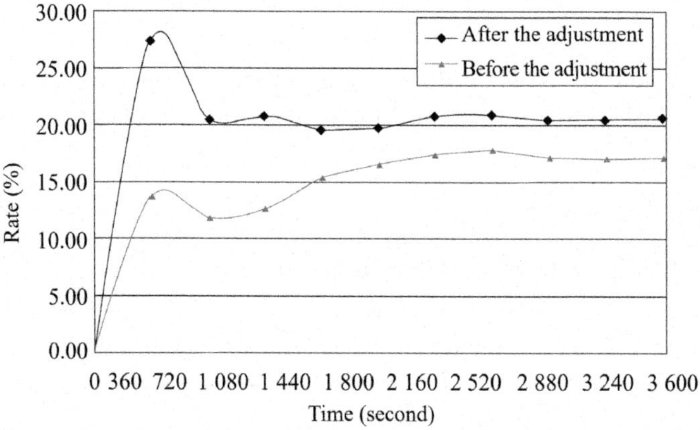

Fig. 10.7 Store entry rates

Part IV
Service Innovation and Future Life

Chapter 11
Service Innovation and Future Life

Provisions in the traditional service sector are composed of "four major items", which are also the four factors of services that concern the customers most, namely, price-performance ratio, convenience, reliability and abundancy of choices. But what do today's customers care about? Or should we ask, what are their expectations on perceptions of service?

An advertisement by Apple may shed some light on the answer: "We used to believe convenience is fun, abundance equals choices, and design needs a focus. But now we start by asking what we want to make people feel: happy, amazed, with their passions connected."

In other words, the old belief that all customers need is convenience has been proved wrong today, since it does not equal fun. We have to think deeply about the feelings and experience we are offering to our customers and innovative services catering to their feelings and experience are also defining our life in the future.

11.1 Curiosity

Fab.com is a flash sales site of creative products in the U.S., with its home page shown in Fig. 11.1. The picture on the left looks like a row of beach chairs at first sight, but if you look closely, you will find they are only chair backs. Now that we are on the beach, for what do we need the bottom half of the chair? We could totally sit on the beach while being amazed by the ingenuous design of the chair back.

The chair backs in the sand arouse people's curiosity on this website and encourage them to look for more interesting products. The product on the top right corner of Fig. 11.1 that looks like a Ferris wheel is actually a towel hanger, a romantic festoon to one's daily life! And the lower right corner shows a special wine opener. In a word, the most outstanding characteristic of the site is that 90% of the products they sell

L. Li, *The Era of New Services*, Management for Professionals,
https://doi.org/10.1007/978-981-99-9565-3_11

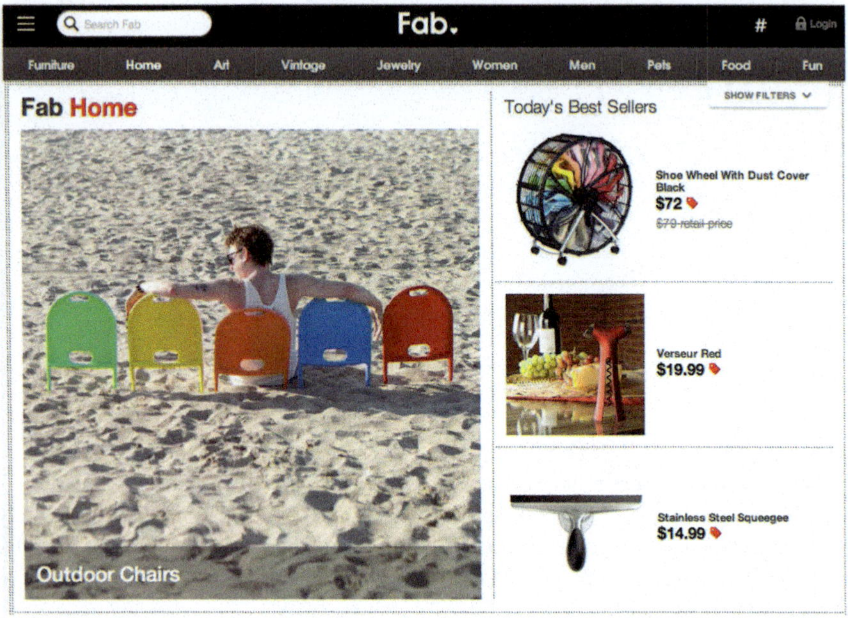

Fig. 11.1 Beach chair backs sold on Fab.com. *Source* https://fab.com/

can never be found anywhere else, so it serves exactly the curiosity of users. When someone wants to buy a surprising gift for a friend, Fab.com becomes a solid choice.

11.2 Fun

I once had a very interesting experience. A friend of mine is a garment retailer. He asked me if I wanted to take part in a Nike event: spending 800 yuan on a box of Nike products that included eight items—two hats, three T-shirts, a cotton-padded jacket and two pairs of shoes.

I figured that each item costed only 100 yuan, not expensive. But the interesting thing was that, as my friend told me, he knew nothing about the products, their colors, styles, sizes or were they for men or women. I had to find them out at the time of unboxing.

Seeing that the deal was interesting and inexpensive, I bought one and got strangely excited when I took things out of the box: I got a red cotton-padded jacket from Manchester United that fit me well, making me delighted. The T-shirts all looked fine, though the shoes were a bit smaller for me. But that was okay, I could send them to somebody else.

As I opened the packed items one by one, I realized that it was similar to the stone gambling someone attends in Myanmar. The gamblers do not know if the stone contains jade or not. The only way to find out is to buy the stone and cut it out. That must feel the same as when I unboxed the Nike items. I called my friend right after I finished the unboxing and asked for another box, but he said, "Sorry, they are all sold out. I'll tell you next time when we do this again."

I thought about it again as my excitement faded. What was it, actually?

In fact, the retailers were disposing of their obsolete inventories, but in a masterly way. Obsolete inventories are one of the most painful spots in the clothing, shoes and hats industry. They are normally sold at discount stores or outlets, but spaces have to be taken, customers need to pick one by one and put down those they don't like, which have to be put in order afterwards by employees according to colors, sizes, specifications and for men or women. All these are quite labor-consuming and the inventories may still be left over.

But the approach recommended by my friend—putting eight items of surprise in one box regardless of their models, sizes and styles—solves all the problems at one go. And customers, finding enough fun from it, would buy a second box, making this a smart disposal of obsolete inventories—taking advantage of customers' curiosity to bring them fun in experience.

The online version of this approach can now be found everywhere on the Internet. The "lucky bags" offered by various e-commerce sites fall in this new marketing mode. Without knowing the contents within the lucky bags, customers are buying them, as driven by curiosity, to see what surprises they may find. The principle is completely the same as my Nike box.

Speaking of fun, I had another special experience to share.

I have been a great fan of Haidilao hot pots. As we know, there are many things to do when we wait for the table at Haidilao. They offer free tea, soybean milk, chess and card games, even manicures for ladies. However, the novelty of these services soon wears off.

Once when I sat in a corner, playing on my phone to kill time, a Haidilao waiter came to me and asked, "Sir, are you interested in the mobile game made by Haidilao?" That was really surprising, since I'd never thought that as a hot pot restaurant, Haidilao would develop a mobile game. She explained to me that they developed a farming game for customers to grow vegetables and grass and feed cattle and sheep. Amused by the news, I asked: "I am a loyal user of the game Happy Farm, why would I turn to play the same game of Haidilao?" Seemingly prepared for such a question, she told me, "Our game is different from Happy Farm. You could raise your cattle in the game and exchange it for real beef at our restaurant."

Winning beef by simply playing a game? How could I ignore such a good deal? So I downloaded the game right away and took my cattle-raising cause seriously. It was not long before I realized my naivety, it was really hard to raise a calf to its maturity! You had to sow the seeds of grass, spray fertilizers and pesticides to make sure they grow well, then vaccinate the calves, so on and so forth. I'd never raise it up in the half-an-hour waiting time.

That calf hung in my mind when I was on my way home after the hot pot dinner. When it grew into an adult three days later, my first thought was to exchange it for beef at Haidilao. Actually, I ate at Haidilao once every two or three weeks before that, but the fun of the game attracted me there only three days later. I went there spontaneously and happily since my need for "fun" was satisfied. From this view, we may find a broad space for service innovation.

We may name a trend to apply this approach more extensively, which is to "Game Everything!" The fundamental logic of the trend is to integrate the mode of strongest customer stickiness—games—with traditional services, to form unique attractiveness and capture the huge market consisted of all customer groups interested in games, the essence of which is to precisely introduce the fun of high stickiness into services.

For example, Duolingo enables users to learn English, Spanish, French or German through playing games several minutes a day, without the need of textbooks or teachers, and all are for free! The application of research achievements of the Behavioral Science and principles of game-makers has helped Duolingo improve its Day 2 retention rate of users from 13 to 55%. Users can also get virtual coins in the process of playing. Now think about it, haven't the films *The Da Vinci Code* and *Ready Player One* revealed the future to us?

11.3 Passions Connected

WeChat may be the best example of having people's "passions connected" as mentioned in the Apple advertisement.

As a social communications product, WeChat is undoubtedly a legend since it has pervaded all aspects of people's life.

Its biggest characteristic is the mining and maintenance of social relationships. It "activates" schoolmates of the same primary school or kindergarten who have not seen each other for years. Friends who have lost communication for decades are in contact again on WeChat, even gather for dinner the next day. How amazing it is.

Starting from social relationships, WeChat has permeated into all aspects throughout people's life, including payment. Its users are connected in the most convenient and interesting ways (WeChat red packet, for example), which makes it, in no doubt, a signature service that changes people's life and even production organizations.

11.4 No Need to Choose

The food delivery market in China has maintained rapid growth in recent years, hitting a market scale of RMB 204.56 billion in 2017, with an increase of 23.1%. Many outstanding food delivery platforms also emerged in this period, including the well-known Ele.me and Meituan Delivery.

There are hundreds of restaurants offering delivery service near my university, so I have to spend 10 to 15 min choosing the food I want to have and wait for another

40 to 50 min after ordering online. If the delivered food does not taste well, I would consider it as not worth the candle. To put it another way, the diversity in choices provided by these food delivery platforms to users has actually made it more difficult for them to "choose".

A more typical example is given in Fig. 11.2, with the list of shops on each floor of Chaoyang Joy City in Beijing shown in the elevator. The paper is fully dotted with logos of all the shops in the department store, but if anyone wants to find an ideal place to dine from the paper, he'd be trapped in the elevator for forever.

Joy City, indeed, has offered abundant choices to its visitors but is also putting people with decidophobia at a loss. Therefore, abundant choices do not necessarily mean the best services.

Do we have better offers then? There is an interesting mobile application named "ONE", whose core idea is "one is enough in the complex world". It operates in a simple way by pushing one picture with one piece of text to its users each day, along with a short passage or several lines of poem. That is all. Users don't have to make any choice.

The text in Fig. 11.3 was for Chinese Valentine's Day: "A pig is a pig, black or white. Two pigs are not alone, stupid or not." How sweet it is.

Himalaya is another popular mobile application that offers abundant audio resources to its listeners. However, among the sea of choices, users can select and

Fig. 11.2 The list of shops printed in an elevator of Chaoyang Joy city

Fig. 11.3 A push message of "ONE". *Source* http://www.wufafuwu.com/a/ONE_tupian/2015/0326/69.html

subscribe their favorite channels and listen only to updates in these channels by clicking into "my subscriptions".

Therefore, for today's services, the best choice may just appear when people have no need to choose.

11.5 Multifunctional Spaces

The place to analyze here is a department store called "Hi General Merchandise", whose most outstanding characteristic is the full utilization of space. Special handmade products, toys for children, a book store and a café are integrated in the multifunctional space that accommodates all types of services to attract curious customers with the unique scenario and business model. A small space with multiple functions integrated can better satisfy the increasingly comprehensive and diverse demands of customers.

People are more willing to visit places that can satisfy different demands at the same time, so as to cope with the accelerated pace of life. A place has to be attractive enough to lure visitors if it serves only one kind of demands. In the most ideal circumstance, a place that caters to multiple demands at one go would generate a powerful attraction to users since it saves the time cost for them, improves their work and life efficiency, and thereby allows them more time for something else.

The Helsinki Central Library Oodi in Finland (Fig. 11.4) is an impressive case that I must introduce to you. It has adopted VR, online service, book sorting robots

Fig. 11.4 Helsinki Central Library Oodi in Finland

and other advanced technologies to improve citizens' experience, implant innovative designs and endow the library with multiple roles. Only one third of the space at Oodi is used for book shelves, with the rest undertaking more functions for citizens to, in addition to acquiring knowledge, enjoy public life, spark new ideas and practice interesting thoughts.

The ground floor of Oodi provides open functional areas like café, cinema, canteen and inquiry desks, giving citizens a free space for communication. The more attractive part is the open horizon with beautiful views that extends from the spacious ground floor to the city square. Small spaces for people of different interests are set on the second floor, where citizens can experience music making, sound recording, electronic games, 3D printing, sewing and other interesting activities. There are also makers' spaces, conference rooms and coworking spaces for entrepreneurs. The third floor is the library for citizens to slow down their pace and silently read a book. The children's section nearby is considerate enough to lower the shelves to suit the height of kids, making it easy for them to fetch books and put them back.

This charming library is the result of the innovative designs made by the city of Helsinki based on a large amount of surveys. Citizens can enjoy multiple benefits and the fun of a fantastic life by simply visiting a library. This sublime multi-functional building now plays the role of "the living room of the city", accommodating all kinds of functions including reading, gathering, entertainment and recreation, and offering citizens a place to acquire knowledge, skills, experience and stories.

The "multi-functioning" trend is also common in product innovations. The founder of Tesla and SpaceX, Elon Musk, seeing that many American families installed solar panels on their roofs to save energy and protect the environment, wondered why they had to keep the tiles and roofs as long as the solar panels had been installed. Musk then developed a solar roof that carries multi-functions but costs only 42 dollars per square meter. The tiles are solid, with a heating function and can be penetrated by sunlight. This innovation turns a house into a solar-power-bearing building, uses its walls as batteries to store electricity for Tesla electric vehicles and thereby, constructs a complete ecosystem. This case proves that a product endowed with various functions not only brings convenience to consumers' lives, but also inspires our way towards future with product and service innovations driving behind it.

11.6 Tips

Some tips given to customers in service can also be taken as tips for modern service innovation.

For example, the Chinese restaurant chain Din Tai Fung, while selling Shanghai hairy crabs, designed an "appreciation" handbook that illustrated the home cooking recipes of hairy crabs with comics, teaching buyers to cook and enjoy the delicacy in an engrossing way.

The way Din Tai Fung shows its customers how to cook the crabs they bought correctly and decently is a silent psychological hint that suggests to the customers: for one, they are capable of accomplishing the "tasks followed"; and for two, their cooking skills would be improved. The two things are equally important, because the former relieves customers from the worry about the "risks" resulting from their poor crab-cooking skills, while the latter caters to their "desires" to grow knowledge and competence.

Haier has provided us with another example. If you put Tong Ho (garland chrysanthemum) into the latest-generation Haier smart fridge, you will see a picture of Tong Ho in the display on the door, telling you about the content within the fridge, even showing its nutrition analysis and cooking recipes. The fridge is delivering customers knowledge and tips. When we empathize with our customers and offer them useful tips, they will understand our commitment, get a better experience and return us with sound feedback.

The widely used WeChat Official Accounts and WeChat Mini Programs have brought about a new model of tips-based retailing. For example, "A Glass with Ken" is a WeChat Official Account run by a whisky collector named Ken. On this account, he opens courses like "Ken's Drunk Talk" on Whisky appreciation on the one hand, and offers Whisky buying channels through functions like "online store" and "bar reservation" on the other hand. The introduction of authoritative knowledge and further experience based on users' trust have formed a perfect service loop. Such a "non-mainstream" mode would probably become the "mainstream" in the future.

11.7 Scenarios Triggering Tender Feelings

Some scenarios are designed to trigger tender feelings in customers as they enjoy the services.

Fig. 11.5 Greetings printed on the bottom of bowls

A restaurant that serves takeaway food is distinctive for serving not disposable dinnerware but porcelain bowls and plates for home use. They also considerately provide reusable plastic covers to ensure the sanitation of food in the delivery process. Deliverers will come to the door to collect the used dinnerware afterwards. It obviously increases the delivery costs for the restaurant, but the life idea they convey is well received by the customers—eating takeaway food though, I am living a valued life. The disappeared plastic takeaway boxes also remind them they are contributing to the cause of sustainability.

One sweet and heartwarming move of the restaurant is to print different greetings to the bottom of bowls. Customers finishing their food would find funny words like "Keep staring at me and I'll bite" and "I need a hug" within the bowl, as shown in Fig. 11.5. Heartening designs like this are clearly a practice of differentiation in modern fast food business. Such an innovative idea in service would easily attract loyal customers since they can taste home and love in the food, and all the restaurant has to do is to ensure the quality of food and speed in delivery.

11.8 New Interactions

Interaction is the essential activity of a service.

Apart from satisfying users' explicit demands on services, providers have to add joyful, intriguing new experiences to interactions. This trend of service innovation is growingly important under the ever-booming technological advances.

As a common experience in fine museums, visitors can touch the floating bubbles on an interactive screen to get all kinds of interesting information. Users are offered a way to acquire information services suitable for their personal interests.

Here is the interaction process: You just have to click a graph to trigger bubbles containing related subjects and stories, and a click on a certain bubble will unfold it into detailed information shown on the screen, while shrinking other graphs to the corners. The information is presented in both text form and videos.

This novel interactive mode encourages users to explore proactively and participate in the service process, making the service experience even more attractive. It not only provokes the thinking of service designers, but also provides a chance for information technologies to play their roles.

Also, new interactive modes are blurring the distinction between videos and games. Viewers of Netflix's interactive film *Black Mirror: Bandersnatch* can change the narrative structure of plots by clicking options on the screen. It can be taken as an invitation for viewers to personally participate in the film after passively receiving the filming service for nearly a century. Maybe the next step more exciting than deciding the story development is that viewers can put on VR rigs and become characters in films. If this comes true, who would be able to predict the story of a film in the future?

11.9 Word-of-Mouth Economy

Word-of-mouth communications are a vital element in service management, for they, on the one hand, consist of an important dimension of service that concerns customers, and on the other hand, are a basic element that influences consumers' expectation of the service. The gap between their expected and perceived service qualities will turn directly into a satisfaction or dissatisfaction of the service.

In some service areas, these communications have even become a core service content, like in the example of Dianping. Data of users' reviews and comments on most e-commerce websites are also a part of the word-of-mouth communications on services and products, serving as references for others' buying decisions.

Now that word-of-mouth communications are playing importantly in all aspects of services, how can we guide them towards a positive direction in the process of service design and management? As the old saying goes, "good wine needs no bush". If the quality of a service or product is fine enough, it won't need other marketing channels nor a good store site, for word-of-mouth communications are the best promotion to attract enough customers.

Therefore, a business with strong enough confidence in its services and products may well take word-of-mouth communications as the major marketing approach. In fact, the prevalence of social media has provided such communications with ideal platforms whose speed of propagation is without parallel in any previous times. And video platforms like Tik Tok have significantly boosted the efficiency of word-of-mouth communications.

So the most convenient, but also inconvenient, way to make an Internet-famous shop is to maintain a fine quality of products. The first comers would naturally spread, through social media, good words about the fantastic experience they enjoyed. With the help of proper incentive mechanisms, such positive communications would achieve better results.

One thing that cannot be ignored in word-of-mouth communications is the scale of service. When the service is at a small scale, word-of-mouth communications can bring enough amount of consumers with operational risks well controlled. But if the service capacity has not been expanded when the number of consumers soars, the quality of service experience may deteriorate.

Businesses at this point would either develop horizontally, to cover more customer groups with chain stores and extend the service scope; or use a reservation system to balance the demands. If the service quality is on the rising path, they can even moderately increase the prices to release the burden caused by high demands.

For large companies above a certain scale, people's familiarity with the main features of their brands and services would make word-of-mouth communications no longer applicable. There are two strategies for them. One is innovating and updating some elements in the current service system to surprise existing users and stimulate a new round of word-of-mouth communications while satisfying their curiosity. The other is taking existing users as the base points to develop new users through social media marketing. Positive and active word-of-mouth marketing and reputation maintenance are an effective way to sustain the company's vitality and develop new users for services both in start-up and mature scaled stages.

Negative word-of-mouth communications are fatal to players in the service sector, for the quality management is different from in the manufacturing sector. Manufactured products will experience multiple links of inspection before delivery, to minimize the possibility of quality problems and unqualified products can be unshelved or recalled, to avoid substantial losses to users. However, in the service sector, the intrinsic attributes of services make it impossible to inspect their qualities before usage, and inferior service experience cannot be replaced or recalled. Considering this, service providers have to study the mechanism of information flows and the ways to control them, so as to tackle negative word-of-mouth communications well.

We have to imagine the motives that drive consumers to share a poor service they've experienced and their way of sharing. Upon receiving such a service, consumers would normally expect the business to make remedies first. When the expectation goes in vain or the remedies are not good enough, the motive of spreading this unsuccessful service experience would grow in their mind.

Therefore, in the face of failures in services, providers have to, on the one hand, prepare a systematic remedy plan or a remedy system; and, on the other hand, encourage, through making unconditional promises or other means, customers to feedback on the problems, rather than spreading words about the unsuccessful experience in online or offline service networks or social networks.

The process of controlling negative word-of-mouth communications in the age of IoT and Big Data contains both opportunities and challenges. The opportunities come from the IT-based acquisition methods of users' data in key links, and their state and affective data that allow service providers to understand their experience and reactions in service process more precisely and carry out possible in-process interventions to ensure a general control.

As for challenges, fanned by developed social networks and decentralized media, micro communications can blaze seemingly indisputable, or even lopsidedly exaggerated scenes of failure in service provision to the wide public in a fast and graphic manner, stirring up discontents.

In view of these, here is what we should do when returning back to the perspective of service providers. Firstly, clearer service standards have to be defined at the design stage to ensure the consistency of service delivery along the dimension of time or the full lifecycle of a service system. Methods like the quality integration model of service packages or gap model of service quality can be used at the design end to improve service quality and retain the possibility of error. Secondly, precise acquisition and analysis of process data have to be carried out during service operation to strengthen process control. Lastly, in case of negative events, systematic remedies should be made, based on empathizing with the customers, as an apology and to provide tangible or valuable mending.

If users of our services are abstracted and simplified into a huge social network, which includes two types of users—existing ones and those have not yet used our services, positive and negative word-of-mouth communications can both be seen as information flows in this network.

All the methods to be used in service design and management in the above discussions are efforts to adjust and control the direction and speed of these information flows, as well as their influences on each node. The conception of this network and its visualized presentation in the future mean significantly to service designers and managers, because through revealing a clear view within the organizations of service providers, it helps us detect internal problems and risk points, inspire excellent employees and encourage excellent performances.

11.10 Service Boosts "Rural Vitalization"

Rural revitalization has always been more than just the economic resurgence; it's also about rejuvenating and passing down cultural heritage. Chenjiapu Village in Songyang County, Zhejiang Province, and Dali Dong stockaded village in Rongjiang County, Guizhou Province, stand out as two vivid examples demonstrating innovative services in the process of rural revitalization.

In Chenjiapu Village, located in Sidu Township of Songyang County, Zhejiang Province, a blend of traditional and contemporary service design has crafted a unique rural tourism model that combines economic and cultural elements. The establishment of the bookstore, Nanjing LIBRAIRIE AVANT-GARDE, in the village pays homage to the ancient architectural aesthetics of the area while infusing it with modern design, turning the bookstore into a remarkable landmark that merges history with the present. Meanwhile, the Stray Birds Hotel offers tourists an in-depth experience of rural life, allowing them to truly immerse themselves as part of the Chenjiapu Village community. Here, the countryside serves not just as a backdrop of natural beauty but also as a vessel for culture and daily life.

Dali Dong stockaded village in Rongjiang County, Guizhou Province, emphasizes the protection and preservation of the Dong ethnic group's traditional culture as the cornerstone of Dong stockaded village's development. The Well House bed

Fig. 11.6 Dali Dong stockaded village

and breakfast, which symbolizes a harmonious blend of the modern and the traditional, draws its architectural inspiration and materials from the locality. It maintains aesthetic consistency with the stockaded village landscape and ingeniously incorporates the Dong's traditional indigo dyeing and textile crafts into its product designs, showcasing how ancestral culture can be seamlessly integrated with modern-day living (Fig. 11.6).

11.11 "New Infrastructures" Boosted by "New Services"

Nowadays, new infrastructure construction has become China's key strategy that develops vigorously at state and regional levels to lay a solid foundation for a wonderful life in the future. The scope of the "new infrastructure" is large enough to cover all aspects of the national economy and people's livelihood. It includes three broad aspects: information infrastructure, represented by 5G, industrial Internet and AI; integrated infrastructure, represented by intelligent transportation and intelligent energy; and innovative infrastructure, represented by infrastructures supporting science and technology, scientific education and industrial technological innovation. From a systematic view, "new infrastructure" not only creatively updates the very fundamental concept of "infrastructure", but also opens up unprecedented design spaces for the society and economy of the future. It is an overall acceleration towards a "better life".

In this overarching strategy of great weight on the future of a country, how to master the direction and standards of "new infrastructure" construction well and how to assist and even lead the construction with appropriate encompassing innovative thinking have become issues of vital importance.

"Plan before you act" has long been the essence of the system thinking in Chinese culture. To find clues for the "plan", we have to return to where we started in this book and learn from the S-D Logic, to step on a more reasonable, conducive, organic and ordered approach: "To satisfy the people's aspirations for a better life" should be taken as the utmost demand to plan about "new infrastructure" as led by "new services". The linear logic that progresses alongside a single technological direction should also be broken through so as to construct a systematic scenario-based design space of "new infrastructure" from the four perspectives of service.

Following such an encompassing thinking, the QFD tool in SERVINO Methods can be borrowed to establish interrelation matrixes as the core link, which can be understood as the "middle-stage" or "middleware". Specifically, people's demands and their requirements on new infrastructures will compose matrix A; and the new technologies (to be included in the enabling technology library of the SERVINO Methods) that can satisfy or support these requirements will compose Matrix B. The interrelation matrixes will soon establish effective connections between people's essential demands and the goals of "new infrastructure" construction. It is predictable then that all long-time pain spots will be solved promptly and all newly-built infrastructures will be soon well applied.

For instance, the low-latency 5G technology should be able to activate demands that cannot be satisfied by traditional communication infrastructures with high latency. For example, doctors of Chinese PLA General Hospital in Hainan have successfully manipulated surgical robots through 5G technology to implant a PINS-branded brain pacemaker for a patient in Beijing. From the view of medical service, operations of this kind require precise real-time manipulations over surgical instruments, so the communication infrastructure in support of tele-medical services has to bear an "excellent real-time performance", which relies on the "low latency" feature of the 5G technology. In this case, 5G is serving the latest demands of telemedicine as an important technological direction of "new infrastructure" construction. Similarly, if the next-generation tele-surgeries need to use AI technology to monitor the patient's vital signs before and during the operation in real time and make risk predictions, or robots are needed for nursing services, new demands over "new infrastructure" would arise from these new surgical needs. And such demands would, in turn, point to directions for the development of medical and communication technology innovations in the future.

It can be seen from these examples that the cross-disciplinary integration of demands at the medical frontier and technological advances in Science and Engineering is the key issue in constructing "middleware" and transforming the powerful potential of "new infrastructure" into reliable capacities in future medical services in similar scenarios. Therefore, the "middleware" of "new infrastructure" and their supportive systems have to be based upon strong and well-organized cross-disciplinary integration and innovation. For example, the newly-founded Institute for Interdisciplinary Medicine and Engineering at Tsinghua University is a collaborative innovation platform that serves the "industry-education-research-practice" demands of hundreds of faculty members in over ten Medicine and Engineering departments. Through this platform, many latest technologies are stepping out of laboratories to the clinical stage and towards industries, to make their contributions to the construction and promotion of "innovative infrastructures" in the "new infrastructure" construction strategy.

It is hopeful that the contradiction matrix of service systems described in the SERVINO Methods may provide important guidance to the design of "new infrastructures". That is, infrastructure innovations making the best use of innovations in enabling technologies to build new service models will, ultimately, transform our input in "new infrastructure" construction into tangible benefits to the people's production modes and life styles.

Now, suppose that we can study and construct the "middleware" well, where do we get the ideas for a "better life", or what are the real sources of such demands? The answer lies in the imaginations of life and society in the future as described in this chapter.

Just as the design of a Disneyland starts from "scriptwriters" and "creative thinkers" who give birth to the stories, and is then handed over to artistic designers, engineering designers and practitioners for actualization step by step, the "new infrastructure" construction also needs a batch of "creative thinkers", "urban designers" and "industrial system designers" to propose insightful, even overthrowing, conceptions on our future life (future economy and society, at large), with the help of laws of service systems evolution and other thinking approaches introduced in this book, then clearly define the demand spaces delineated by these "future scenarios" and use the SERVINO enabling technology library and interrelation matrix to preliminarily identify the design space of "new infrastructure", so that the technological R&D and engineering practices followed can easily put the conceptions of "new infrastructure" into reality and infuse them with everlasting vitality through reasonable and effective iterations.

Afterword

The era of new services is too grand to be scrutinized in merely 11 chapters. The firm belief that drives me to accomplish this book derives from the sense of mission motivated by transformations surging in the new era, from the excitement of standing on the shoulders of giants and catching a glimpse of the enchantment of service innovations, and from the resonance aroused within me upon witnessing the ingenuity of service innovators.

Let alone the infinite business forms in the service sector that enchant researchers with dazzling postures, the analysis of a small store may still be difficult as it can "look like a range when viewed in face and a peak when from the side". My hope is to sort out clues from complexity and put forward principles that may withstand the test of time. If you crave for more service management theories or tricks that can be put into immediate practice, please stay tuned for my incoming online course.

My years of teaching standing behind the podium of Tsinghua University has made the gestation and preparation of the book possible. The book is finished under the support of the Special Program of Innovative Methods of the Ministry of Science and Technology of the People's Republic of China. My gratitude goes to Professor Zheng Li, the Vice President of Tsinghua University, who has guided and pointed to me the research direction of service innovations in Industrial Engineering; Zhao Lei, Wang Chen, Yu Ming, Yan Jingbin, Ma Liang, Jia Jia and other dear fellows who have accompanied with and encouraged me greatly in my study and teaching of service innovations; leaders and teaching faculty members of Department of Industrial Engineering of Tsinghua University who have always supported and taken care of me; students and friends that used to join me in my classes and reward me with passionate discussions; students of the Service Innovation Laboratory of my Department, who have probed with me the mystery of services, especially, Cui Fengming, Shi Jing, Shen Qing, Wang Pidong, Wang Meihui, Peng Yingzi, Ni Shiying, Dai Rui, Zhao Lin, Li Yushan and Wang Ridong, for their hard work in information and documents sorting and collation; and my editor Shao Yue, expert reviewers and the whole team of CITIC Press Group for their professional work and wholehearted devotion.

At last, I am dedicating this book to my diligent, wise, kind and generous grandparents, my father and mother who keep leading and encouraging me with love

L. Li, *The Era of New Services*, Management for Professionals,
https://doi.org/10.1007/978-981-99-9565-3

and trust, my dear wife for always being there for me and taking all the trouble to proofread my writing, and my son who fills me with pride and mental power.

May *The Era of New Services* be a small but warm light alongside your adventure towards the path of innovation and the beauty of life, glittering in the aroma of sandalwood or the sound of a gurgling brook. May your way lead you somewhere lofty, to look far and write a better future with the pen named "service" in your hand.

SPRINGER NATURE

GPSR Compliance

The European Union's (EU) General Product Safety Regulation (GPSR) is a set of rules that requires consumer products to be safe and our obligations to ensure this.

If you have any concerns about our products, you can contact us on ProductSafety@springernature.com

In case Publisher is established outside the EU, the EU authorized representative is:

Springer Nature Customer Service Center GmbH
Europaplatz 3
69115 Heidelberg, Germany

The manufacturer's authorised representative in the EU is Springer Nature Customer Service Centre GmbH, Europaplatz 3, 69115 Heidelberg, Germany. If you have any concerns regarding our products, please contact ProductSafety@springernature.com

Printed and bound by CPI Group (UK) Ltd, Croydon, CR0 4YY
01/10/2026
02225883-0016